THIS SCHOOL BELONGS TO YOU & ME

THIS SCHOOL BELONGS TO YOU & ME

Gerald Newmark, Ph. D.

HART PUBLISHING COMPANY, INC.
NEW YORK CITY

CONTENTS

This book is dedicated to Charles E. Dederich, founder of Synanon Foundation, to his wife, Betty Dederich, member of the Board of Regents, and to all members of the Synanon family, who have created a drug-free, non-violent, totally integrated learning community. This community daily demonstrates to the world that people of different races, religions, and walks of life (including ex-prostitutes and dope fiends, lawyers, secretaries, scientists, cooks, educators) can live together in peace and harmony and experience life joyfully, productively, and creatively, while maintaining the highest ethical principles.

Throughout my work to bring about change in public education, Synanon has been a major influence on me and has been my inspiration for the concept of a vibrant living-learning community. I like to call the Synanon community "A Community of Big Shots" because it is a community where everyone is included, where everyone experiences closeness and affection, and where everyone can feel powerful by participating in his own evolution.

ACKNOWLEDGMENTS

Many people played an important part in the development of the Tutorial Community Program (TCP) concepts described in this book. Foremost among them was Dr. Ralph Melaragno who shared the directorship of the Tutorial Community Project with me. Ralph Melaragno has been a valued partner, advisor, critic, and friend. Although Dr. Melaragno contributed to the development of the ideas in this book, he is in no way accountable for these particular formulations, for which the author bears sole responsibility.

The Ford Foundation deserves much credit for supporting the long range developmental effort that was necessary for the full implementation of the Tutorial Community Project. Many school projects are supported for only one or two years and stop at the point when real progress could be made. Marjorie Martus, the Foundation's program officer for the project, deserves particular credit for her backing throughout the six years of the project. She was our chief supporter and critic. Many thanks also go to Nancy Boggs of the Ford Foundation for her assistance in arranging for the production of a documentary film on TCP. Her consistent support, encouragement and suggestions during the writing of this book were much appreciated.

The cooperation of officials in the Los Angeles City School System, especially former Deputy Superintendent, Graham Sullivan, was important in getting the pilot project off the ground.

Principals, teachers, parents and children at the five project schools were, of course, the ones most directly involved. Their willingness to experiment, put in extra time and energy, and confront and overcome numerous difficulties were responsible for breaking new ground in education. The concepts and procedures described in this book are the results of their efforts. We owe all of them a special debt of gratitude.

Much appreciation goes to Charles and Tina Carey who showed great enthusiasm for the notion of TCP from its inception and later backed this up by having their non-profit organization, Educational Communications Corporation, sponsor the project during its last three years. The schools involved were: Pacoima Elementary School, Wilshire Crest Elementary School, Dublin Avenue Elementary School, Plainwood Elementary School, and Norwood Elementary School.

Many persons served with distinction as staff members and consultants during the various stages of the project. I would like to express my appreciation to all of them, and particularly to thank JoAnne Polite, Dorothy Posnick, Don Watson, Phoebee Nalls, Jean Miller, Betty Brady, and Dr. Carl Sewell. Dr. Larry Solomon's contributions to the ideas concerning feedback, team building and shared planning-and-decision-making during the final two years of the project were exceptional.

The advice and support of Dr. Harry Silberman and Dr. John Coulson of the System Development Corporation during the first three years of the project were extremely helpful. Suggestions received in the early stages of the project in the areas of feedback and community building from Dr. Bill Coulson, Dr. Carl Rogers, and other members of the Center for the Study of the Person at La Jolla, California, were highly valued.

A special thanks to Mary Conway Kohler, director of the National Commission on Resources for Youth, whose pioneering work in the field of "youth serving youth" has been an inspiration to all of us. Many thanks, too, to Peggy Lippitt, one of the leaders in the peer tutoring movement, whose assistance, encouragement and materials were very much appreciated.

Special thanks go to Helen Brush and Lou Delgado for the exceptionally fine photos of TCP in action. Appreciation also goes to Bill Jersey whose sensitive documentary film "Tomorrow We'll See What Happens" reflects the spirit and essence of the project.

Thanks, also, to Al Bauman for his valuable suggestions and moral support throughout the project.

I am also much indebted to Ed Siegel for permitting me to be his "only friend" at a time when I needed to be needed.

Many people rendered invaluable service in the preparation of this manuscript and I would like to thank them all, notably: Lois Braun, Joan Cernov, Dr. Betty Jones, Yo Marujama, Julie Walden for reading parts of the early drafts and making comments which were useful in making revisions; Nina Bauman for her painstakingly careful typing of the original draft, her conscientious attention to detail and her numerous helpful suggestions; Lois Frazzano for her care and accuracy in typing parts of the final draft; Dan Stein for his fine initial editing and continuous interest and assistance; Beatrice Hart for her intelligent and helpful final editing; and finally, my cousin, Betty Grossman, whose generous sharing of her home, food, typing, and warm personality made final revisions a pleasant experience.

A special word of gratitude goes to my brother and colleague, Dr. Irving Newmark, for his unwavering support and his contagious optimism and enthusiasm.

These acknowledgments would be incomplete without mention of my son, David, who was the captive subject of my early educational experimentation; and of my mother, Esther, whose unconditional love and chicken soup were always sustaining.

Finally, a warm, heartfelt thanks to my wife, Sandy, for her encouragement, support, ideas, concern, prodding, "gaming," and love that made the completion of this book possible.

FOREWORD

People interested in improving schools have accepted as gospel for many years the importance of the teacher in the learning process. Indeed, a great deal of effort to produce useful changes in schools has focused upon retraining or changing the teachers. Sometimes this emphasis has led to the simplistic and mistaken notion that colleges and universities pour knowledge into teachers and teachers pour it into children. Such views pay inadequate attention to the complexities of the human relationships that have so much to do with whether anything is learned and with the attitudes and behaviors that are such an important byproduct of formal learning.

The tendency to see the teacher as a model and as the sole source of learning and the student as the vessel into which the teachers' knowledge is poured avoids the reality of what we now know really goes on in schools and, indeed, outside of them. It is common knowledge today that children learn from everything they see, hear and do; that they learn as much or more from their parents, their friends and their fellow students as they do from their teachers; that the television is a new, stimulating and sometimes disturbing source of learning; that the school paying attention to nothing but the pupil-teacher

11

relationship probably won't serve its students as well as it might; and that an important element in improving the effectiveness of teachers is helping them to ally their work with all these other sources that stimulate children.

These lessons were brought home to me dramatically several years ago when I visited some elementary schools in Los Angeles. In those schools, an effort was being made to take advantage of all the sources of teaching and learning that are available within the school and that the school can command from outside itself. The most visible activity giving evidence of this wide-ranging approach was the system whereby children taught one another. There were organized periods of time in which fifth graders, who had been trained in certain techniques of teaching, were carrying these through with second or third graders. But beyond this, there were parent volunteers performing a variety of important functions and teachers working with each other and with parents and students in ways which went far beyond the usually assumed role of the elementary school teacher. In effect, the schools I visited were a new kind of learning community, which I found exciting and which were even then beginning to produce measurable results that looked promising.

The person whose thinking, persuasion, and infectious low-key enthusiasm lay behind the activities in the schools I visited was Gerald Newmark, the author of this book. Skillfully working with his colleague, Ralph Melaragno, and others, he stimulated them to create an environment for learning which enhanced the roles of principals, teachers, students and parents and gave to each a new dignity, new dimensions, and new responsibilities. Most importantly, the schools involved in this effort knitted together the persons who work in them in a way that made the school more of a community than it was before.

Guiding this process and building progressively on day to day experience took some extra time and effort and some additional expense, and we in the Ford Foundation were glad that we could assist with the project. As is frequently the case in the relationship between the Foundation and a grantee, we, too, learned a great deal about what might be done in schools through the skill with which Jerry Newmark, his associates, and school staff used our resources. At the same time, we wondered whether the entire enterprise was one that depended on the unique combination of stimulating leadership and the responsiveness, special interest, and contributions of teachers and administrators in the schools. Was there any possibility that what was achieved in a few schools in Los Angeles could happen elsewhere?

This book of Jerry Newmark's is a response to that question. It tells in simple and clear terms how to create schools in which everyone is a learning resource and everyone shares in running the institution. I am sure that Jerry would not argue that this is the only way to achieve these ends. As others ring changes on it in the gradual process of making schools more effective places, I am sure that he will be delighted, for the essence of what is outlined here is the process of people working together rather than an exact prescription for everything they do.

HAROLD HOWE II
Vice President for Education and Research
The Ford Foundation

❧ NOTE ❧

Regrettably, the English language does not offer a pronoun without gender, except for the frequently inappropriate "one." To fill this void, some people in recent years have advocated the use of "he/she," "s/he," and other rather awkward locutions. In this book, we generally use the traditional male pronouns because they present less stylistic difficulty. We hope that readers will understand that "she" could be substituted for "he" in most instances in this text.

1 OVERVIEW

The School as a Vibrant Living-Learning Community

MOTIVATION

A popular story is making the rounds about the mother who jumps out of bed when her alarm clock goes off in the morning, rushes to her son's bedroom, shakes him, and says, "Get up, my son! Get out of bed. You're going to be late for school! Hurry, son, it's late. Get up! You're going to be late." The son sleepily but stubbornly replies, "No. I'm not going to school! I hate school! I hate it! I hate it and I'm just not going!"

Alarmed, the mother shouts, "What do you mean you hate school? What's got into you? Get out of bed! You're going to be late."

The son doesn't budge. "I hate school and I have three good reasons. First, all the teachers in school hate me. Second, all the kids in school hate me. And, third, even all the cafeteria workers hate me. I'm never going to school again. And that's it."

"Don't be ridiculous!" exclaims the mother. "You have to get up and go to school."

"No, I hate it and I'm not going. Why should I go?" replies the son adamantly.

The exasperated mother responds, "Okay, I'll give *you*

15

three good reasons why you have to go to school. Number one, you have to go to school because I am a taxpayer and my taxes support the school. Two, you are fifty-two years old. And, three, you are the principal of the school. So get out of bed and go to school."

This story evokes unrestrained laughter at gatherings of principals and teachers. Apparently they strongly identify with the principal who did not want to get out of bed in the morning.

While many people may be ambivalent about schools as they function today, it is generally agreed that the school is probably the most important social institution. Everyone goes to it. Thus, it provides continuity for the nation and serves as the training ground for future mechanics as well as presidents. It should be the most interesting and exciting environment in every community. But, alas, as Charles Silberman finds in *Crisis in the Classroom,** too often students, teachers, and administrators are bored, frustrated, and unhappy. The vexing problems common to many inner-city schools: low achievement, poor school-community relations, declining student and staff morale, are widespread.

I have a dream which I think many people share about what a school should be. In my dream, the school is a fantastically exciting place where everyone is turned on to learning and to each other. When the alarm clock goes off in the morning, teachers and pupils eagerly jump out of bed, excitedly looking forward to the day at school. When Friday comes, instead of "Thank God it's Friday," it's "Gee, is it Friday already?" Everyone comes to school in the morning with that feeling of exhilarated anticipation of engaging in a favorite sport in the company of friends.

---

* Silberman, Charles E., *Crisis in the Classroom: The Remaking of American Education*, New York, Random House, 1970.

REALIZING A DREAM

In recent years, there has been a steady stream of books which describe what is wrong with education and present a vision of what schools should be like. But rarely has a book spelled out in any useful form how to get from where we are to where we want to be. *This School Belongs To You and Me* does just that. It describes a new kind of learning community, an exciting school where students, parents, teachers, staff, and administrators are turned on to learning and to each other. Further, this book offers a step by step blueprint for creating this kind of school.

This School Belongs to You and Me is not a theoretical treatise. It is for people who are tired of *talking* about the problems of our educational system and want to *do* something concrete to solve them. It offers a systematic, detailed plan for the total redesign of a school, incorporating the highest humanistic and practical goals. Carl Rogers in the preface of his book *Freedom to Learn** states, "Here is a vision of what education can become." This book is a practical resource or blueprint for people with visions.

THE SCHOOL AS A COMMUNITY OF LEARNERS

The basic idea is a simple one. It involves using the wealth of human resources already available in the school and in the community to revitalize the educational process. This is achieved by instituting in the school what I call a Tutorial Community Program (TCP).

There are essentially four cornerstones to the Tutorial Community Program:

---

* Rogers, Carl, *Freedom to Learn: A View of What Education Might Become*, Columbus, Charles E. Merrill, 1969.

The dream and the challenge.

1. Peer Tutoring and Self-Learning—individualized instruction through helping relationships.

2. Shared Planning-and-Decision-Making—creating a sense of community and proprietorship in the total school community by involving everyone—

students, parents, teachers, administrative and non-teaching staff—in the planning, teaching, and management of the school.

3. Parent Involvement—expanding the learning community and increasing the resources available to facilitate and stimulate learning.

4. Feedback and Team Building—self-correction through open dialogue.

The Tutoring Relationship

In the usual program, the teacher establishes daily learning objectives, chooses activities, obtains and prepares materials, does the teaching and keeps records. The student has little opportunity for initiative in learning, for making genuine choices, for self-learning, for questioning, or for facilitating the learning of others (although he frequently can and does hinder it).

In a tutorial community, everyone (students, parents, teachers, administrators) is a learning resource for everyone else. Students teach students; teachers help teachers; parents train other parents; and all groups interact with each other to foster and improve helping relationships and teamwork. In this environment, learning and teaching are inseparable. Everyone learns to teach and teaches to learn.

Shared Planning

Because in the traditional school students have little experience in making large numbers of small decisions, they are ultimately unequipped to make larger ones. Tasks are generally imposed by the teacher as the authority figure. The student takes little responsibility for his own learning or classroom. Many tasks imposed by the teacher have little meaning for the student or do not coincide with his own perceived or tacit needs and wants, so he may become disinterested, frustrated, and sometimes rebellious.

In a tutorial community school, shared planning and shared decision making are fundamental processes. Through direct participation in lesson planning and in managing the classroom and school, students develop initiative and self-reliance. They become increasingly competent and confident in exercising judgment and making decisions. As they are treated as respected people their positive self-concepts and emerging sense of power give them a stake in their community and they need no external spur to motivate them. The schoolwide philosophy of shared management among students, parents, and school staff is reflected in the feeling of ownership experienced by all.

Parent Involvement

Parents frequently have been thought of as outsiders in the education of children. As one teacher put it, "We wanted to close the school doors and keep the parents out." But this cannot work. Where parents and teachers are not supporting each other, or are working at cross purposes, education suffers.

One goal of a tutorial community school is to bring the school and community closer together—to create a cooperative atmosphere in which school personnel and parents share responsibility, concern, and pride in a school they feel they own and run. It involves teachers and parents becoming more knowledgeable about school and community, getting to know each other as people and not as stereotypes, sharing in planning and decision making and offering assistance where needed.

In the Tutorial Community School many channels are established for back and forth communication. Parents are members of the committees that plan and manage instructional and support activities. Parents participate in open forums, in training sessions, in tutoring, in special projects. Report cards go both ways, with parents giving their own evaluations of the school program and their children's needs and progress.

Interaction flows in both directions—not only do parents participate more actively in the school program, but school and teachers move more and more into the community. Teachers make home visits, to the delight of the children. Children go on trips and use the resources and work with the people of the community. As the goal of community is realized, school becomes an exciting, stimulating and joyous experience, a place you don't just *have* to be but *want* to be.

The helping relationship.

Feedback

In the usual school, the student does not feel "this is my school, my class, my education, my educational community where I come for important reasons, where I am an important and respected component, where I can get help in accomplishing important tasks, and where my behavior can influence others." Older and younger students have little feeling of belonging to the same community. Contacts between students of different grades are infrequent. When they occur, students often treat each other with disdain. Competition among students is fostered and one student's success may be bought at the expense of another. Many of the rewards for success are based on the satisfaction of feeling better than someone else.

In the tutorial community school open, direct, honest feedback sessions are built in as a regular feature. The mutual concern and accountability that develop from these discussions provide the school with the capability for self-correction.

The feedback session is an attempt to provide an atmosphere that encourages frank expression of thoughts and feelings. It is an opportunity to get to know oneself and to understand the effects of one's actions on other people. It is an occasion for making contact and getting to know people better, for developing a familiarity that can build trust and confidence.

The feedback session consists largely of persons giving each other positive and negative reactions about things that are helping or hindering achievement of school goals. It is a time when people can share problems and ask for and offer help and suggestions. It is a place where every decision and action, including the principal's, can be questioned openly and where everyone's voice is equal.

THE TUTORIAL COMMUNITY PROGRAM AND EDUCATIONAL PROBLEMS

Why should educators and the lay public be interested in TCP? In recent years education has witnessed many changes. Earlier attitudes of non-intervention and lack of interest have been replaced by increased public concern and extensive government financial support. We have seen a proliferation of learning and research laboratories and materials development centers. The attempt to modify and improve instructional goals has resulted in the augmented use of audio-visual aids and in the introduction of programmed instruction. Other trends using new curricula, team teaching, open schools and alternative schools have been experimented with.

Despite all the ferment, however, results have not fulfilled expectations. Too many students leave elementary school with minimal mastery of the basic skills of listening, speaking, reading, and writing. Few students have developed enthusiasm for learning or for school, or possess any capability for self-directed learning. High achievers often become bored and are underachievers in relation to their potential. Many children become early dropouts, especially minority or "disadvantaged" children.

The educational goal of treating people as individuals has become a cliché without ever becoming a reality. In the average first grade class there may be a range of three years in achievement by the end of the school year. This range increases through the years, so that in the sixth grade of the typical urban school there may be a six-year range of achievement. A teacher with a class of 30 or more students finds it almost impossible to attend to such wide ranges of individual differences in aptitude, ability, interest, motivation, problems, and achievement levels.

This discouraging situation is unlikely to change until educational programs become truly responsive to individual needs and until the entire school atmosphere changes significantly. Meeting this challenge is the aim of the Tutorial Community Program.

TCP is highly cost-effective. It achieves its objectives through the creative use of human resources. It relies not on special materials, equipment, buildings, visual aids, computers and the like, but rather on tapping into, developing, and expanding the latent talents of teachers, parents, and children. TCP is based on the helping relationship: people-helping-people.

In the age of "future shock," everything changes constantly and the only constant is change itself. New information becomes dated or obsolete almost as fast as it is discovered. Today's solutions become tomorrow's problems. Under these conditions, learning how to learn and self-directed learning are important educational objectives. The development of these capabilities, and practice in meaningful endeavors that foster them, should not be delayed until the student is in college or graduate school. Self-learning should be encouraged and planned for from the earliest possible moment (beginning in the kindergarten or preschool) and should continue throughout the student's school career.

Improvements in materials, equipment, facilities, and teaching procedures will have little effect as long as students feel no responsibility for learning, do not care about the school, the teachers, each other, and (worst of all) themselves. What is needed is a total change in atmosphere. The school must become a learning community with its various members joined in a common effort to improve the learning of all.

THE ORIGINS OF THE TUTORIAL COMMUNITY PROJECT

In 1968 my colleague, Ralph Melaragno, and I completed a small-scale study of several Los Angeles city schools under a

Ford Foundation grant. In trying to discover ways to individualize and improve classroom instruction in predominantly Mexican-American schools, we found that the most significant resource was the student himself.

To help first-grade Mexican-American children in the area of reading, we had fifth and sixth-graders tutor the first-graders and first-graders tutor each other, with considerable success. With training, elementary school pupils were able to assist other pupils in achieving specific objectives. A positive relationship developed between the learner and tutor. The learner not only profited from the instruction, but enjoyed receiving help from schoolmates. Tutors took their roles seriously, had a sense of importance and seemed to derive pleasure from the success of the learner.

Teachers reported that some of the older students who were doing poorly in their own class and were considered discipline problems, improved in their work and attitude toward learning as a result of assuming tutoring responsibility. Parents of tutors told school administrators of their pleasure at the students' participation in this project. Parents also received training as tutors and worked with their own children with positive results. The project demonstrated that children, with proper training and support from adults, were able to function effectively as helpers and teachers of other children to their mutual benefit.

As this small-scale project (we worked with a few first-grade classrooms and with a limited portion of the regular curriculum) neared completion, we asked ourselves, "So what?" As we analyzed the results and evaluated the significance of the project, we concluded that it was another case of "The operation was successful but the patient continued to die." There were too many other variables having greater impact and influence on the total atmosphere and outcomes of the school.

The tutorial process as we used it was an appendage to the

regular curriculum. It involved a limited number of selected students. As long as it was a piecemeal remedial program, its impact had to remain limited. It was further hampered by a lack of teamwork and by poor communication among teachers and between them and parents and administrators.

We therefore decided against simply expanding the original project. We wanted to do something more ambitious. We asked, "If we could develop our ideal school, what would its main features be, how would we go about it, and how long would it take?"

Out of this came a proposal for a research and development project to create a model school with the following main features: tutoring and self-learning, shared planning-and-decision-making, parent and community involvement, and self-correction through task oriented feedback.

THE MODEL: GRADUAL DEVELOPMENT OF A TUTORIAL COMMUNITY PROGRAM (TCP)

The conversion of an entire elementary school to a *first* Tutorial Community School had to be accomplished gradually over a considerable period of time. We therefore proposed a seven-year project, which would enable us to use the experience of each year to appraise and revise procedures and design plans for the year ahead. Under such a plan, school personnel would assume new responsibilities and roles gradually. They would have considerable time to familiarize themselves with new procedures before becoming deeply involved in their use. The pressure to produce instant miracles would be minimized and there would be leeway to try out many different approaches.

The major goals for students, as well as for the school staff and parents were:

1. The acquisition of basic knowledge and skills.

2. Development of the capacity for independent, self-directed learning.

3. Cultivation of positive behavior and attitudes toward self and others, toward learning and school, toward the helping relationship.

4. Increased confidence in one's ability to learn.

The Ford Foundation supported our audacious request for a seven-year grant. The initial school selected had 1800 students representing three ethnic groups (45% Black, 40% Chicano, and 15% white). Classified as a "poverty" school, it had all the problems typical of such a school, including low and declining academic achievement, high transiency, limited parental involvement, faculty cliques and conflicts, and community disapproval. Two more schools were added to the project in the third year. Each enrolled 600 children, predominantly black. They were not considered "poverty" schools, but had problems similar to those of the initial school. In the fourth year an additional two schools joined the project—one middle-class Caucasian with about 500 students and the other predominantly Mexican-American with approximately 1000 students.

The four major parts of the Tutorial Community Program (tutoring, shared planning-and-decision-making, parent involvement, and feedback) are an outgrowth of the research and development activities conducted at the five schools involved in the project. Although all of the concepts, procedures and activities described in this book evolved in these schools, not all of the schools used all of them. Tutoring was present in all the schools. The other elements were implemented to varying degrees in different schools. One of the schools implemented all of the four major elements to some extent.

Despite many difficulties (including conflicts between teachers and parents who volunteered for the program and those opposed to it, inconsistent support from higher administration, and problems with time and schedules), dramatic changes occurred in the atmosphere, operation, and learning in the schools. Academic achievement improved and affective growth took place. There were gains in reading on standardized tests. Children read more books and enjoyed reading more. Other accomplishments included: improved communication and cooperation among personnel; a reduction in racial tensions on the staff; improvement in interpersonal relations and development of an *esprit de corps;* student initiative in taking responsibility for learning; student skill in serving as learning resources for each other on a one-to-one basis and in teams; and the development of pride and positive attitudes toward school, self and others.

THIS SCHOOL BELONGS TO YOU AND ME

The experience with the Tutorial Community Project led to the conviction that our model was transferable to all schools seeking improvement. *This School Belongs to You and Me* describes in detail the rationale and assumptions, the methods and procedures, the goals and strategies that go into the establishment of a Tutorial Community School. The goal is to help other schools adopt these concepts, totally or partially.

This book offers a sequential approach for implementing each of the major TCP concepts. It describes a gradual transition from a traditional teacher-directed classroom to a student-directed self-learning, helping relationship environment. Proceeding in systematic small steps, the program provides successful experiences for both the experienced and inexperienced teacher and avoids the chaos, confusion, and failures that occur when change is too hastily pursued.

What follows is a blueprint for a gradual but total redesign for a whole school. It is also a rich resource book of ideas and practices which can be used by individual teachers and schools to improve almost any existing program. I call it a blueprint because it is practical and detailed. However, it is not hoped or expected that the blueprint or model described in this book will be transferred totally without modifications to any school. A school will adapt and further develop the model to meet its own conditions, requirements and goals.

Whether the Tutorial Community Program is adopted entirely, or in part, or not at all, by a given school, the concepts should be of great interest and importance to everyone involved with education—as a parent, a teacher, an administrator or a citizen. The cornerstones of TCP—the helping relationship, shared planning and decision making, self-learning, proprietary involvement in the community, self-correction through open dialogue—are not new concepts in a democratic society. But making these concepts a reality to children in their daily educational experience is new. Teachers will find that these ideas can be translated into practical and feasible procedures in the classroom. We hope they will be inspired to try them and to urge their wider adoption in their schools.

Over and above the actual steps and procedures is the prevailing philosophy. It is hoped that educators who read this book will be influenced by these concepts of the role of the student, the role of the teacher, the nature and goals of learning, and that these ideas will affect their teaching whether or not they make use of the specific procedures presented here.

THE ORGANIZATION OF THIS BOOK

Chapters II through V are comprehensive "how to" manuals for the four major concepts involved in a Tutorial Community

School. These manuals provide parents, teachers, administrators with enough detailed information to begin implementing specific features of TCP. Included in the discussion of each major concept are the goals, underlying assumptions, general and special considerations, methods, procedures, materials, personnel, time, costs, and potential problem areas or pitfalls and how to avoid or overcome them. Each chapter describes frankly what anyone undertaking an authentic Tutorial Community Program is getting into.

Chapter VI discusses implementation strategy and procedures. The tutorial community concepts can be implemented in a variety of ways to meet different conditions. Both traditional and alternative schools will find some or all of the TCP concepts compatible with their own philosophy and goals. Some schools may choose to adopt the entire program, moving gradually but systematically into it. Some schools may wish to adopt it on an experimental basis by creating a "school-within-a-school" giving parents, students and teachers a choice between TCP or the usual program. Some schools may want to select only certain features for adoption throughout the school. Some schools, or teachers, may adopt certain TCP features within specific classrooms. Whatever method is chosen, Chapter VI describes what resources are required to achive the desired goal.

THE DREAM AND THE CHALLENGE

From one point of view, TCP is a highly ambitious and idealistic adventure. It takes the notion of the university as a community of learners and scholars seeking the truth together, and attempts to apply it in the elementary school. On the other hand, as ambitious and idealistic as it may seem, it is not unrealistic. In fact, it is a very practical handbook for survival in our modern, alienated, strife-torn world. What our schools

Building a sense of community.

and our society need most is a sense of community, of sharing, of working together, of people helping people. That's what TCP is all about. A teacher teaches not just by what he says, but also by what he is. The student observes and learns from what the teacher does, believes and feels, from the teacher's nonverbal as well as verbal behavior. The student learns not only subject matter, but values, habits, attitudes, and beliefs.

Moreover, the child learns from everyone he comes into contact with—the librarian, office clerks, parent aides, custodians, cafeteria workers, nurse. He learns from the environment—whether it is dull, drab and dirty or bright, warm and clean. He learns from the total atmosphere—from the spirit of the place. He learns from observing how adults act with each other, whether they role-model mutual respect, teamwork and cooperation or guardedness, isolation and competitiveness.

Although the tutorial community approach was developed in elementary schools, the philosophy, principles and methods are applicable to all levels of education. At secondary and college and university levels these concepts may be even more critical. "Community" is universal. A brief definition of community by a colleague* and former consultant to TCP captures the essence of the tutorial community school:

> *'Community' means not literally teaching anyone, not literally learning from anyone, but teaching and learning at the same time, all mixed up. It means reciprocal yielding, it means influencing and being influenced at the same moment. It means not always having the right answers. It even means not always having a grip on the best questions. It means coming to someone when you are not ready to come to him.*

---

* Coulson, William, *Groups, Gimmicks and Instant Gurus*, New York: Harper and Row, 1972.

It means not deciding everything for yourself. It means letting others have a say in who you are and it means asking others to let you in, too. (As I say these things about community, it feels like that would be a very safe place to be and to grow.)

In such a learning community, the hypocrisy of preparing children to take part in a democratic society by schooling them in an autocratic environment that promotes followership and dependency begins to disappear. The school is not preparation for life, but living. The life and functioning of the school are inseparable from the curriculum and education of the children.

2 TUTORING and SELF-LEARNING

Educating for Self-Direction and Creative Learning Through the Helping Relationship and Individualized Learning Experience

How many times do teachers bemoan the fact that their pupils do not take responsibility for learning or for remembering what they learn? When learning is a passive act this is a common result. A teacher is distraught with his pupils' achievement test results—it is as if he had taught nothing. He had taught, but his pupils either failed to learn or did not retain what they learned. What is wrong? Is he a poor teacher? Are they poor pupils? Perhaps. But perhaps not. Perhaps there is something wrong with the whole learning environment.

Converting learning from a teacher-directed activity to a pupil self-directed activity is a major goal of the Tutorial Community Program. Setting up a tutorial system in which there is individualized instruction and self-learning through cooperative help and sharing is the means for achieving this goal. As tutor or as tutee each pupil learns as he teaches and teaches as he learns. Not only does each student feel responsible for his own learning; he also feels responsible for someone else's learning, and takes pride and pleasure in this role, as illustrated in the following situations:

> It is not unusual for a student to play sick to miss school. But this might be considered unusual: a sixth grade

student reported to his teacher, "I was really sick, but I made believe I was well so I could come to school and tutor."

A mother says that her son talked her into changing a dental appointment from a weekday to a Saturday so he would not miss school. "I did not want to cop out on my tutee," he said.

An elated mother remarks, "My son actually comes home and asks me for advice. He wants to know how to get younger children to listen better. We are really starting to talk to each other."

The kindergarten and first grade teachers were amazed when they were ultimately told that the eight upper grade students who had been tutoring their children were "social-adjustment" students, considered to be the worst problem children in the school. The teachers had not been told this in advance and judged them by their performance. As tutors in the younger classroom, these children were responsible, dependable, well mannered, concerned, and effective. The upper grade teachers reported that the tutors' work and attitudes in their regular classroom improved tremendously.

A substitute teacher told upper graders arriving for their daily tutoring assignment to return to their regular class. The tutors responded indignantly, "We can't do that. These children need us."

Science fiction? Someone's fantasy of what school should be like? Not at all. These are examples taken from a TCP school where children were given responsibility for their own learning and for assisting others in the learning process.

Examples of how this learning environment develops self-reliance and initiative are numerous. In one classroom, a tutor having trouble helping a Spanish-speaking child said, "I'm not helping you enough. I better find someone who speaks Spanish to help us." The tutor found another tutor who spoke both Spanish and English. The bilingual tutor then acted as a translator for the other two. This proved to be awkward. Finally, the original tutor said to the bilingual tutor, "This isn't working out. You can do a better job of helping him than I can. I'll go find someone else to help."

A fifth grade teacher, returning to school after having been sick for a day, was surprised to find a friendly, appreciative letter from the substitute. This had never happened before. The letter stated:

> *I truly enjoyed working with your class today. It has been quite an experience for me. I like the way they worked together and along with the second graders.*
>
> *In the afternoon they worked independently, and of course some tutored the second graders, after which they interviewed me.*
>
> *They also had a discussion on the type of setup that they are working in. And they all love it.*
>
> *It is so pleasing to see a situation where teacher and pupils are really working together in what seems like a meaningful relationship.*

BASIC CONCEPTS

Individual vs. Group Instruction

Children are by nature good learners—active, curious, information and experience seeking creatures from birth, with strong desires for independence and self-reliance. In their early years they master some of the most difficult skills they

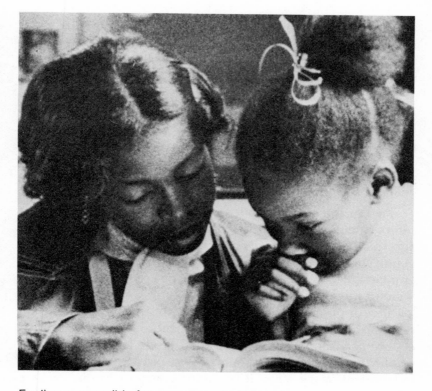

Feeling responsible for someone else's learning.

will ever learn: understanding speech and speaking, walking, feeding themselves, and controlling bowel movements. Much trial-and-error independent exploration goes on, and each child progresses at his own rate. Parents, in a one-to-one relationship, attempt to assist the child without stifling his independence.

Then the child comes to school and is put in a class with thirty other children. He spends a good part of the day sitting still listening to the teacher. He learns only when told to and only what others want him to learn. He is expected to progress at the same pace as others in his mastery of materials and skills. He has little responsibility for, or influence over, what happens in the classroom. He gets individual attention mainly when he misbehaves.

TCP attempts to change this and to further self-learning and helping relationships through a planned program of peer tutoring, student learning teams, and individualized and independent learning activities.

Tutoring as a Central Instructional Procedure

Peer tutoring is not new. (As used in this book, peer tutoring refers to children tutoring other children irrespective of the age span.) It is going on in different forms throughout the country. One unique aspect of TCP is that tutoring is not an appendage to the regular curriculum, or a remedial program in which a few of the highest achievers tutor some of the slowest learners or poorest achievers. In TCP, tutoring and the helping relationship are developed as the central instructional procedure of a school. Everyone, at all grade levels, becomes a teacher and a learner. Although it is an old idea, it is nevertheless revolutionary when it becomes a way of life in a whole school.

The practical results (which include higher achievement) are gratifying, but perhaps even more important are the personal and social gains in terms of character and values. *People helping people* is a value that society must develop to survive.

The Tutoring Relationship Enhances Learning

As Lippitt and Lohman* point out, peer tutoring is an

---

* Lippitt, Peggy; Lohman, John E., "Cross-Age Relationships—An Educational Resource," *Children*, Vol. 12, No. 3, May-June, 1965.

effective learning experience for both tutor and learner for these reasons:

1. Children can communicate effectively with each other because their communication styles are alike; the tutor speaks the learner's language.

2. The older child serves as a model that is appropriate to the younger child's level of aspiration. An adult's abilities, skills, and standards may seem beyond the learner's reach.

3. The older child is less likely to be perceived as an "authority figure" with the inhibiting effects this evokes.

4. Being placed in a position of responsibility motivates the tutor. Assisting other children to learn helps him to develop, internalize and test his own knowledge.

5. The tutor gains insights into the learning process and acquires a better appreciation of the progress he has already made in school.

6. The younger child has an opportunity for positive relationships with older students and develops a more realistic image of the next steps in the growing-up process.

7. Using children as tutors gives more children the opportunity to receive more individual attention and guidance as they engage in learning activities.

New Concepts About Teaching and Learning

Moving into a tutorial system involves readjustments in consciously and unconsciously held attitudes and viewpoints.

Concepts about the role of adults, the role of children, the helping relationship are reevaluated.

The teacher begins to develop a new role as guide and facilitator of learning rather than as sole dispenser of knowledge. Instead of teaching students directly, the emphasis shifts to helping children learn on their own and from each other. The teacher becomes a learner-facilitator.

Teachers are compelled to move from working in isolation to working closely in cooperative relationships with other teachers. Not only do they spark each other with ideas, but they learn to trust, respect and communicate with each other.

As children become involved in teaching other children

The tutor speaks the learner's language.

they begin to feel good about asking for and offering each other help. Competitiveness is replaced by cooperation as students work together on learning teams.

Students are more motivated and take greater responsibility for their own learning. The tutor tries to find the best possible way of reaching his pupil; and not only does the pupil have a stake in showing how apt he is, but he wants to reward his tutor by making him feel that he has been an effective teacher.

Gradual Progression or Phasing

When a new approach is introduced into a school, it should proceed at a pace that is comfortable and will guarantee success. The tutoring program is best developed in four phases, moving gradually from simple to more complex activities in carefully designed, sequential steps. This procedure maximizes the probability of success for both teacher and student at each step. The progression from teacher-directed to student-directed learning moves from a basic structured tutoring program, through a less-structured advanced program to increased student choice, learning teams, interest centers, and independent learning.

Obviously, for a pupil (or parent or trainee or aide) to become a tutor is not a simple matter at all. He has somehow to absorb the insights, knowledges and skills acquired by teachers over long years of experience and training. Likewise, for a teacher to make the transition from director of learning to guide and facilitator is not easy or automatic. These changes do not come about overnight, or simply by willing them. However enthusiastic everybody involved may be, they need practice and experience in relating to each other in their new roles and jobs. Specific provisions and procedures have to be built into the program for sequential training and evaluation as each successive stage is reached. *(See Form 1, Basic Tutoring Program, p. 311; and Form 2, Sequence of Steps in Developing Tutoring, Self-Learning Program, p. 313.)*

The four major phases involved in achieving a tutorial system as a central instructional procedure of a school program are:

> Phase I: Basic Tutoring
>
> Phase II: Advanced Tutoring
>
> Phase III: Learning Teams
>
> Phase IV: Self-Learning

Progress within each phase, as well as from one phase to the next, is achieved through planned activities and procedures which are detailed in this chapter. As a rule, new activities begin with a limited number of teachers and students. When the activity is running smoothly, more teachers and students are gradually added until the whole school is involved. As teachers and students gain experience in the activity, they help train and act as resources for the others.

PHASE I: BASIC TUTORING

A first step in initiating the concept of the helping relationship in a school is the setting up of a structured tutoring program. Within this carefully defined framework the dynamics and procedures involved in the new relationships between paired teachers, teacher and pupil, parent and pupil, and pupil and pupil are worked out. The basic, structured program is not an end in itself. Once the basic, structured program has been established, the teacher can move comfortably into more and more dimensions of the helping relationship and into both formal and informal approaches to self-directed learning, team learning, and classroom self-management.

The tutor serves as a model.

Intergrade Tutoring

The basic intergrade tutoring program starts by having students from one class tutor students from a class at a lower grade level regularly for a specified period of time. The teachers of both classes develop their own plan.

In intergrade tutoring, at first each class either sends or receives tutors, but does not do both. Usually, grades four through six serve as tutors, while kindergarten through second grade receive tutors. Third grade classes may opt either to send or receive tutors.

Each teacher is paired with one other teacher in a tutoring relationship; a teacher sends to or receives from only one teacher. At the outset the older children are assigned to help the younger with oral reading, with emphasis on vocabulary building. Later tutoring extends to all areas of the curriculum.

In order for tutoring to operate successfully as a central instructional procedure in a school, extensive training of tutors and teachers in the philosophy and methodology of the tutorial community program is required. The following steps are generally followed:

1. Training students

2. Training teachers

3. Paired teacher planning

4. Teacher resource groups

5. Teacher observation of tutoring

6. Teacher-tutor feedback sessions

Training Students for Tutoring

We readily recognize the need for teachers to understand the *why's* underlying the what's and how's of teaching. Without a basic philosophical understanding and orientation, teaching can become mechanical, uninspired and uninspiring. Rarely, though, do we try to transmit our ideology of education to our students. Generally the only schools that do this are the experimental or alternative schools, and usually the students in these schools have a greater sense of community because they understand what their school is about and how it differs from other schools.

In TCP the students and teachers are in a close partnership relationship. It is as important for the students to understand and believe in the concepts underlying TCP and the helping relationship as it is for the teachers.

Tutor training takes two forms: general orientation training deals with the underlying philosophy and goals of the tutorial community approach, and specific training explains what to do to achieve these goals. The sending teacher usually has the main responsibility for orientation training and the receiving teacher for specific training. However, it is important that both teachers be thoroughly familiar with both types of training and participate in both.

The training program consists of activities designed to teach the tutor to:

> Understand and value the helping relationship.
>
> Establish a friendly, supportive relationship with his tutee.
>
> Make the learner feel important and successful.
>
> Know the objectives his learner is to achieve.
>
> Know the procedures he is to use as he works with his learner.
>
> Anticipate the kinds of problems his learner may have.
>
> Know some techniques for overcoming those problems.

To keep track of steps taken in training tutors, teachers should complete Tutor Training Checklist. *(See Form 3, Tutor Training Checklist, p. 315.)*

GENERAL OR ORIENTATION TRAINING   In the orientation training sessions, brainstorming, role playing, problem solving, and discussion are used to explore the nature and importance of the helping relationship. Getting to know the tutee and establishing a learning climate that meets his needs are stressed.

The following nine activities, conducted during five to seven sessions of 30 to 50 minutes each, have been developed.

The Lippitt-Eiseman* materials developed at the University of Michigan Institute for Social Research are an important source for these activities.

Activity 1: Introduction to Tutorial Community Concepts and the Helping Relationship

A good way to start, if possible, is to show the TCP film "Tomorrow We'll See What Happens."* After a short general discussion, show the film a second time. *This time* stop after scenes showing students helping other students. Begin the discussion by asking questions such as: Did the students seem interested in what they were doing? How could you tell? Was there anything the tutor did that you particularly liked? How does this approach differ from what you are used to in school?

Another effective activity is to conduct a short demonstration lesson which will show the shortcomings of group instruction and the advantages of tutoring for both tutor and learner. The teacher presents some phrases in Swahili to the class as a whole. He then tests them. This usually shows that they are now at different levels. The teacher asks what would happen if the class pushed ahead as a group. It is pretty clear that if the teacher followed the pace of the average student, some students would fall hopelessly behind and others would become bored.

The teacher demonstrates one-to-one tutoring. The class is then divided into tutors and tutees, or the entire class may be

---

* Lippitt, Peggy; Lippitt, Ronald; Eiseman, Jeffrey, *Cross-Age Helping Program: Orientation, Training and Related Materials*, Ann Arbor, Center for Research on Utilization of Scientific Knowledge, Institute of Social Research, University of Michigan: 1971.

* This 30-minute documentary film which shows what happens as students, parents, teachers and administrators attempt to develop TCP concepts of education is available for purchase or rental from: Films Incorporated, 1144 Wilmette Avenue, Wilmette, Illinois 60091.

tutors and invite another class in to be tutees. They discuss what they must know and do as tutors. They then proceed with their lessons. The lesson in Swahili presented here *(see Form 4, Demonstration Lesson in Swahili, p. 316)* may be used, or any other lesson which presents new material can be used.

Following these activities, a discussion of the tutorial community idea is conducted in which the following basic concepts are developed:

Why change in the instructional program is needed: Traditional schools with one teacher to 30 or more students cannot be sufficiently responsive to individual differences in learners. Group instruction casts the teacher in the role of sole disseminator of information and the student in the role of a passive receptacle.

The direction of the change: Everyone serves as a learning resource for everyone else. All persons feel free to ask each other for assistance. Asking for help when needed is a sign of strength, not weakness. Tutoring helps one become a better learner. Tutoring between classes and within classes benefits both tutor and tutee.

The new learning climate to be established: Cooperative learning replaces competition. Respecting individual differences in rate and style of learning assumes that every student is a capable learner. This becomes obvious when we remember that prior to entering school everybody mastered such complex skills as understanding speech, talking, walking, feeding oneself. Parents helped when it was needed and then withdrew as children became independent. Some children learn some things earlier or faster than other children. This is not necessarily an indication of superior intelligence or a guarantee that the early starter will always remain ahead.

The new roles for students and teachers: The student takes greater responsibility for his own learning. Self-directed learning is a major goal. The teacher becomes a learner and experimenter as his role changes from sole disseminator of infor-

Here, let me show you.

mation to resource person and facilitator of learning. Students learn the skill and art of teaching.

The importance of the helping relationship: Developing a sense of community where everyone cares about everyone else and feels responsible for their learning and welfare has important implications not only for school, but also for family, city, country, world. The goal is to achieve peace and friendship instead of constant hostility and war by replacing suspicion and competition with mutual trust and cooperation.

Activity 2: Tutor-Learner Socialization

Getting the paired classes (upper grade and primary) together to get acquainted with each other increases rapport between the two classes. Later when they get together for tutoring the feeling of "I know you" will be a great advantage. It is the first step in breaking down the isolation of the self-contained classroom. Socialization activities develop mutual respect and camaraderie across age levels. They lay the foundation for building a caring learning community in which people helping people is a primary value.

Although initial tutoring may involve only part of each class, the socialization activities should include all students in both classes. The two teachers begin to establish rapport with, care about, and take responsibility for the children in both classes. The teachers have a chance to observe how specific children interact with each other and may in part base the

Now *you* do it.

selection and matching of tutors and learners for initial inter-grade tutoring on these observations.

In the first few months of the tutoring program, the two paired classes should get together at least two or three times. The classes may be combined, with both teachers supervising together or they may be split, with each teacher taking half of his own class and half of the other. Subsequently, the teachers should have joint whole-class activities as frequently as they deem it desirable and profitable. These get-togethers may be informal and social or they may be more structured. Some sample activities are:

> Lunch in the park.
>
> A field trip.
>
> An art or music session.
>
> An outdoor or indoor game.
>
> A crafts or hobby session.

Each class could brainstorm activities they would like to engage in together and make their selections from among the various student suggestions.

Activity 3: Ways to Help Learners Feel Important and Successful

This activity uses the technique of brainstorming to find as many ways as possible to help tutees feel good about themselves and to motivate them to greater effort in learning.

When people feel appreciated, liked, useful, successful, important, and included it improves morale and stimulates learning efforts. Helping relationships should emphasize the positive.

The teacher may begin by relating something someone did that made him feel any of the above emotions.

Tutors are asked to think of situations in which someone made them feel any of these emotions.

The teacher leads the group in a brainstorming session. Students are asked what kind of actions or situations can evoke each of the feelings mentioned above. All suggestions are listed on the board or on newsprint paper. Students choose the ideas they like best and role play them. The emphasis is on how the learner felt in the situation. The list may be duplicated for student notebooks and posted prominently in the classroom.

Activity 4: Understanding the Role of the Teacher and Tutor

The receiving teacher and tutors work as a team to help the learners. The teacher has the primary responsibility for diagnosing the learners' needs and training tutors in ways of helping. The teacher is available to help when things go wrong. The tutor is encouraged to ask for help when necessary and to discuss his ideas with the teacher.

In his relationship with the tutor, the teacher role models the behavior the tutor should exhibit with his tutee. The teacher praises the tutor at every appropriate opportunity; expresses his own ideas and feelings and elicits the tutor's opinions and responses. The teacher emphasizes that asking for help is not a sign of weakness but an intelligent way to use available resources to solve problems.

To demonstrate and encourage an open exchange of ideas the teacher may have students role play the following situations with each other or with the teacher:

Asking teacher for help.

Giving information about the tutee.

Offering ideas about things to try.

Handling misbehavior.

Activity 5: Difficulties Children Have Learning

To help students understand why some children have difficulty learning, to help them diagnose learning problems and think of ways to help learners overcome these problems, they need to understand that most children *can* learn. Blocks to learning may come from within the child or from external conditions such as teacher behavior, other children, or materials. Understanding the difficulty makes it easier to devise solutions. Patience and interest are very important. Observing and discussing problems with other tutors and teachers may yield suggestions for developing better relationships with learners.

To begin, the teacher asks the tutors to recall any difficulties they may have had as younger children. He may have tutors act out these situations after he has demonstrated role playing with another teacher or with a student.

Role playing can show a situation from various vantage points. Vicarious experience can be gained by playing a specific role. The insights gained are valuable when the experience is encountered in real life situations. Role playing permits trying out and practicing new roles without risk of punishment. It avoids damaging others by providing safe opportunities for making mistakes.

Cartoon pictures are available in the Lippitt-Eiseman materials* showing children having trouble in the classroom. The teacher may also have the children draw their own pictures of a child having difficulty. The pictures are used to stimulate analysis and discussion. The following questions are posed to the tutors:

What is the nature of the problem? *(facts)*

---

* Lippitt, Peggy; Lippitt, Ronald; Eiseman, Jeffrey, *op. cit.*

Why is the child having this problem? *(inference, assumption)*

What is your opinion of the situation? What are your feelings about the child's or the teacher's behavior? *(value judgment)*

The teacher may discuss one situation with the total group and then have the students analyze other situations in smaller groups or in pairs, reporting back to the total group. Some situations may be selected for role playing.

The pictures the teacher or students have drawn on the difficulties children have learning (or the cartoon pictures from Lippitt-Eiseman) may also be used to focus on the teacher's behavior to see in what ways it blocks or facilitates learning. Some suggested questions:

Did the teacher help the child?

What might the teacher be feeling about the child?

How might the teacher feel about his own ability to cope with the problem?

Activity 6: Interviewing the Younger Child

Tutoring is not just a job but a relationship between two people. Knowing each other better facilitates the learning process. A direct way to get to know someone better is to ask questions.

Using the interview form *(see Form 5; Tutor Interview of Tutee, p. 318)*, tutors role-play this activity with each other prior to meeting with their tutees. Following the interview, they discuss their feelings and reactions to the interview.

For the actual interview the two classes split up, with half the tutors going to the receiving teacher and half the tutees going to the sending teacher. At the end of the interview, the tutor asks the tutee what he would like to know about him.

Activity 7: Analyzing Data From Interview

Tutors develop an understanding of the tutees by analyzing answers to the interview questions. They make inferences about how the tutee feels about himself and about other children, school, and teachers. Tutors examine and compare their own feelings with the feelings of the tutee.

Each tutor fills out a data analysis sheet. (See Form 6, Tutor Analysis of Tutee Data Sheet, p. 320.) In small groups (two to four per group) the tutors compare their findings. The groups report back to the whole group and summarize their findings on the board. This summary indicates how many learners like school, how many dislike school, and so forth.

Activity 8: Observation of Tutee in Classroom

This activity provides tutors with first-hand experience about how the younger students act in their classroom. It introduces tutors to procedures, standards, and the atmosphere of the classroom in which they will work.

They may observe that when students are occupied with interesting work within their capabilities they are usually content and do not misbehave. When students cannot do the work, or find it boring, or cannot get help when needed, they become restless and may behave disruptively.

The older students spend at least one hour in the younger students' classroom. The younger students are told in advance that the older students are there to observe how their class works. The older students (no more than ten at one time) sit off to the side and for the most part observe by watching one child at a time. They may be directed to observe from one to three children during the visit. They make notes on their observations (see Form 7, Tutor Observing A Younger Student in Class, p. 321). Tutors discuss observations with sending and receiving teachers shortly after their visit (same or next day).

Activity 9: Preparing the Younger Class to Receive Help

To create a positive and receptive atmosphere for receiving tutors, the teacher lets his class know that he regards being helped as a privilege and an opportunity. The importance of getting individual help in learning is stressed. It is pointed out that the tutor is doing what the teacher would do if he had the time. The benefits of having an older friend are stressed. (The teacher may use the Swahili lesson or any other lesson introducing a new skill to demonstrate the need for individual help.)

Clarification of the teacher's and tutor's role is necessary.

Role play is used to train tutors in their new roles.

The teacher should explain specifically what tutor and learner will be doing. It should be emphasized that the teacher retains responsibility for control in the room and for evaluating each child's progress.

The teacher should not overly stress obedience to the tutor because this represents the tutor as a possible threat. Instead, the emphasis should be on the cooperative nature of the relationship. The tutor should be seen as a potential friend and a supporter.

SPECIFIC TRAINING Specific training prepares the tutor for exactly what he does when he sits down to work with a learner. Usually, with new and inexperienced tutors, three major training activities are conducted in four to six sessions of 30 to 50 minutes duration.

Activity 1: Introduction to the Receiving Classroom

The receiving teacher meets with the tutors in the classroom. He briefs them on his philosophy of teaching, the curriculum for the class, and materials used. They tour the classroom, with the teacher pointing out furniture and seating arrangements, where materials are kept, use of bulletin boards, and the reasons for these arrangements.

Activity 2: Training with Tutor Reading Kit

In the basic intergrade tutoring program in reading, the main emphasis is on vocabulary building. To some extent, the tutor also helps the learner develop word attack and comprehension skills. Vocabulary building is emphasized because it is a relatively simple task with which to develop the helping relationship.

Each tutor is provided with a Reading Kit (*see Form 8, Tutor Reading Kit, p. 322*) which presents the exact procedures, holds materials (flash cards) and provides teachers with a means of checking progress. The tutor also lists words the tutee mastered and missed, logs pages read, and evaluates each session on forms provided in the Reading Kit.

The teacher explains each of the following five parts of the kit:

1. Word Review.   The tutor has prepared study cards with the words missed in previous reading sessions. Before the learner starts to read, the tutor has him read the study cards to see if he has mastered these words.

2. Reading Phase.   The tutor reviews with the learner the part of the story read in the previous session. He then gives the book to the learner who reads as the tutor listens, helps with unknown words and records them on the Word List of the Reading Kit. *(See Form 8, Word List, p. 324.)* When time is up, or five words have been missed, the tutor and learner review what was read.

3. Word Study Phase.   As the learner watches, the tutor prints the words missed on flash cards, spelling each word aloud. He then tests the learner on these new words and places the cards in the kit.

4. Supplementary Activity Phase.   During the last ten minutes of the session, the tutor engages the tutee in a fun reading activity—he may read to the learner or they may play a word game.

5. Evaluation Phase.   The tutor enters comments about the session in the Reading Kit Daily Log. *(See Form 8, Tutor's Daily Log, p. 325.)* He may record problems, successes, feelings about the tutoring and about his relationship with the learner.

The teacher and student role play the entire tutoring sequence using the kit and a sample reading assignment. The sequence begins with greeting the learner and establishing good rapport. The teacher plays tutor; the tutor plays learner. Other tutors observe and take notes. The teacher holds a discussion with all tutors after the role play.

Then student pairs role play the reading sequence before the group. Different pairs take each phase. The teacher leads a discussion after each phase. Then student pairs practice the total sequence with each other. The teacher circulates and gives assistance. Several sessions may be required until students are thoroughly familiar with the materials and procedures.

Activity 3: Training in Positive Reinforcement

Positive reinforcement techniques are discussed and role played with the tutors. The first prerequisite is to develop a friendly atmosphere. The tutor can accomplish this if he: calls the learner by name; smiles; acts friendly; sits close to the learner; engages in informal friendly conversation at the start of each session.

A second positive reinforcement procedure is for the tutor to give support to the learner through the following behavior and attitudes:

> When the learner responds correctly, give him positive feedback by saying something encouraging. People like to know how they are doing and enjoy sincere praise. Vary the feedback. For example, "Right. That's very good." "Correct. You're doing very well."
>
> When the learner responds incorrectly, do not tell him he is wrong or say anything that will make him feel bad. Give the correct answer and then ask the question again, providing the learner a chance to respond successfully this time.
>
> When the student does not respond, wait a few seconds, then give the correct answer. Repeat the

question and have the student respond before going on. If a learner does not know the answer and you wait too long, he may become frustrated or embarrassed.

Do not do the work for the student. If you give the answer too soon, he loses the opportunity to show what he can do.

A third reinforcement procedure aims to encourage independence in the learner. The tutor tries to help the learner find the answers himself instead of giving them to him. He praises the learner for doing the following without being told: asking questions, turning pages, marking answers, locating information, studying independently in an area of need.

Teacher Training

This training involves both orienting teachers to the Tutorial Community Program and teaching them how to train students in the necessary knowledges and skills.

Teachers have to be thoroughly grounded in all major concepts of TCP: need for individualized instruction, importance of the helping relationship, the new roles of teachers and students, the advantages of a learning community where everyone is a learner and a teacher, and so forth.

An overview of different types of tutoring is presented: intraclass, interclass, self-tutoring, formal, informal, structured, unstructured, one-to-one, small group. The four phases from basic to most advanced aspects of self-learning through the helping relationship are described.

The progression from immediate to long-range goals is discussed, starting with the initial basic, structured tutoring program with limited content and time, and moving to the advanced program where everyone is a learning resource for everyone else in all areas of the curriculum throughout the day.

Teacher training includes explanatory presentations, dem-

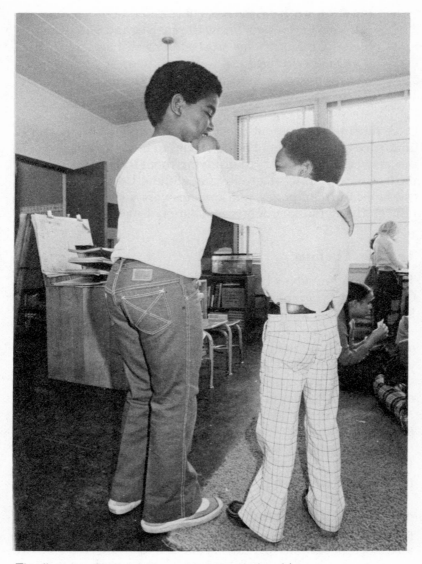

The first step is to develop a friendly relationship.

onstrations, discussions, and role playing. It is similar in content and activities to the tutor general and specific training program. Teachers learn the theory and philosophy of the program and become familiar with the actual materials and methods in order that they may in turn train the tutors.

When the Tutorial Community Program is first introduced to a school, it is important to have one person who is free from full-time teaching responsibilities to coordinate and supervise program development in the initial stages. This person, called the TCP coordinator, may be an experienced teacher, supervisor or principal. The first training workshops may be conducted by this TCP coordinator, or by an experienced consultant, with the school coordinator serving as an apprentice. The teachers who undergo the initial training will, as they become more experienced, serve as resources for new teachers.

Paired Teacher Planning

Vital for the success of a tutoring program is regular communication between the paired teacher team (i.e., the sending teacher whose class will do the tutoring and the receiving teacher whose class will be tutored). The paired teachers need a regularly scheduled period of time to get together for planning. Before each meeting, both teachers should write down an agenda of specific questions and topics to be covered.

Before the tutoring actually begins, these meetings are devoted to planning the specific arrangements. For example, teachers need to decide how many tutors to start with; which students to select initially; where and when the tutoring and the tutor training will take place. Each teacher pair makes its own decisions. *(See Form 9, Paired Teachers' Tutoring Plan, p. 327.)*

Once tutoring is under way, paired-teacher meetings are used to evaluate the program to see what is going well and should be expanded and what is not going well and needs to be strengthened, revised, or eliminated. New ideas and practices develop from these meetings.

Teacher Resource Groups

A resource group consists of from four to six pairs (8 to 12 teachers) of sending and receiving teams. The group meets regularly (at least monthly) with the TCP coordinator to discuss the overall program and to: share information about successful and unsuccessful experiences; ask for and offer each other help; formulate new ideas; and receive feedback from the coordinator based on the latter's first-hand observation of the classroom programs.

As the program expands, teachers will be at different stages in the program and should be able to help each other anticipate and overcome problems and move more smoothly into the advanced phases.

Practical Arrangements

In designing the tutoring program there are many decisions to be made and options to be exercised. There is no ideal set of arrangements for all schools and teachers. Procedures derived from past experience are offered here. The suggestions are largely for the beginning stages of the program. Once the program is fully established and tutoring is pervasive and natural, changes and improvements will be made as needed. Some of the decisions will be made by the total staff, some by teacher resource groups, and many by the paired teachers themselves.

TEACHER PAIRING   Pairing of teachers is generally by mutual consent. Especially in the early stages, it is important to pair persons who want to work together. Establishing an effective program and moving it forward creatively depend on a close and positive working relationship between the two teachers. Once the program is well established and teachers are comfortable with the methods, it should be easier for everyone to work together in all kinds of partnerships. Staff feedback sessions and other mechanisms are designed to resolve communication problems and to bring about a sense of community among the entire staff.

ADJACENT CLASSROOMS   Paired teachers should be in adjacent classrooms to facilitate communication and frequent contacts between both teachers and students. Proximity also makes it easier to extend the helping relationship throughout the day and to other aspects of the curriculum.

PAIRED TEACHERS PLANNING MEETINGS   At the outset, it is important to allow for a minimum of one weekly meeting of 45 minutes to an hour for planning, evaluating, and revising procedures. Teachers have held these meetings before school (sometimes in two half-hour sessions), after school, or (less preferably) during lunch hour. Ideally, planning time should be allotted during the school day. Some schools shorten the lunch hour or begin school earlier, leaving time at the end of the school day. Some schools arrange for early dismissal one afternoon a week to allow time for paired teacher and resource group meetings and feedback sessions. If paired teachers have a good relationship and are in adjacent and connecting classrooms, they have frequent daily contact during tutoring and independent activities. Once the program is well established and teachers have daily informal contacts, the more formal planning sessions may take place less often.

GRADE SPAN   Initially, a span of at least two grades between sending and receiving classes is desirable. This assures that tutors are not so removed from the level of the material as to be bored. At these ages, a two year difference is enough for a younger child to look up to an older child as a role model. Once the helping relationship concept is well established in a school, and everyone is a learning resource for everyone else, the age span becomes less significant. All students will serve as both learners and tutors simultaneously, and combinations may include younger children tutoring older children and low achievers tutoring high achievers in a specific task where the tutors are more knowledgeable or skilled.

NUMBER OF TUTORS   It is best to start with a few children in each class. When the first tutors are trained and functioning effectively, other children are gradually added until all children in both classes are involved. Initial tutors are usually involved in training subsequent tutors under the teacher's guidance. After the first year, when teachers and students are experienced, the program operates on a larger scale. Starting small (with from four to eight tutors) allows the teachers and tutors to gain experience with the program without undue pressure. The full range of problems emerges and can be worked out more simply with the smaller group.

TUTOR-TUTEE RATIO   Usually one tutor is assigned to one learner for an extended period of time. However, when tutors are doing well and request it, they are sometimes assigned to several learners.

SELECTION OF TUTORS AND LEARNERS   To maximize the probability of success in the beginning, pupils should be selected who seem most ready and eager. Observing students during the socialization activities gives the teacher some clues. Leader types (not necessarily the high achievers) are effective in spreading and popularizing the helping relationship concept. Some teachers have started successfully with children who were behavior problems in their own class. Avoid choosing tutees who are the lowest achievers or those with severe learning problems. This could discourage tutors in the beginning. The first tutors should be volunteers. Emphasize that everyone will eventually be involved. The concept of the helping relationship as the major direction for the whole school must be continuously reinforced until it becomes the norm.

MATCHING TUTORS AND LEARNERS   As much as possible, they should be matched for compatibility—including social and achievement factors. Clues as to how they get along may be found during the socialization activities. It is advisable to avoid pairing low achieving tutors with high achieving tutees. Some teachers like to match the top half of the tutoring class with the top half of the receiving class and the bottom halves of each. Special learner needs and tutor strengths are also considered.

Initially, it may be advisable to pair children of the same sex. Boys sometimes resist tutoring or being tutored by girls, although the reverse is usually not true. When both classes are totally involved in tutoring this is generally not a problem. If problems arise with a tutoring pair, changes may be made. However, they should not be made lightly, but only as a last resort after discussion in feedback sessions with other tutors. Problem solving is an important part of the tutor's curriculum.

LENGTH OF TIME TUTOR ASSIGNED TO SAME LEARNER   If the relationship between the tutor and tutee is good, usually one semester is appropriate. Working with one learner over an extended period of time fosters a personal relationship between tutor and learner, facilitates tutor-teacher exchanges concerning specific learners, and promotes tutor understanding of learner needs enabling them to develop effective ways of working together.

However, when other factors (personality problems, boredom, and so forth) make it advisable, vary the stretch of time the same pair works together.

TIME AND FREQUENCY OF TUTORING SESSIONS   Five days per week is recommended: one day for preparation and training; three days for tutoring; and one day for tutor feedback session. After the program has been under way for awhile, a preparation day is needed only when new material or tasks are introduced. Then the tutoring is extended to four days.

Sessions should be kept short at first, about 30 minutes. The tutoring session usually includes 10 minutes at the end for playing a learning game. It is better to have tutor and learner feel the sessions are too short rather than too long. At first, teachers tend to prefer to schedule the sessions during the morning when children are fresher.

LOCATION OF TUTORING   When only part of the class is involved, tutoring usually takes place in the receiving classroom. Pairs may work in the classroom, corridor, library, or outside yard. As the program develops, more options providing variety in locations are actually utilized.

When the entire classes are involved, it is recommended that tutoring take place in both the sending and receiving classrooms (half of the tutors and half the learners in each room). This involves both teachers in observing and supervising. It also avoids overcrowding in one classroom. Teachers can exchange rooms periodically so as to observe all students in action.

KEEPING TRACK   Tutoring schedules are usually posted in both classrooms, listing tutors, the learners they are paired with, where they go, when, and for how long. It should be possible for the program to continue as usual when a substitute teacher is present.

CONTENT OF THE TUTORING   In the tutorial community school, all subjects and activities eventually come within the scope of the helping relationship. Everyone is a learning resource for everyone else in the total curriculum. Initially, however, it is advisable to aim for simplicity and minimize the load on the teacher. The first tutoring tasks should not require an excessive amount of training or preparation of materials. However, it is important to select a task that will have ongoing usefulness. For example, skill in listening to a child read, asking questions or developing sight vocabulary, has ongoing usefulness. When a specific developmental task is assigned to a tutor, such as teaching the alphabet or a specific skill in math, the emphasis should be on developing good study techniques rather than on just mastering the specific skill. It is not the content but the process of learning that is stressed.

MATERIALS   Each teacher should be provided with books and manuals which offer specific and general training in the principles of learning and relationships in a tutorial community. *This School Belongs To You and Me* as well as *Cross-age Helping Program** are helpful. Other recommended books are listed in the Selected Bibliography *(p. 407)*.

Each tutor should be provided with the material (e.g. basal reader, library book) to be used with the tutee, as well as with specific directions spelled out by the teacher for tutoring activities and sequences and ways of recording progress. The Tutor Reading Kit *(see Form 8, p. 322)* is an example of such material.

TUTOR RESPONSIBILITY FOR DISCIPLINE   Tutors should not be expected to discipline learners who misbehave. Tutors are encouraged to discuss discipline problems at teacher-tutor feedback sessions and get suggestions. If a problem arises that requires immediate attention, tutors consult the teacher.

When a tutor is absent, his tutee can join another learner

---

* Lippitt, Peggy; Lippitt, Ronald; Eiseman, Jeffrey, *op. cit.*

The tutor tries to find the best possible way of
reaching his pupil.

and his tutor, or work independently. When a learner is absent,
his tutor can observe others tutoring and make notes for a
feedback session or he can do independent work.

TIME AND PLACE OF INITIAL TUTOR TRAINING   Paired teachers

can exchange classes for training purposes, with the sending teacher providing the general training in principles of learning and the concept of the helping relationship, and the receiving teacher conducting the training in the content to be taught. Or, if the primary class is on a shorter schedule, the training of tutors can take place at the end of the day in the sending teacher's classroom, with the receiving teacher participating. Training sessions may be scheduled at other times if release time is made available through the use of a special teacher or other resource person.

Teacher Observation of Tutoring

During the tutoring period, the classroom teacher must be free to observe the tutors in action. The teacher assists tutors with immediate problems, provides on-the-spot training, and makes notes of things to praise, criticize, or question during feedback sessions with tutors. Both teachers should observe tutoring in action. This is facilitated by dividing the tutoring between the two classrooms.

The teachers look for the following: Are tutor and tutee relaxed with each other? Have they established a friendly rapport? Are tutor and tutee sitting close enough to each other for good vision and hearing and easy comfortable manipulation of materials? Are tutors following the correct sequence of steps as they use the tutoring kits? Are tutors writing legibly enough on the flash cards? Are the tutors encouraging independence in the learners and not doing the work for them? *(See Form 10, Teacher Observation of Tutor, p. 329.)*

As the teacher moves around, he has a good opportunity to give honest and specific praise to tutors and tutees. Periodically, the teacher sits down and follows a tutoring pair through their entire tutoring period. Tutor strengths and weaknesses, and ways of improving are discussed in feedback sessions.

The Coordinator also observes the tutoring sessions periodically *(see Form 11, Observation of Tutoring by TCP Coordinator, p. 330)* and discuss his observations with teachers and tutors.

Tutor-Teacher Feedback Sessions

An important way to guarantee tutor effectiveness is for the teachers to hold feedback sessions with the tutors. Tutors meet with the sending and receiving teachers separately or together, to discuss things that are blocking or facilitating the tutoring process and to share ideas. Meetings take place regularly (once weekly at a minimum). A good time for the feedback session is immediately after tutoring. Sessions should not be held with the whole class at the same time. It is too large for adequate discussion. Half of the class (15 to 16 tutors) for at least 25 minutes at least once a week is recommended. Some teachers prefer shorter sessions more frequently. Teachers may also schedule time to meet with each tutor individually.

During the feedback session, tutors are asked to comment on what went well, what problems they had, and what could be done about them. Tutors are encouraged to offer suggestions to each other. When suggestions are accepted they should be discussed at the next meeting to see how they worked out. Periodically, tutors discuss their tutees' overall progress and their feelings about it. Sending and receiving teachers sometimes exchange classes so that the receiving teacher can conduct feedback sessions with the tutors.

Occasionally, when the tutoring has been divided between the two classrooms, each teacher may conduct feedback simultaneously with a mixed class of tutors and learners. About once a month, both teachers (sending and receiving) try to meet with the tutors during lunch time or at the end of the day.

Feedback sessions are a vital part of the tutorial community concept. They are the means for both personal growth and overall improvement of the program.

One teacher described how these sessions function: "Right after the tutoring with the younger children, we get together and talk about what happened and how we can make it better. I treat them like fellow teachers, and we share ideas, concerns, problems, and suggestions.

"This is a very important part of their own learning. They sharpen their thinking. They learn how to identify problems, evaluate results. They learn about human relations. They learn how to ask questions and how to ask for help and use other people's ideas. It does a great deal for their self-image, and they really start identifying with the whole learning and teaching process."

Potential Problem Areas

The following obstacles may interfere with developing an effective tutoring program:

UNREALISTIC EXPECTATIONS   To develop a new program, especially one that requires significant changes in the roles of students and teachers, takes considerable time and systematic attention. When problems arise, as they assuredly will, some teachers may become discouraged and wish to revert to traditional methods. During the orientation workshops, and all along the way, it must be emphasized that new programs are not perfected overnight. Whenever possible, problems should be anticipated. Realistic expectations and goals should be stressed. It generally takes teachers at least a year to become comfortable in a new role, and a few years to iron out all the bugs and become creative using an approach stressing peer tutoring and self-learning.

TEACHER ATTITUDES   Some teachers find it difficult to change from their traditional roles to becoming a guide or facilitator of learning. These teachers need support and help from the administration and other teachers. They also should be reminded that the school is committed to the concept and the question is not will it work, but rather how to make it work. Also, in the beginning it is advisable to select teachers who believe in the TCP concept and are committed to make it work. As they gain experience in using this new educational approach they are better able to transmit their enthusiasm and know-how to the more reluctant teachers.

ERRATIC PAIRED TEACHERS MEETINGS   If paired teachers do not meet regularly to share observations, evaluate progress, and make necessary adjustments and revisions, the program usually suffers. The value and importance of joint planning and evaluation must be continually stressed.

LACK OF ORIENTATION TRAINING   If the general orientation training for tutors is scant, students do not see the big picture and fail to develop proper attitudes toward the helping relationship. They tend to treat tutoring mechanically.

INADEQUATE TEACHER INVOLVEMENT   If the sending teacher does not observe the tutors in action or hold regular feedback sessions, tutors do not get a feeling of importance. They treat the tutoring as an appendage to the regular program rather than as a major new thrust.

When the receiving teacher does not observe tutors, and spends the tutoring time teaching the part of his class that is not being tutored, the tutors do not receive on-the-spot assistance and the teacher is not effective during feedback sessions with tutors.

INSUFFICIENT TEACHER PLANNING TIME   The load on teachers in any new program is great. In TCP, teachers put in many after-school hours to meet, plan, and develop new ideas, receive training, provide training for others, work out differences, solve problems and prepare materials. The administration should provide release time during the regular school day for some of these activities by arranging for a shortened school day, class coverage by a specialist or substitute teacher, combining classes, and so forth.

MAINTAINING HIGH TUTOR MORALE   During the early stages of the program, when tutoring tasks are highly structured and

The tutor encourages independence in the learner.

largely teacher planned, some tutors may become bored. A good way to alleviate this is to introduce new tutoring tasks which can be alternated with the reading kit. Other techniques to improve tutor morale are: making the tutor feedback session a more social occasion with refreshments being served; providing visible evidence of learner's progress through charts or graphs; daily encouragement and positive reinforcement from teachers; sharing experiences with the entire class; praise before the class; pasting pictures of tutor and learner in both classrooms, with a print to take home; encouraging parents of learners to send notes of thanks; inviting parents of learners to a joint class party or picnic.

Effectiveness Features

Positive, supportive, cooperative attitudes by the principal, coordinator and teachers are crucial in developing a successful and effective program. *(See Form 12, Staff Responsibilities for Tutoring Effectiveness, p. 332.)*

PRINCIPAL'S ATTITUDE   The principal must demonstrate by words and actions his interest in and support of the program. He must be the prime mover and advocate. The principal must be knowledgeable about all aspects of the program. He should periodically observe tutoring, attend paired teachers and resource group meetings, and offer assistance in solving logistical and other problems. He provides feedback and encouragement to the teachers and supports experimentation and risk-taking. He must present the overall picture and long-range goals so that TCP is looked upon as a new way of life and not just as a minor appendage to the regular school activities.

PAIRED TEACHERS AS ROLE MODELS   Both teachers must believe in the importance of tutoring and convey this to their students by words and actions. They must meet regularly with each other and with the tutors and show concern and interest in the children of both classes. The teachers' friendliness and cooperation with each other model the helping relationship.

POSITIVE TEACHERS' ATTITUDES Lippitt and Eiseman* have described some of the teacher ingredients that contribute to successful tutoring programs. Receiving teachers should welcome the program because it provides their students with individualized instruction. They should view tutors as valuable partners. They should share their ideas with the tutors and ask them for suggestions, opinions, and criticism.

In working with tutors, the teachers consciously try to role model the behavior that will help the tutors relate constructively to their learners. The teachers' directions to the tutors are clear and they check to make sure they are understood. They frequently voice their appreciation for the tutors's efforts.

Sending teachers believe they are providing opportunities for their students to feel important, to gain confidence and skill in relating to others, and to improve their capability for self-directed learning. They view tutoring as a way for their students to gain a greater feeling of adequacy, and to grow in self-esteem. They believe their students' own academic work will improve because they are using what they are learning and because explaining something to another deepens one's own understanding of it.

GRADUAL PROGRESSION/SELF-RENEWAL STRATEGY The probability of success is maximized by beginning with a limited number of enthusiastic teachers. The TCP coordinator can give them sufficient attention and follow-up. Once their programs are operating smoothly, they become models and re-

---

* Lippitt, Peggy; Lippitt, Ronald; and Eiseman, J., *op. cit.*

sources for the rest of the staff who are gradually phased into the program.

The peer helping relationship concept applies to teaching staff as well as to students. New teachers are trained by experienced teachers and the more experienced serve as ongoing consultants for the less experienced. One school started with two teachers the first year and had the entire staff involved by the end of the second year. As teachers take over more and more responsibility for each other and for program development, the TCP coordinator position is gradually phased out. The goal is to develop a self-renewing institution which is cost effective and is not dependent on outside resources.

Intraclass Tutoring

In order for the notion of tutoring to have immediate schoolwide impetus and impact, intergrade tutoring is usually undertaken first. Thus the tutoring program begins with significant interaction between children and teachers at different grade levels. This points immediately to a major change in the school's instructional philosophy and program. If the school started with intraclass tutoring and children within the self-contained classroom tutored each other it might not signal a significant change.

Intraclass tutoring usually is initiated when intergrade tutoring is functioning smoothly. The overall philosophy, goals, techniques and procedures for intraclass tutoring are basically the same as those for intergrade tutoring.

The notion of the helping relationship, begun with the basic intergrade program, is reinforced by the teacher's emphasis on students within a class helping each other and working together cooperatively. Initially, the cooperation may be informal rather than planned or structured. For example, children are encouraged to ask other children for help whenever they need it before going to the teacher. Later, the helping relation-ship is systematically developed.

Within a given classroom, time is scheduled for students to help other students with a specified task or activity. The following approaches may be used:

Students are paired to work together in a buddy system for a prescribed period of time on specific assignments in a subject area. Each pair may consist of a low achiever and a high achiever. Pairs are encouraged to seek help from other pairs when needed. Tutoring usually begins with reading and ex-pands to other subjects.

High achievers in a given area are designated as helpers for that area (e.g., reading, arithmetic, spelling, art, music, and so forth). All class activities and areas of the curriculum are covered so that each student is a helper in some area. Names of all helpers and their designated areas are clearly posted on the blackboard. Students go to designated helpers when they have a question or a problem in a given area.

Some teachers have free choice periods where students are all working on different activities That way, helpers in one area do not become overloaded.

The teacher may involve students in the joint establishment of criteria for selection of tutor-tutee pairs. Self-selection may be an important element in initially establishing the buddy system. The teacher makes final decisions and changes as necessary after the program is underway.

The teacher observes the tutoring, offers help when needed, gives frequent encouragement and honest praise, and makes notes for use in feedback sessions.

Interschool Tutoring

A special form of intergrade tutoring involves junior high school or high school tutors coming into elementary school classes. Many of these older students will be returning to the elementary school from which they graduated.

This program has the special value of providing opportunities for students to continue in the positions of responsibility, with the attendant feelings of importance and self-worth, which they experienced in the elementary school.

Interschool cooperation among teachers and administrators allows for an integrated program from kindergarten through ninth grade. It also facilitates the students' transition from elementary to junior high. It gives fifth and sixth graders contact with junior high students who can tell them "what the score is." Reducing the unknown and providing some personal contacts prior to their arrival at the junior high diminishes their anxiety and concern. Further individualization of instruction through intra- and intergrade tutoring within the junior high itself may be promoted.

Because of special logistic problems (for example, busing tutors to and from elementary school, physical separation of paired teachers), this program should not start until the cross-age tutoring within the elementary school is operating smoothly.

The general goals are to:

Provide individualized assistance to elementary school students in reading.

Provide experiences that enhance junior high students' sense of self-worth and their skill in thinking, planning, problem solving, and oral and written expression.

Further the concept of mutual support and peer co-operation among students, both within and between schools.

The basic elements of intergrade tutoring are all applicable: teacher training; training of tutors; observation of tutoring; tutor feedback sessions; paired teacher planning; teacher resource groups.

Specific arrangements include:

Tutors volunteer by enrolling in a special English class at the junior high, for which they receive regular course credit toward meeting the English requirements for graduation.

Seventh, eighth and ninth grade junior high students tutor third to sixth graders.

The tutors receive training one day a week (Monday); tutor the younger children three days per week (Tuesday, Wednesday, Thursday); and have feedback sessions one day per week (Friday).

The junior high teacher provides the orientation training on principles of learning and interpersonal communication and relations.

The elementary school teacher provides specific training in what is to be taught and tutoring procedures to be used. Tutoring usually involves reading and language arts skills, with emphasis on improving comprehension and increasing interest in reading.

Feedback sessions are conducted alternately by the sending and receiving teachers. Occasionally, they hold them jointly.

Tutors keep a diary of their experiences which becomes part of their written English work. Also, they write periodic reports and evaluations of the tutoring.

Minimizing problems that may arise is extremely important. With haphazard scheduling, transportation problems will cause cancellation of tutoring sessions or reduce time for tutoring.

Lack of coordination between sending and receiving

teachers can create differences in expectations and confusion among tutors. Because the teachers are not in the same school and do not see each other daily, it is even more important that they meet regularly to plan, evaluate, and revise procedures.

PHASE II: ADVANCED TUTORING

Getting Started

Phase II is begun when the basic intergrade tutoring program has been implemented effectively. This means that most children are involved in the paired classes, students and teachers are comfortable in their new roles, and the intraclass tutoring program is under way.

When the advanced tutoring program begins, previous procedures and processes—tutor and teacher training, observing tutoring, tutor feedback sessions, paired teacher and teacher resource group meetings—are continued and expanded.

Teachers and students should be ready for the intergrade tutoring to take place for longer periods of time, for more frequent informal contacts between children of paired classes, for tutoring to be extended beyond reading to other curriculum areas. A variety of tutoring tasks and activities will be introduced and developed. Students will have more choices and create their own materials and methods. Classes may have multiple tutoring relations—for example, the same class tutors a lower grade and receives tutors from a higher grade. Paired teachers share greater responsibility for the learning of both classes.

The basic helping relationships will occupy longer periods of the school day, with teacher doing less and less group instruction and students working together and independently (under teacher observation and supervision) more and more.

Expansion of the Basic Tutoring Program

Variety of Tasks

At this stage, the initial tutoring in reading—using the structured tutoring kit, is expanded into other reading activities (reading stories to each other, dictating original letters and stories to the tutor, helping the tutee with library skills). Tutoring also expands into other curriculum areas (writing, arithmetic, social studies, science, physical education, music, art, dance). The following are examples of different tutoring activities and areas:

A learner needs encouragement.

1. Tutors and tutees can make educational games and play them together. They may invent their own games or make adaptations of commercial board games; or they may go to the library to look at game books which contain directions for constructing games. (For example, The National Commission for Resources for Youth has published several such booklets— "Tutor Tricks," "For the Tutor," and others. *See Bibliography, p. 407.* Herbert Kohl describes home-made games in his book *Math, Writing and Games in the Open Classroom.**)

Tutor and tutee obtain whatever materials they need to make the selected game and construct it together. The tutor teaches the tutee or a small group of tutees how to play the game.

These games improve reading, reading readiness, math, and other skills and are usually fun to play for both the tutor and tutee. Constructing games provides experience in planning and decision making and in manual skills, and is an outlet for creative imagination. Sharing is encouraged as tutor and tutee exchange their games or invite others to play their games and develop variations to the basic game.

Some examples of games made by tutors are:

Anagram Opposites: The tutor made up a set of cards with words the tutee had learned in the reading sessions. The tutee picked a card, read the word aloud, and then spelled out the opposite word with anagram letters the tutor had provided (in alphabetical order in egg cartons).

Hidden Words: The tutor made up charts consisting of grids with letters in each box. Each chart had words in a particular category (animals, foods, etc.) hidden vertically, horizontally, diagonally, backwards or forwards, up or down. The tutee chose a category and was shown that chart. He had a

---

* Kohl, Herbert, *Math, Writing and Games in the Open Classroom*, N. Y., Random House, 1974.

given amount of time to point to and pronounce as many words as he could find.

The Price Is Right: The tutor made a large chart of pictures of common school and household objects. Each picture had a price tag. The tutee threw a rubber dart at the chart and counted out the exact price using play money.

Dice High: The tutor threw five dice, kept the highest one and threw four, kept the highest two and threw three, etc. until he had thrown five times. He totaled his score. The tutee then had a turn. Higher score won.

2.   Tutors and tutees can create their own picture booklets about the tutoring. They can take their own photos and together write captions. They will learn a little about photography. In laying out the booklet to show a sequence of activities, they learn how to create a story. Writing captions provides experience in pinpointing and communicating ideas and feelings in writing. These booklets enhance reading practice because there is a high interest level in the content. Sharing is promoted throughout the classroom as students exchange booklets. Contact with parents and opportunities for positive feedback are fostered if the children take the booklets home and parents write thank-you notes to the tutors.

If the students enjoy this activity, they may do other booklets about the teacher, principal, etc. If taking photographs is impractical, students may draw their own pictures or use a collage technique using magazine pictures.

Tutors and tutees can read stories to each other from library books. The tutor and tutee go to the library and the tutor assists the tutee in selecting a book that he wants to read and can understand. If the tutor selects a book to read to his tutee, it should be a story of interest to the tutee. Tutors sometimes have tutees draw pictures that depict their impressions of the story.

3.   Reading to the tutee develops the tutee's listening and language skills as well as reinforcing speech and reading skills for the tutor. Interesting discussions can develop between tutor and tutee as they begin reacting to their stories.
   Other reading activities are:

> Tutor and tutee may read a play together, or a small group of tutors and tutees may read and enact a play together.

> Tutor and tutee read various articles in the tutee's *Weekly Reader* magazine.

> Tutor and tutee read comic strips to each other. Tutor and tutee create their own comic strips.

> In intraclass tutoring, students may be paired to read library books to each other in a buddy system.

4.   Tutors can help tutees learn new songs. The tutor might use a record to teach the words and tune of the song. Tutee and tutor may enjoy working out the melody on the xylophone. Later, tutors and tutees can form singing groups, and both classes may have a joint singing festival. This learning activity helps in vocabulary building and sight reading, and is also fun.
   Variations on this are:

> Tutor and tutee listen to a recording of a favorite song, stopping periodically to write down catchy words, or words that rhyme, etc.

> A trip can be planned for both classes to the public library. Tutors can take tutees to visit the record room.

> Tutor can try to find records with catchy lyrics and rhythms that his tutee might like. Tutors can type the

song on ditto masters and teach the words to their tutees. Copies can later be passed out for a song fest.

Tutors and tutees can try to write their own songs, or write their own lyrics to known songs.

5.   Tutor and tutee can go on a walking trip through the local community. They may collect leaves for nature study. While walking, they read signs, watch men working in the street, and discuss what they see. When they return to class, they can talk, write, paint, make a booklet or a collage about their trip. Looking at familiar scenes in a new way, trying to discover fresh scenery and explore unfamiliar corners of their neighborhood help the students develop observation skills and enrich their vocabulary. Students find this stimulating. It also stresses the idea that the whole community is a source of learning and that the classroom is an integral part of the community. The students may use a camera on their walking trip.

6.   Tutors can assist tutees in using various learning centers in the tutee's room (math, science). The teacher explains the use of the centers to the tutors, and they, in turn, help the tutees use the centers. Tutors learn to explain and give directions.

  The teacher might also have the tutors help make some of the materials for the centers and assist in updating material for the center. Tutors learn how to plan and organize materials for setting up centers and observe and evaluate the use of the center. A group of tutors and tutees might plan and create a center together. Tutors may invite tutees to their room and show them their center.

7.   Tutors can assist tutees in many art-related activities, such as making puppets, cardboard carpentry, painting, assembling a collage, creating a mural, clay work, etc. The teacher meets with the tutors and explains the art activity. Teacher and

The tutor gains insight into the learning process.

tutors plan the materials needed, and the teacher explains how to work with the children in the specific art activity for that week.

If the tutee has made a puppet, he can use his puppet to tell a story, act out a role, or just to talk about himself to his tutor or classmate. If tutor and tutee paint pictures, they may exchange them as gifts for each other or for each other's parents. Art activities lend themselves to socializing and fun, as well as being a source of learning. They help develop warm relationships between tutor and tutee and enable them to learn more about each other.

Eventually the tutor or a team of tutors might plan an art-related activity for the week. Tutors and tutees may work together drawing a mural. They plan their drawing, sketch their ideas on paper and then project their actual work on a mural.

8. The tutor may work on library skills. The tutor who has received training in the use of the library, may periodically take his tutee to the school library and teach him simple library skills (e.g. using the card file). Occasionally they may visit the neighborhood library branch.

Tutor and tutee might work together to set up a miniature library center in the classroom. Thus, as he teaches, the tutor is reinforced in his own learning and improves his own library skills. This kind of individual instruction and follow-up helps both tutor and tutee retain the knowledge acquired.

9. A tutee who is having trouble with reading may dictate stories to his tutor, creating them out of his own imagination. Sometimes a tutee finds it easier to draw a picture sequence and then dictate a story about it. The tutor records the tutee's actual language and helps the tutee read what he has written until the tutee can read it on his own.

Typewriters are excellent devices for stimulating children to write their own stories. Tutors and tutees enjoy typing stories. Tutees are often motivated to write stories and letters just because it is fun to pick out words and to see their own words appear in official-looking type.

Variations on this activity are:

> Tutors help tutees write or type letters to various friends, relatives or teachers and staff.

> When they have written and illustrated a story, tutors might use colorful yarn to outline those words which were difficult for the tutees.

> Tutors help tutees make a comic strip. Tutees draw the pictures and the tutors help with dialogue.

Tutors and tutees write poems, rhymes.

10.   Tutors may assist with physical education by teaching tutees playground games. Tutors serve as play leaders during the physical education period. Play leaders are taught the game by the teacher and later they teach it to small groups of tutees. They may also supervise team games. Play leaders can supervise play areas during lunch and recess time. Tutors may assist tutees in dance activities. Tutees like to emulate the older students.

11.   The tutor writes a note to the tutee's parents to introduce himself and to let the parents know that he is tutoring their child. Periodically the tutor can write to inform the parents of their child's progress.

Many times the parents will take the time to write to the tutor to thank him and to encourage the tutor to continue to work with their child. When the parents do this, it boosts the tutor's ego. He feels good knowing that he is supported by his tutee's parents.

When the tutor and the tutee's parents begin writing notes and calling each other on the phone, this is a high point in the tutoring program. Both tutor and tutee become excited and happy when they see this interaction. Sometimes the tutor's parents get to know the tutee's parents through telephone or face-to-face contact at school or home. The tutor may visit with the tutee and his parents or invite the tutee to visit with him and his family.

12.   The tutor makes a gift for his tutee. A tutee likes to receive gifts from his tutor; the gift has a very personal meaning to him. The tutor takes pride in what he makes for his tutee and feels good about his tutee's satisfaction. If the tutee shares the gift with his parents, they begin to sense the close and warm feelings between the tutor and their child.

The gifts may be items that the tutor has crocheted. Tutors may make objects of wood for their tutees; the gift may be a picture drawn by the tutor; tutors may give a favorite book to their tutees, usually a book that the tutor read when he was the tutee's age; the tutor may make Easter baskets or other appropriate holiday items.

Sometimes the tutees may ask to learn a skill (crocheting, carpentry) in order to make gifts for their tutors.

Longer Time for Tutoring

Formal teacher group instruction is gradually replaced by individualized learning through the helping relationship.

Initially, formal basic tutoring sessions were scheduled for 20 to 30 minutes two or three times a week. In the advanced tutoring phase, this may be expanded to 40 to 60 minutes daily (two or three 20-minute, or two 30-minute sessions).

Intraclass sessions are also held more frequently and for longer periods. The two classes hold intraclass sessions at the same time so younger students can consult both their classmates and their tutors for help as necessary.

Greater Student Initiative and Choice

In the basic program, the tutoring was highly structured with very limited student choice. In the advanced program, student initiative and choice are encouraged:

> Tutors and tutees are offered suggestions for many different activities and can make their own choices.

> Within an assigned activity tutors and tutees have a choice of materials to work from (for example, reading from books of own choice instead of from assigned reader).

Tutors are given a goal and encouraged to develop their own methods and materials. For example, tutors assigned to teach direction words to first graders— over-under, right-left, top-bottom, in-out—develop their own games and physical activities.

More Contacts Between Paired Classes

Students are encouraged to go back and forth between adjacent rooms at various times throughout the day (e.g. during independent activities). A younger student who needs help will go to an older student's room. The older student, when finished with an assignment, may go to the younger classroom to see if he can help. These interactions are facilitated by having both classes schedule independent activities, intraclass tutoring, or team learning at the same time. As these activities take up more and more of the school day, contacts between children in the two classes occur throughout the day.

In addition to formal and informal tutoring, the two classes come together periodically or regularly (weekly, monthly) for joint projects and social activities such as:

Planting vegetables in the school garden

Taking a walking field trip in the community

Having a picnic (parents of both classes are included)

Producing a puppet show

Group singing

Playing games outdoors (mixed teams)

Art-related activities (painting, collage, murals)

Celebrating special events (holidays)

End of year party

Presenting a performance or a demonstration (e.g. gymnastics, play, science experiment, magic show) for the other class or for other invitees

Multiple Class Relations

Initially, a teacher served as either a sending teacher or a receiving teacher, but not both. Students were either tutors or tutees (except for intraclass tutoring, where they may be both at different times).

In the advanced program, as the tutoring sessions are extended, a teacher may serve simultaneously as a sending and as a receiving teacher (for example, a fourth grade class may tutor in the second grade and be tutored by sixth graders; and the second graders may tutor in kindergarten). That is, after the first tutorial relationship is well established, a second relationship may be added. It may be formal with specified tasks, time, and materials; or it may be informal with the older class available to the younger pupils during independent activities and intraclass tutoring periods; or it may be arranged only for whole class joint activities such as those described above; or it may be some combination of these arrangements.

Cooperative Teaching

In the advanced tutoring program, the teachers take more responsibility for the learning of the children in both classes.

During informal tutoring contacts between classes throughout the day, when adult assistance is needed students go to either teacher.

Teachers exchange classes for the presentation of certain lessons, projects, and activities, taking advantage of each other's talents and skills (for example, one teacher conducts art with both classes, the other teacher does music).

Teachers diagnose and plan jointly for special children in both classes (low achievers, gifted, behavior problems).

Potential Problem Areas

Gradual progression is important. Before going into the advanced program, the teacher should make sure the major elements of the basic program are operating effectively. For the advanced program one major new activity should be introduced at a time, and usually with only part of the class at first.

Teachers may move into the advanced program prematurely because they feel tutors are bored (indicated by carelessness, coming late, fooling around). However, these problems usually arise not because the tutoring tasks are boring, but rather because the tutors have inadequate grasp of their role because of insufficient feedback sessions.

Introducing too many new, varied and complex activities simultaneously may not allow sufficient time for planning, training, observation, follow-up and encouragement. Things may begin to fall apart.

As students are given freedom to move more freely between classrooms, some children may misuse it and occasionally become disruptive. Some teachers may want to stop the interaction rather than viewing it as a problem to be solved with students, especially through feedback sessions. If the teacher is process rather than content oriented, he will regard the working out of problems with the students as an opportunity to promote initiative, thinking, self-management. It will not be viewed as taking away time from the curriculum, but rather as an important part of the curriculum. Addressing any problem can involve all the skills of listening, speaking, reading, writing, and thinking, and should be so used.

PHASE III: LEARNING TEAMS

Phase III broadens intraclass tutoring into various team efforts. Learning teams offer students greater opportunities for self-

Camaraderie extends beyond the classroom. Tutors
walk their young friends home.

direction and independence; help them develop higher-level
thinking and planning skills; improve their ability to work
cooperatively and effectively with each other; and provide for
basic skill development in reading and writing, not as isolated
subjects but as an integral part of curriculum projects. Practice
and improvement occur through using basic skills to accomplish a meaningful end, rather than as ends in themselves.

Development of team efforts proceeds from a structured,
teacher-directed form to more flexible student-directed procedures. The TCP coordinator should start slowly with one or

two teachers, adding others afterwards. Teachers also are encouraged to start slowly with one team and expand gradually, enlisting students to train subsequent teams. Just as every individual (student or teacher) is considered a learning resource for every other, so is every team. Learning teams can be conducted at all grade levels. Obviously, action planning techniques will be simpler and less sophisticated with younger students. Also, teams in paired classrooms can use each other as resources. Some teams eventually cut across grade levels.

Unlimited variations in the types of teams are possible. The teacher should maintain an experimental attitude and feel free to try new things.

Intraclass Learning Teams

The intraclass learning team is designed to free students from dependence on the teacher and to foster student cooperation. Initially, the learning team is fairly well structured and uses materials and assignments provided by the teacher.

Getting Started

An orientation session is held with the entire class to stimulate enthusiasm about helping relationships and teamwork. A sports analogy can be used to illustrate the team concept. A good learner utilizes all available resources. Asking other students for help when needed is a sign of strength, not weakness.

To form teams, start with one skill area such as math or reading. Discuss with students the criteria for team makeup, including the need to achieve appropriate mix of skills and ability levels. Have students make suggestions for forming teams with the understanding that the teacher has the final say.

Explain the steps in carrying out a learning task as a member of a team *(see General Procedures below)*. Hold a question and answer period to see if students understand the sequence of steps as well as the rationale for each step:

1. Why check your own work first?

2. Why not look at the answer first?

3. Why ask a team member for help and not the teacher?

4. What is the teacher's role?

Role play all steps, using a brief math lesson as an example.

General Procedures

Within a given class, four to six children of different achievement levels in reading and/or math form a learning team for mutual support. The team procedures are:

1. Each student works on assignments individually. Materials provided must facilitate individualized learning and self-pacing. Programmed materials are helpful.

2. Each student checks his own work. Answer sheets (or booklets) are provided.

3. Each student reviews his own incorrect responses and tries to discover by himself the reasons for his mistakes.

4. When the student can't do a problem or can't discover the reason for the mistake, he seeks assistance from one of the team members.

5. If nobody on the team can help, he seeks assistance from special student helpers (usually two to

four students who are high achievers in specified areas are designated as special helpers).

6. If student assistance is not sufficient, he seeks help from the teacher.

7. Each student keeps records of his own progress.

8. Each team keeps records of team progress (charts, graphs, etc.)

9. The teacher observes and gives assistance where needed.

10. Feedback sessions are held regularly with each team and periodically with the whole class.

11. Procedures are revised as needed.

Potential Problem Areas

Some students will ask team members for help too quickly, without first trying themselves to determine the cause of errors. Before helping, the helper should ask the student questions which will help him to find the source of the problem by himself; e.g. "Did you check your work?" "Did you look in the dictionary?" "Did you read it again?"

Some students will copy the correct answers without trying to rework the problem because they are eager to keep up with or ahead of friends. Without criticizing, the team member or teacher should emphasize the negative consequences of this behavior by pointing out that the student is preventing himself from learning. The self-defeating aspect of this behavior becomes clear if the teacher provides intermittent criterion tests.

If sufficient sets of answers are not available, problems are created. All children must be able to check their own work easily.

Students will sometimes come to the teacher without first trying to get help from other students. The teacher should ask the student seeking help if he has checked with a team member or special helper.

Effectiveness Features

Teachers should observe the teams in action and offer suggestions and help daily, especially at the outset. The benefit of cooperation must be continually stressed. As problems arise, they should be taken up with the whole group.

It is helpful if learning team activities of adjacent classes are scheduled at the same time. Begin with one team in each class. Work out and refine the procedures. When the initial team is functioning smoothly, add other teams until the whole class is involved. When a team is functioning effectively, learning assignments in other subjects may be added. Different teams may be organized for different subjects, but no student should be on more than two teams because it gets too complicated. When the same team takes on different content areas, the operation is simplified.

For students to derive satisfaction from the achievement of other members, it is important to record team goals and post an ongoing, visible record of progress. Display evidence of the quantity and quality of work accomplished by individuals and by the team as a whole.

Tutor Teams

In the tutor team concept, five tutors comprise a team to jointly select, plan, conduct, and evaluate tutoring activities designed to improve the reading skills of their assigned learners.

General Procedures

Materials are provided to the tutors which contain numerous learning activities and simple, self-explanatory instructions. These materials may be teacher-made, or they may be commercial materials such as are contained in:

> *For the Tutor*, National Commission on Resources for Youth, New York, NCRY, 1970.

> *Individualized Instruction: Games That Teach*, King, Hopson P., Encino, California, ICED, 1971.

When the tutor team is experienced, it develops its own learning games and activities.

Each tutor reads through the materials and selects four or five activities he would like to try. Each tutor discusses his choices and the advantages and disadvantages of each activity with the group. The group decides which activities to try and lists them in order of priority.

The group discusses how to conduct the first activity and prepares a simple lesson plan. They attempt to anticipate factors which will inhibit success and suggest ways to overcome them. They also try to identify factors that will facilitate achievement of lesson goals and plan to emphasize these.

Each tutor conducts the same activity with his learner and records the results achieved. The group then evaluates the tutoring process and makes recommendations for revisions. The revised lesson is then repeated.

The group spends some time at the end of each planning session critiquing its own process. *(See Form 13, Group Process Questionnaire, p. 334.)* The teacher observes the students plan together and makes notes. He may tape record the sessions for use in feedback sessions. He offers support when the group requests it or if the group gets bogged down. At the conclusion, he helps students evaluate the group process and recommends improvements.

Potential Problem Areas

Student teams may do a superficial job of shared planning, decision making, and evaluation of their own group process if not initially supported by the teacher. The teacher must provide feedback to the group on their effectiveness. This activity requires a high level of student functioning and the mastery of new skills in group process. To be effective, it is essential that the teacher arrange his schedule so as to be able to give the group suitable attention. It is not an activity that can be started and then neglected.

The teacher's own in-service training sometimes gets slighted because of time pressures. Sometimes teachers initiate team activity with little preparation. The teachers' own experience in group action planning may be limited, and they need ample training and practice to develop enthusiasm and confidence.

Effectiveness Features

Tutor teams should be introduced after the basic intergrade tutoring program (with the whole class involved) and the intraclass learning teams are running smoothly. This allows the teacher time to select and train the initial tutor team while the other activities are going on without his close supervision.

A teacher who is experienced in the tutor team activity trains other teachers. The teacher in training learns what to do and how to do it through direct experience with the materials and procedures to be used with his own tutors. In addition, where possible, the teacher-trainee should also have the opportunity to observe a tutor team in action prior to initiating the activity in his own class.

Sometimes the sending and receiving teachers
observe and consult together.

When a tutor team is functioning effectively, tutors should
conduct training of another team under teacher guidance, or
assist as apprentices when the teacher trains another team.

Student-Initiated Curriculum Teams

A group of students, under the teacher's guidance, decide
together on things they want to learn. Using action planning
procedures, they jointly develop, implement, and evaluate
ways to achieve their objectives.

Action planning is a carefully designed system that can be
used by an individual or a group to move more effectively

toward the solution of problems. In action planning one learns how to define a problem and state objectives, how to brainstorm, how to refine ideas, establish priorities, test for agreement, develop alternative strategies, choose a final plan, assign the right personnel, and establish realistic target dates. Once under way, evaluation and revision procedures keep the work effort focused on achieving positive final results.

Action planning is simply good thinking organized into a series of procedures. It is a major approach used by all planning groups in the school to develop the tutorial community programs. It is also an important part of the curriculum for student learning teams and a significant factor in developing the self-directed learner. *(For a detailed description of Action Planning see Chapter III.)*

Some broad purposes of student-initiated curriculum teams are to:

> Provide rich curricular units of two to four weeks' duration which are developed around students' interests (things about which they are curious and want to learn more).

> Work together as a team to gain increased effectiveness and knowledge through sharing ideas and resources with others.

> Through participating in joint action planning, develop such higher level cognitive skills as thinking, planning, decision making, and evaluating.

> Provide skill development (reading, writing, arithmetic, listening, speaking) not as isolated subjects, but as an integrated part of a curriculum project.

General Procedures

The teacher starts with one team of about five students. The teacher trains the students in action planning techniques through:

Presentation, discussion, and example.

Guiding the students through the entire sequence once, from brainstorming to final implementation and evaluation of a short unit of study.

Observing the students use the process on their own, offering support and feedback when the students request help or get bogged down.

Each team planning meeting should conclude with a brief evaluation of the session: What were the goals, to what extent were they achieved; what factors facilitated or blocked group effectiveness; what suggestions can be made for improving future sessions? A more detailed evaluation using the same basic questions should occur at the conclusion of major phases of the project. At the completion of the project, the teacher helps the students to evaluate the total process and to make recommendations.

Team activities will vary in duration. A team may be organized to accomplish a single, short activity within a few days (for example: find out all you can about traffic problems in this neighborhood), or the learning task may extend over a longer period of two to four weeks, until certain information is obtained; or it may take an extended period (two to four months) to accomplish a project in depth requiring considerable research (for example: plan a model city and prepare a scale model). Complex materials and the use of the outside library and community may be required.

The number of students on a team (usually from three to five), and the criteria for grouping students will vary. The teacher should experiment with different size groups and

The tutor can construct his own games and materials.

arrangements and should involve students in discussions about size and selection.

End products of student curriculum teams may be reports, displays, and interest centers. Sometimes a project results in the creation of an interest center or workshop with the curriculum team serving as facilitators for other students to explore the topic.

Once one team is operating smoothly and has completed the action planning sequence for at least two units of study, a second team is organized and trained. The members of the first team assist the teacher to organize and train the second team. The process is repeated until all students are members of a student-initiated curriculum team.

Potential Problem Areas

In the beginning, students tend to rely on teachers to make decisions and solve problems. Also, teachers are apt to guide too strongly; the tendency to want to "teach" and take over is formidable. Teachers must resist this and encourage students to use their own resources as much as possible.

Evaluation of the group process often gets slighted. Teachers should see to it that time is set aside for evaluating each planning meeting and the various stages of the project.

The teacher may try to impose his curriculum ideas on students or push them prematurely to a decision. The emphasis should be on developing the group process and problem-solving ability of youngsters and not on turning out a report.

A teacher who has insufficient experience with action planning may skip steps and take short cuts. Teachers should develop knowledge and confidence by observing and/or assisting an experienced teacher before initiating this activity.

PHASE IV: SELF-LEARNING/INDIVIDUALIZATION

Underlying Concepts

One of the major goals of education is to produce self-learners, persons who can learn on their own. A self-directed learner has a growing ability to independently formulate problems and goals, consider alternatives, make choices, develop plans, use human and material resources effectively, evaluate his own progress, revise objectives or methods, and work at a learning task alone or with peers as co-partners without the direct and continued supervision of an adult. These skills are gradually and systematically developed in a tutorial community school through one-to-one tutoring relationships, student team experiences, and, at the advanced stages, through independent projects.

Quality education which would produce self learners cannot take place in a classroom in which 25 to 35 children with a wide spread in achievement in all areas are treated as a group and are required to cover the same content at the same pace in the same way, rarely if ever receiving individual attention or instruction.

The best learning takes place when instruction is organized to consider learners' individual differences in ability, interest, motivation, learning style, and level of achievement. This requires treating each child in a classroom as a unique individual, adapting instruction to each child, and providing a variety of choices in goals, materials, procedures, pacing, instruction, and setting.

"Individualized instruction" and "individualized learning" are not synonymous. All learning is individual. Instruction can be varied to suit different students. However, individualization is not synonymous with self-learning. Self-learning includes both working alone and making choices. It is possible to individualize instruction while giving students little opportunity for free choice, and it is possible to give a student complete freedom of choice without individualizing instruction. Many people have tended to equate the two, believing either that individualization of instruction means students must be given total freedom of choice in what they do at school, or that allowing students to do whatever they choose means instruction has been individualized. These interpretations are not valid. For example, if the student is working with programmed materials or computer assisted instruction, he may be working independently at his own pace without ever having any choices to make. Also, if all the choices available are beyond the student's present skill level, he has no genuine choice at all. Also, when a student is being tutored by another student, he is receiving individual instruction, but not necessarily growing in his ability to become a self-learner (to work alone and to make choices). On the other hand, when a student functions as a tutor, he is also developing his ability as a self-learner.

In a tutorial community all aspects of the instructional process are subject to individualization—objectives, content, materials, instructional assistance, methods, pacing. However, individualization is not an all or nothing situation. We can approach the ideal by dealing with one aspect at a time. Self-learning skills must be developed gradually under guidance. Self-learning does not mean *complete* freedom of choice and *always* working alone.

If students are to become capable self-learners, experiences that foster the ability should be encouraged and planned from the earliest possible moment, beginning in kindergarten and preschool and continuing throughout the student's career. By giving students continuous practice in making a large number of small decisions, they will be better equipped to make larger decisions and assume more and more responsibility for their own learning.

There is no easy blueprint or guide to what decisions and tasks children at different ages are ready to handle on their own. Teachers at each level will have to experiment and constantly keep in mind the goal of making children independent of the teacher.

Interest Centers

An *interest (or learning) center* is a territory set aside where a student may explore a given aspect of the curriculum (science, math, art, sports, animal life, reading, and so forth). A variety of materials at varying levels of difficulty related to that aspect are concentrated in the designated area. Emphasis is on student experimentation and discovery, although some centers may be highly structured. The students can work independently or with one or more classmates. Materials may include everything from standard texts to programmed materials, live animals, geometric shapes, cuisinaire rods, and junk.

Centers may be teacher-initiated or student-initiated. Usually, the program starts with the former and moves toward the latter. Eventually both of these are in the classroom.

Teacher-Initiated Centers

Planning: Teachers who want to provide a rich environment responsive to individual differences must first become familiar with their children's interests and styles of learning. The teacher should keep a list of ideas for potential centers which can be developed through action planning with students. Ideas can also be obtained from books on individualized learning. Centers should be diverting and also provide learning experiences. Ideas for materials and activities, as well as step-by-step procedures for planning, organizing and evaluating centers can be found in various books on student-centered learning, such as the following:

> Darrow, H. F., and R. Van Allen, *Independent Activities for Creative Learning*, New York, Teachers College Press, 1961.

> Glasser, Joyce F., *The Elementary School Learning Center for Independent Study*, West Nyack, New York, Parker Publishing Co., Inc., 1971.

> Lorton, Mary B., *Workjobs: Activity-Centered Learning for Early Childhood Education*, Menlo Park, California, Addison Wesley Publishing Company, 1972.

> Stohl, Dona K., *Individualized Teaching in Elementary Schools*, West Nyack, New York, Parker Publishing Co., Inc., 1971.

Taylor, Joy, *Organizing the Open Classroom: A Teacher's Guide to the Integrated Day*, New York, N.Y., Schocken, 1974.

Skill Development: Students will be exploring, inquiring, discovering, observing, and reporting. The skills of reading, writing, listening, and speaking will develop as a by-product of these tasks. However, some centers may involve direct training and drill in one or more of these skills. For example, a center may be an IBM terminal hooked up to computer-assisted instruction (CAI) programs. Also, students may use various kinds of programmed materials and workbooks. The students may assign themselves to these centers when they are aware of needs, or the teacher, making his own diagnosis, may assign students.

Gradual Progression: It is wise to start slowly and expand gradually. Begin with one or two centers; then increase choices available at each center. Then add one new center at a time.

Teacher training:

1. Initial orientation about centers is received from an experienced teacher, either one-to-one or as part of a group workshop. Sometimes the workshop is organized as an after-school or evening or weekend course for which teachers receive credit towards salary increments.

2. Opportunities are provided for observation of interest centers in an experienced class, followed by questions and discussion.

3. The new teacher plans and implements a center, using the experienced teacher as a consultant when necessary.

A tutor and her pupil work in a learning center created
by a student team.

Cooperative teaching (paired teachers):

1. A new teacher may be paired with an experienced
    teacher at the same grade level to get started. The
    first center may be borrowed entirely from the
    other class. By replicating a center which has been
    successful in stimulating student interest and learn-
    ing, the new teacher can get the feel of a center and
    have some assurance of success without the pres-
    sure of detailed planning, organizing, and develop-
    ing or obtaining materials.

2. Later, paired teachers can exchange centers and
    share materials. This reduces the amount of work

and effort required of each teacher and increases the variety of experiences for the children, as well as the probability of success. The paired teachers meet periodically to evaluate the centers, exchange ideas, and make new plans, focusing on how they can cooperate to facilitate and enhance each other's work.

3. Initially, students use centers within their own room. Gradually, arrangements are made for students to have access to centers of paired classes. The pairing and sharing can be with the same grade level or between two classes paired for tutoring.

4. Teachers observe in each other's classrooms and offer comments and suggestions.

5. Three or four groups of paired teachers (tutoring pairs) meet periodically as a teacher resource group. (This is usually the same group that meets to improve the tutoring program.) They share successful and unsuccessful experiences, ideas, and materials. Further exchanges of centers take place. They list problems and seek solutions together. A group of six or eight is small enough for everyone to participate and large enough to be a rich source of ideas and assistance. They use action planning to develop ideas for new centers.

Training students:

1. Students must receive orientation and training in the purpose and use of centers. Orientation may involve all the students in the class, but should be conducted with small groups. They must learn to use one center at a time. The first students to use it can be used to train other students.

2. Students from within the class or from another class may be trained to tutor at the center and will then help teach students to use the center.

Teacher observation of centers:

1. The teachers observe children at work in the centers; help them stretch beyond where they are; ask them questions; help them formulate better and better questions; see what basic skills they are lacking; and direct them to experiences that will fill the gap.

    The teacher is himself an experimenter and a learner. The teacher observes whether the center is stimulating student interest and learning, and must change centers when they have outlived their usefulness. The teacher must learn from the students, listen to them, tap into their interests, find out what turns them on, and thus gain clues for new projects, centers, and environmental changes that will promote learning.

2. The teacher encourages children to work independently, but is available as a resource when needed. He gives on-the-spot help and praises and encourages. He models the role of an interested, excited learner. The teacher may himself work on a project at a center—whether weaving or fixing a clock or writing a story—and share his work process with the students by verbalizing what he is doing as students observe and question him at work.

3. The teacher creates an atmosphere and environment in which children want to learn and have the resources and materials to do so. He attempts to have the children participate increasingly in creating that environment.

Feedback sessions:

> The teacher meets periodically with the whole class or with small groups or with individual students to share impressions and observations. He gives students both positive and negative feedback and elicits the same from them.

Student-Initiated Centers

Student-initiated centers are developed by students under the guidance of the teacher using brainstorming and action planning methods. The teacher helps the students to plan, to make decisions, to obtain materials, and to pursue learning activities.

When centers are developed by the student-initiated curriculum teams, the team trains other children in using or expanding the centers.

Potential Problems

Teachers frequently start too many centers at one time and cannot follow up properly with materials, observation, and student training. A gradual approach is needed.

If students are prematurely given complete freedom of choice, the result is generally chaos in the classroom. There must be a gradual increase in freedom of choice of centers, materials, amount of time, manner of reporting, and so forth.

If training of students to use the centers is slighted, it may result in misuse or lack of use. Teachers must constantly observe students at work in the centers. Do not equate presentation with learning.

If teachers do not share ideas and materials, centers will become a drain on their time, energy, and emotions.

Teachers may abandon a center prematurely, or keep one after it has outlived its usefulness, if they do not pay attention to student needs and ideas and discuss problems and seek feedback from other teachers in paired teacher and resource group meetings.

When teachers have put energy into preparing a center, they may sometimes be reluctant to change it even though students show little interest.

In observing and facilitating the work of students, some teachers interfere too much and do the work or thinking for the students. This may be the result of an overemphasis on the product rather than concentration on improving the student's learning process.

Teachers may mistake fun and diversion for learning. The teacher should be clear about the main objectives and have a check list and a means of evaluating progress. However, it is true that many by-products or unplanned results may be as or more important than the anticipated goals, and may be difficult to measure.

Effectiveness Features

The teacher must be willing to be a learner and experimenter. There is no hard data on the ideal kind and number of centers, number of activities at a center, frequency of change, or duration of a student project. These vary for different teachers and for the same teachers at different times and with different students. It is important to be open and flexible.

Teachers should not compare or measure their rate of developing classroom centers by that of other teachers; they should be guided by their own needs, styles, and sense of well-being.

Record keeping and evaluation should be simple. Students should keep their own records of progress and results, with the teacher checking periodically through his own check list, special tests, and individual conferences.

Parents can provide another adult resource in the room,

obtaining materials, and evaluating the progress of individual children.

The principal must be the main facilitator in helping teachers find time to plan, observe and obtain materials, and in providing space, materials, and encouragement.

Independent Study

Students vary in their ability to work independently at self-originated projects. Generally, a student who finishes assigned work by himself and is a high achiever may be encouraged to move ahead in independent work.

Such students are then given great leeway to work by themselves and plan their own weekly and daily activities. They continue with team efforts or tutoring assignments (and a few whole class activities), but are free to work independently on activities of their own choice for a few days of each week.

Gradual Progression

Initially, the teacher will work out with the student his broad goals for the week (for example, what type of reading or writing project and how the teacher will evaluate progress). The student makes his plan and discusses it with the teacher, who may suggest some revisions.

The student keeps a daily log of what he did.

The student writes a weekly report answering the following process questions:

Did you have a good week or bad week and why?

To what extent were objectives achieved?

How closely was your learning plan followed (time, place, content, activities, materials, and so forth)?

What caused deviations from plan? Were they beneficial?

What did you learn about your own working habits, attitudes, learning process?

What did you like most about the week's experience?

Least?

What changes do you plan?

What kind of help do you need to do a better job next time?

The report is submitted to the teacher, who reads and discusses it with the student. The teacher makes suggestions and provides assistance when needed.

When the student appears ready (he is using time effectively or requests more time), independent study is expanded to the entire week.

Gradually, more students begin working on independent contracts. As the process continues, the number of students and the amount of time they work independently increase. The schedule may begin with three mornings per week, increasing to five mornings weekly, then to three full days and two mornings, and finally to five full days.

The teacher confers with each student at least once weekly while other students are engaged in intraclass tutoring or learning teams. Students may suggest curriculum projects or studies or the teacher may offer suggestions.

Potential Problems

The main problem is loss of confidence by the teacher when things go wrong, if for example, the student doesn't accomplish much work and appears to be "wasting time." The tendency is to believe the student is not learning anything if he is not "busy" every minute. Although daydreaming has no measurable learning value, the teacher must realize that not all random activity or inactivity is a waste of time and that some "goofing off" may be valuable. However, where it seems to be out of proportion, it needs to be confronted. Each student's ability to function independently develops differently. The teacher's job is to keep experimenting with new ways of fostering independence.

Similarly, administrators must realize that the teacher's progress in promoting independence will be uneven and they should provide constant encouragement, training and support for the teacher.

A student curriculum team engaged in a self-initiated baking project.

Effectiveness Features

Eventually, all students will be working most of the day without direct supervision and teacher control, independently, as part of teams, in tutoring relations, or at interest centers— with ever increasing student choice of content studied and methods used.

As the number of students working independently increases, the amount of time the teacher can spend with each one in individual conference diminishes. It is very important that teachers train students to criticize and evaluate each other's work and to give each other feedback both about the results of their efforts and about their learning process. Students on independent contracts may be trained to use process questions (see p. 334) in pairs and in small groups. The teacher may also begin to have the pairs administer tests to each other, score them, and interpret and discuss the results.

Students working independently may at first miss things that the teacher would have called attention to, but they will get better and better at getting the most out of what they are doing. The payoff in improved self-confidence, self-concept, responsibility for learning, and understanding of the learning process will be enormous if this process is started early and continued.

Student Self-Management

The goal of self-management is to develop in students a sense of proprietorship of their school. The classroom is not isolated from life, it is life itself. The school is a community of people living together, not merely preparing for life. The mottos of the classroom community are: Don't do anything for the child that he can do for himself. Give children as much responsibility as they can successfully handle in developing the classroom community.

The challenge in child rearing is to give children as much

freedom as possible so they can become self-directed and self-confident persons, while providing as much structure and guidance as necessary to prevent them from hurting themselves and each other or from being insensitive to the needs and rights of others.

Involvement in planning and decision making and self-government cannot start too early. People do not become wise overnight, nor does wisdom come just with age. Giving children choices and responsibilities that are age appropriate prepares them to become self-directed, responsible, cooperative decision makers.

The following activities have been tried out in TCP schools to develop self-managing and self-governing skills and to promote a sense of community in the classroom. (They complement the other student-centered activities such as student tutoring, team learning, and independent study.) The list is not exhaustive. Teachers and students are encouraged to use the action planning process to develop as many ways as possible for students to take responsibility for managing their own classroom to make it a living-learning community.

Classroom Activities

Getting Acquainted: The teacher uses the first day to get to know the children informally and to introduce them inductively to the notion that they are to have choices and decisions. At the outset the classroom is emptied of furniture, or all furniture (desks and chairs) is pushed to one corner or against the walls, so that the center of the room is clear. The teacher prepares six or seven different activities which students can work on in teams of four to five on the floor.

After greeting the students and introducing himself, the teacher describes the activities and has the students choose the ones they want to work on. (For example, in one corner there is a pile of junk: buttons, bottle tops, etc. The task is to sort the items according to size, shape, color, etc.). Meanwhile, the teacher roams around the room observing how the students work, making comments, asking questions, finding out something about the students and their interests.

Room Arrangement: A class discussion is held about the room arrangement and the type of goals it should help facilitate (individualization, teams, interest centers, and so forth). Have groups draw up room plans and be prepared to justify their plans. The class selects the best plan and implements it. After a month, the class meets again to evaluate the room arrangement and to propose changes.

Taking Attendance: A class list is posted where children come in. Children check their names off or they use name tags on nails to indicate "in" or "out." A student is assigned to make up a daily attendance list for the main office.

Check in-Check out: A similar system can be used throughout the day whenever a child leaves the room (for tutoring, to the infirmary, office, bathroom and so forth) and returns.

Morning Activity to Start the Day: The teacher involves students in planning activities to begin each day in an exciting and interesting way. Examples include singing, spelling game, math game, Simon Says, and guessing games. The whole class may decide on activities to be pursued for a week or more, or the class may be divided into five teams with each team responsible for planning and conducting the activity each day.

Activity to End the Day: The day can end as it began, with group games or activities. The children plan exciting or interesting activities to end the day.

Milk and Lunch Money Count: Students record their intention to purchase milk or lunch on a check sheet. Two students are appointed each week to make the tally and give the report to the teacher.

Establishing Classroom Rules and Standards: The class discusses what they like and dislike about classroom life, what works and doesn't work, and the reasons for regulations. Students are divided into teams to draw up rules and standards to present to the class which then makes decisions through consensus. The list that results from this discussion is posted in the room. What to do about violations of standards is also discussed. The standards are evaluated and revised monthly.

Electing Class Officers: A discussion is held about classroom jobs and responsibilities and on qualifications of candidates. Rules are set up for nominating, voting, and terms of office. The candidates prepare campaign speeches. The election is held. After each term of office, the total process is evaluated and changes made.

Clean up Responsibilities: Each area of the classroom is assigned to a student team for clean up. Class officers may conduct an evaluation of the effectiveness of each team and maintain an ongoing graphic display of results.

Suggestion Box: To encourage evaluation and constructive criticism, a suggestion box is provided. Suggestions for improvement of the classroom and the school as a whole are treated separately. Class officers screen suggestions and with the teacher decide which should be selected for class discussion. Following the discussion, decisions are made on implementation.

Post Office System: Have individual mail boxes for each student. Encourage the children to write notes and letters to each other, to their tutors or tutees and to the teacher. The mailman of the day or the week can sort and deliver local mail (intra-class) or out-of-town mail (inter-class).

Classroom Bulletin Boards: Assign different wall territories to various student teams. Each team can use its space in any way it decides: to post work, ideas, thoughts, humor, or whatever.

Hallway Bulletin Boards: Assign wall space in the hallways to each class. Each class decides how to use its space. Displays may include the work of children, teachers, parents. Action planning may be used to arrive at group consensus on how to use the space. The class may divide its territory into smaller areas and assign each area to a student team.

Handling Problems: Once a week students discuss class and school problems and how to improve the learning and interpersonal atmospheres. Suggestions may be made in teams and then discussed with the entire class. The class decides on recommendations to be forwarded to the Student Council.

Inputs to School Newsletter: Set aside some regular class time for the children to write brief contributions (anecdotes, notices, jokes, serious, informative, amusing class news) for the school newsletter. The children may read aloud what they've written and decide together what to submit to the newsletter. Primary children could dictate items to their older tutors. Items not sent to the school newsletter may be used for the class newsletter.

Class Newsletter: Students meet regularly in teams to prepare items for their newspaper under designated headings (tutoring, monster jokes, personality of the week, sports, something from home, and so forth). Teams take turns being responsible for putting together the final paper.

Students are encouraged to keep a daily diary and use that as a source for newsletter items. Their diaries may have such headings as: what happened today that was funny, sad, interesting, unusual, exciting, dumb; something I liked, didn't like, and so forth. Primary students could receive help from older children of paired class. The newsletter is sent home to parents. Parents are encouraged to submit items for the class newsletter.

Hosting Class Visitors: A class meeting is held to discuss what the class would like guests to know about the room. A guidebook is prepared for guests on how to observe in the class and what to look for. Guests are asked to fill out a questionnaire afterwards, giving their reactions to what they observed. A weekly host and hostess may be selected to greet guests and show them around the classroom. Parents are encouraged to visit class often. A class goal is for each child to get his own parents to visit at least once each semester.

Citizen of Week: Each week, the class selects one to three students who have performed some outstanding act of good citizenship. A child who wants to nominate someone writes a paragraph to justify the nomination, describing some outstanding action (stopped a fight, showed courage in giving critical feedback to teacher) or some consistent behavior (always on time, keeps area neat and clean). A variation would be for any child who wishes to complete the sentence, "I believe I should be elected good citizen of the week because... " Commendations are read to the class which then selects the three outstanding ones and ranks them. Polaroid pictures are taken and posted in the classroom with descriptions underneath of the acts of the good citizens. Descriptions are also printed in the class newsletter. The first choice is sent to the Student Council to compete for the schoolwide "Good Citizen of the Week Award."

Most Improved Person (MIP): Every so often (eight to ten weeks) the class votes on the MIP in various areas, e.g. feedback sessions, reading, spelling, arithmetic, sports, art. The teacher presents the awards at a ceremony. Students develop criteria and selection procedures with the teacher. Results are publicized in the class and school newsletters.

Most Improved Team (MIT): The same procedure as above for class learning teams.

Grading Tests: Most of the time children will grade their

own tests. Periodically, special progress, diagnostic, or mastery tests will be graded by students trained to do this job. These students will help train other students.

Lesson Plan for Teacher Absence: Students plan and conduct class when the regular teacher is absent. Definite responsibilities are assigned to each student team. Written instructions are prepared describing the roles of the student teams with or without a substitute teacher present.

Holiday Festival Plans: Each student team is assigned to study a different holiday and plan a class celebration. Each team is responsible for planning and conducting the class activities for the holiday on the designated day.

Planning Field Trips: Student teams brainstorm a list of places to visit. They gather information, and make a report to the class using literature, pictures, and other materials. The class decides by consensus which places to visit. The students discuss what they want to find out and plan the trip and the follow-up activities. The students help to recruit parents to accompany them on the trip.

Student Self-Evaluation: At the end of each reporting period, as part of the regular report card, the students evaluate their own progress in all areas—academic, social, physical— and assess their own need for improvement or help.

Students also evaluate teacher performance and other aspects of instruction and class life. Some of the things that students have reported on are:

> Was I able to get help from the teacher when I needed it?
>
> Did I get adequate training to be a tutor?
>
> Did the teacher listen to my suggestions during the tutor feedback sessions?

Was the teacher accepting of criticism during class feedback sessions?

Were the materials available to me for tutoring and self-learning adequate and interesting?

Did the teacher allow and encourage me to make decisions about the content of my learning and my time schedules?

Was the teacher friendly and cheerful most of the time?

Student Record Keeping: Students keep track of their own progress—the quality and quantity of their work—using check sheets, graphs, forms or grade books.

Student Contracts: Each student makes out a written plan to complete certain assignments and responsibilities within a given period of time. Students may plan weekly or monthly goals and activities.

Class Feedback Sessions: Children are provided regular opportunities to voice their opinions and feelings about their school life. Students can express freely what made them feel good or bad, including what the teacher contributed. These feedback sessions can take place daily at the end of the day for 10-15 minutes, or one to three times weekly for a longer period of time.

Student-Parent Council: Student officers meet periodically with the class parent council to discuss ways to improve the class and further the development of the classroom community.

Schoolwide Activities

Hosting School Visitors: On a rotating basis, each upper grade class takes responsibility for selecting students who will show visitors around the school. These students receive training in conducting school tours and in turn train students who succeed them.

School Post Office System: All students are encouraged to write to each other, to the principal, teaching and nonteaching staff, and vice versa. Each upper grade class rotates responsibility for running the postal system. This includes the collection, sorting, and delivery of mail for a month. Mail boxes are placed throughout the school.

Suggestion Box: Students, teachers, nonteaching staff, and parents are encouraged to make suggestions about changes they would like to see made in the school. Suggestion boxes are placed at strategic locations in the school. The Student Council screens the suggestions and decides which ones require action. A list of the suggestions is published in the newsletter, along with the disposition made of the suggestions. Outstanding suggestions are also posted on a hallway bulletin board.

Committee Representatives: The Student Council selects students to serve as representatives on the TCP Committee and on any other faculty committees designated by staff.

Effectiveness Features

Teachers can find many opportunities to develop student initiative, self-management, and decision making skills once they have changed their attitudes about the role of the teacher, about what a classroom is, and about the capabilities of children. Teachers must regard student self-management activities not as peripheral to the curriculum but rather as an integral part of the curriculum itself. In attempting to learn how to govern themselves and take responsibility for their own lives, children will make mistakes. Making mistakes and experiencing the consequences of actions are important steps in learning to make decisions. These skills are hard to learn and teachers must resist the tendency to give up and revert to a teacher dominated relationship when things go wrong.

Most of the activities described can be carried on with almost any age level. Of course, adaptations will be necessary for the younger children. Beginning with the early grades, many activities are repeated each year at more and more sophisticated levels. Older students help the younger with many of these activities.

As this type of classroom community develops, the rewards for the teacher and the payoff for the children are considerable. The teacher no longer has to feel and act like a policeman. The children no longer need to feel as though they are in jail. The adversary relationship between student and teacher changes to one of colleagueship. The teacher becomes a community leader, a guide and, above all, a learner. As the teacher shows greater respect for the children and their capabilities and clearly expects that they can become self-governing and self-directed, it becomes a positive self-fulfilling prophecy.

ADDITIONAL IDEAS IN FOSTERING TCP CONCEPTS

Ungraded or Multiple Age Groupings

Because of wide individual differences in achievement of pupils, almost all classes may be regarded as ungraded. Instruction that treats all second graders as though they were the same is self-defeating. In almost any primary class, the achievement level will span three or four grades by the end of the year. In the upper grades, the range will usually cover four to six grades.

The so-called ungraded schools are those in which instruction is individualized and students progress at their own rate with material appropriate to their achievement level, irrespective of age. Thus, some seven-year-olds may be doing arithmetic at the fourth grade level and reading at the third, and so on. The primary group they belong to or report to the first thing in the morning may be designated by the number of years in school or may have mixed ages together (as in the British infant schools).

In tutorial community schools, at the outset the homeroom groupings are established by chronological age, but this loses its meaning as instruction becomes more and more individualized. As the paired classes (an upper grade and a primary) housed in adjacent classrooms have increased interactions throughout the day, with children sharing both rooms and working more and more with each other across grade levels, a form of multiple age grouping emerges.

A next step, which some teachers have taken, is to mix both classes and have both teachers share total responsibility for all the children.

Other teachers have gone to a family grouping arrangement, with children from three grade levels (1-3) in one homeroom paired with a class having children in grades 4-6. There probably is no single best type of grouping of children. The ideal arrangement is the one that is flexible enough to meet the needs of the particular children in a particular school.

Human Resources Directory

A long-range overall goal of a TCP school is for everyone to be a learning resource for everyone else. As the walls of the isolated, self-contained classroom come down and students interact, learn from, and assist in teaching other students, there could eventually be a Human Resources Directory for the entire school. This would parallel and extend the listing of each

Student teams liven up the hallways with the displays
of their work.

student in a given class as a special helper in some area. The
listing could function in any of the following ways:

1. The directory might list all students in the paired
    classes and what they are good at (school subjects,
    hobbies, and special talents are listed). For exam-
    ple, Jerry Smith—arithmetic, harmonica, baseball.
    The list would be cross-referenced by subject mat-
    ter: Arithmetic—Jerry Smith, Julie Jones.

2. A copy of each class directory filed in a central
    location would become a school directory.

3. Students could utilize resources from other class-
    rooms by communicating by letter through the

student-run intraschool post office system or by contacting other students in person.

4. A Total School Resources Inventory might be developed listing every member of the tutorial community (teachers, children, parents) and his interests, skills, talents, needs. Compiling such an inventory could be an educative experience in itself if it is organized so as to enable members of the community to interview each other, to participate in cataloguing procedures, and to devise a system of retrieval of information. Not only would this provide practice in some valuable cognitive skills, but as a continuing enterprise, it would underline the concept that every member of the tutorial community represents a learning resource and that teachers and books are not to be thought of as the sole sources for knowledge.

The Community as a Classroom

In TCP schools everyone is both learner and teacher and the notion of the classroom as a community is fostered. A further thrust involves the notion that learning is not limited to the classroom. The concept of the "community as a classroom" emphasizes that all the people, places, and events of the community at large represent potentially rich and important resources for learning which can and should be systematically exploited. *The Yellow Pages of Learning Resources,* * a book concerned with the potential of the city as a place for learning, states:

---

* Group for Environmental Education, Inc., *Yellow Pages of Learning Resources*, Philadelphia, 1972.

> *Education has been thought of as taking place main-*
> *ly within the confines of the classroom, and school*
> *buildings have been regarded as the citadels of*
> *knowledge. However, the most extensive facility*
> *imaginable for learning is our urban environment. It*
> *is a classroom without walls, an open university for*
> *people of all ages offering a boundless curriculum*
> *with unlimited expertise. If we can make our urban*
> *environment comprehensible and observable, we*
> *will have created classrooms with endless windows*
> *on the world.*

In TCP schools many teachers have started taking advantage of this resource, beginning with walking trips to explore the local neighborhood and branching out to nature walks in local canyons, bicycle rides to the ocean, and field trips to local organizations of interest (for example, rehabilitation center for drug addicts).

IN CONCLUSION

Our experience suggests that the sequence of activities outlined in this chapter to develop the tutorial, team and self-learning aspects of TCP is applicable to most teachers and schools. It is based on a philosophy of gradual progression from simple to complex which maximizes the probability of success at each step as students and teachers become comfortable and skilled in new roles and activities. However, there exists no linear sequence appropriate for all teachers. Teachers vary as much as do children, so adaptations will be required to suit individual teachers, their learning and teaching styles, their goals, personalities, energy levels, and perceptions of need for change. For example, some teachers may wish to begin with intragrade tutoring before intergrade; others with interest centers and individualization within class prior to tutoring. Others may wish to begin with family grouping or more unstructured tutoring arrangements. They should have a clear rationale for whatever arrangement they choose. They can use the material in this chapter as a guide to be adapted to their own needs.

The duration of any one phase and the number of activities of that phase will vary with: teacher skill, attitudes, beliefs; children's responsiveness and readiness; degree of support for activity by administrators, colleagues, parents; availability of materials and equipment required; administrative factors such as freedom to control time schedules, and so forth.

What has emerged in tutorial community schools is a basic core program which involves all teachers in basic intergrade tutoring, and an advanced program which involves different teachers in different aspects—learning teams, centers, student-initiated curriculum. Some teachers and some schools may not get beyond the basic intergrade tutoring program, others will go for the total program.

There is no one definitive system, but all systems are based on certain principles which make for change through continuous evaluation and revision. At any given time, there will be some things that most, or all, teachers will be doing and other things which only a few different individuals will undertake. In tutorial community schools, activities are evaluated against the standard of how well they contribute to self-learning and mutual learning from and with others. All teachers operate within a framework of the helping relationship, including shared learning and teaching, mutual accountability, and shared planning-and-decision-making. These concepts are spread through a highly individualized staff development program based on peer-helping relationships.

3 SHARED PLANNING-and-DECISION MAKING

Developing a Proprietary Interest Through Shared Authority and Responsibility

INTRODUCTION: A SENSE OF OWNERSHIP

During the teacher strike in Los Angeles in 1969, a teacher, walking back and forth on the picket line in front of the school, was approached by one of her second grade students on the other side of the fence:

STUDENT: Mrs. Jones, when are you coming back? We miss you. We don't get to read our free choice books anymore.

MRS. JONES: Why not, Bobby? Why can't you read your books?

STUDENT: Cause we are in a different room now, and the other teacher says we can't go into *your* room to get the books. She says it would be like going into someone's house when they are away from home—that it would be like stealing.

So there it is! "Somebody else's house," "someone else's school," "someone else's room and books," "someone else's directions and order." Where this attitude exists, children have no sense of: this is *my* school, *my* classroom, *my* education, where *my* ideas, needs, feelings, thoughts are respected and can be explored, where I am able to influence my environment and life in school, where I can continually grow in self-confidence and self-reliance.

Our nation prides itself on its democratic institutions, yet we do not attempt to prepare our children for active and full participation as citizens; we do not afford them adequate opportunities to learn and practice the skills of cooperative planning, decision making and self-government. TCP attempts to change this by creating a learning environment which concretizes basic democratic values. One of the main goals of TCP is to develop feelings among students, parents, teachers and administrators that problems are *our* problems; failures, *our* failures; and successes, *our* successes.

In a school, everyone should feel and take a proprietary interest in what goes on. For this to occur, those most concerned with the effectiveness of education must have some authority. They must have a sense of investment and ownership in their educational enterprise, and an investment in each other. People must actually have the power to influence the conditions and quality of living in the learning community to which they belong. This implies that the school must have mechanisms and procedures that insure real, and not superficial, shared planning-and-decision-making* by students, parents, teachers, support staff, and administrators.

To accomplish this, the tutorial community school creates committees that involve the entire school-community population in running the school. For example, in the traditionally organized school, all hiring was done by the principal alone. It

---

* As used in this book, the term "shared planning-and-decision-making" means shared planning and shared decision making.

was *his* staff and indeed *his* school. Others worked there or sent their children there, but had no sense of ownership. The principal made most of the decisions and received most of the blame when things went wrong.

In the tutorial community school, a Personnel Committee is responsible for decisions related to the hiring and firing of personnel. The Personnel Committee was one of the first steps toward developing "we-ness" and "our-ness." Initially, teachers and parents served on the committee. When student membership was first proposed, there was resistance. "Isn't that going a little too far? What are kids going to do on the committee? They aren't qualified or equipped to evaluate a prospective teacher's qualifications for the job." Nevertheless, two students—a sixth grade boy and girl—were invited to participate in an interview with a prospective teacher. Afterwards the principal remarked, "Wow! That was something else. I wish we had tape recorded that session."

Students have feelings and a point of view that can best be represented by students. The same holds for parents, teachers, and nonteaching staff. Combining these perspectives enriches and makes more effective the planning and decision making process. All participants share responsibility, concern, pride, and satisfaction in the cooperative effort to improve the learning of all.

Having a stake and a say in the running of your school is of enormous consequence to participants. A sixth grade member of the Student Council may be quoted: "This has been the best year I've had in school. I really felt important and that I could get things changed here." A parent said: "The principal used to make all the decisions around here. Now, everyone's involved. Not only the teachers and parents, but also the head custodian, the office manager, and the playground director. We're becoming a total community and that's a good feeling." And the principal stated: "My job is easier in many ways because more people understand what you have to go through to get a decision. You know, now they accept decisions when they're finally made. And I think the faculty should be, and is, doing the same with the children. The same idea applies in adopting standards. If instead of imposing standards, we work together in this area, then children accept and understand. In working with any group, this is a valuable thing. As I say, it isn't easy, and I've got a lot to learn and will continue to go in this direction."

Underlying Concepts

People learn, grow, and participate best in an environment where they have some power and feel they have some control over their own destinies and know that what they say or do counts.

The broader the base of people initiating and reacting to ideas, the greater the likelihood of creative and high quality ideas as different people bring different perspectives and experiences to bear.

The greater the number of people involved in planning and decision making, the greater the commitment to carrying out decisions and to making them work.

People who, as individuals or through group membership, have developed a pervasive sense of powerlessness, may need encouragement and assistance to overcome this feeling and to develop readiness for participating in effecting change. Students, parents, minorities, teachers, nonteaching staff who have never before operated at this level need to develop self-confidence and confidence in the new system.

People who are used to holding power and making unilateral decisions (principals, administrators) may find it difficult and may need time to learn to share this power with others, even when they feel it is in the best interest of the organization.

Gradual Progression or Phasing

Because most schools have hierarchical, autocratic structures, the introduction of shared planning-and-decision-making is a difficult and sensitive undertaking. Individuals must not only take on new roles and behave in new ways, but must do so in collaboration with others. Past habits and attitudes often get in the way. As one principal stated, "I think it's a good idea but I don't know if I can do it."

As in other areas, unrealistic expectations would be a potential blocking factor. Change cannot occur overnight and must proceed slowly. Gradual progression involves moving from simple activities and situations to more complex ones, thus increasing the probability of success at each step of the way. Orientation and training of personnel precede the introduction of new activities. Existing committees are strengthened before new ones are started. Student participation with adult groups is delayed until the adults have organized themselves into an effective functioning team and can serve as good role models for the students.

The background, experience, skill and motivation of the principal, teachers, and parents involved will dictate the pace and sequence. There will be numerous occasions, because of local conditions, where the sequence followed will be different from that suggested here. *(See Form 14, Sequence of Steps in Developing Shared Planning-and-Decision-Making, p. 337.)*

Action Planning

Action planning *(see p. 341)* is a major tool of shared planning-and-decision-making. It is a cornerstone of TCP methodology, used by all the committees involved in the running of the school.

Action planning is nothing more than good thinking, stated

in the form of simple procedures for getting something accomplished. It is a carefully designed system of sequential moves toward solving problems and achieving goals, adaptable to individual and group uses. Action planning teaches how to define a problem and state objectives, how to brainstorm and get many ideas out, how to refine ideas, establish priorities, test for agreement, develop plans, choose a final plan, assign appropriate personnel and realistic target dates, establish evaluation and revision procedures.

In TCP schools, all groups—the SCAC, TCP Committee, Personnel Committee, PTA, Student Council, and Faculty— receive training in action planning procedures. It is through the use of these procedures that the committees function effectively.

OPERATION OF TCP GROUPS

To attain the school's goal of shared planning-and-decision-making, all members of the school community—students, parents, teachers, administration, and nonteaching personnel—participate in one or more of the committees which govern the tutorial community school: the SCAC, TCP Committee, Personnel Committee, PTA, Student Council, and Faculty. Together these committees are involved in:

Implementing the school philosophy.

Designing the academic program.

Planning changes in the school environment and atmosphere.

Establishing the organizational structure and operational procedures that facilitate change.

Developing and implementing plans.

Evaluating progress toward goals.

To develop a cooperative relationship within and among these groups, their roles are defined so that although there is much interaction between the groups no group is in competition with another. All of these groups work together in a mutually supportive way, and the TCP Committee plays a central catalytic and coordinating role. *(For a graphic presentation of the functions and interrelations of the committees see Form 15, Responsibilities of Major School Committees, p. 339.)*

The school slowly begins to reflect a feeling of community among all its members as cooperative effort leads to constructive change. For example, at one TCP school, inter-committee collaboration led to the end of double sessions, a maddening compromise with over-crowding caused by earthquake damage to one of the buildings. The School Community Advisory Council boldly decided to convert a little-used auditorium into learning centers which would house four classes. The Faculty approved of this action. The TCP Committee prepared the initial plans and details of the changeover. The PTA helped obtain furniture, carpeting, and equipment. The principal removed many of the bureaucratic barriers and obtained carpenters and movers from the district office. At a meeting of the faculty, teachers decided which four of them would team together in the new environment. Students offered some interesting designs of their own for utilizing the space and were a great help in preparing materials for learning centers. When the work was done, the School Community Advisory Council and PTA hosted a "school warming" party to unveil the new setting to the community. The whole operation was an example of how a broad base of people initiating ideas can solve problems and bring about a creative use of time, space, materials, and human resources.

Tutorial Community Program (TCP) Committee

Early in the life of a TCP school, the goal of making everyone in the school an owner is implemented by getting more people involved in the process of change. A committee representing all segments of the school population is formed to plan and implement change. This is an action committee, which looks at goals, determines needs, and plans and implements immediate action. It meets regularly and often to evaluate progress and to move the school forward.

Who

Regular members of the TCP Committee are: the principal, the TCP coordinator, the faculty chairman, one parent representative from the School Community Advisory Council (SCAC), and one from the PTA, one primary and one upper grade teacher, two student representatives, the head custodian, and the office manager.

Teacher representatives may rotate each month so that in a year most faculty members will have had this experience, or the faculty may elect its representatives for specific periods of time. Nonteaching staff representatives may also rotate from time to time, so that cafeteria workers, playground aides, and others get to participate. Part-time school personnel (school counselor, nurse, and so forth) are encouraged to attend when they can. Active student representation may begin during the second year, when the adults have smoothed out problems and are comfortable with the process. As more people participate in and become more knowledgeable about what is going on, the "we-they" feeling between the committee members and everyone else in the school begins to disappear.

All sessions are open to visitors. Any parent, teacher, staff member, or community person who is free at the time of the meeting may attend. If anyone wishes to present a topic personally, release time is found for that person. Otherwise, the person passes on the information to one of the committee members for presentation. Visitors to the school are invited to observe. Periodically, district officials are invited to attend, especially when a problem is being discussed that relates to their district responsibilities.

When

Meetings are generally held weekly. One school found 11:00 A.M. to 12:00 noon most appropriate because it allowed for continuation into the lunch hour when necessary. Holding the meeting during regular school hours places this function squarely in the center of school life rather than treating it as an extracurricular, after-school appendage. It also places less of a demand on teachers' time. Release time for teachers to attend can sometimes be handled by having the paired teacher (usually in an adjacent classroom) supervise both classes with the assistance of a parent.

Leadership

Initially, the principal and TCP coordinator take turns conducting meetings. The principal gradually withdraws, and all meetings are conducted by the TCP coordinator. (This is a full-time person, usually from the teaching or administrative ranks, who is responsible for facilitating, coordinating, and acting as a catalyst for implementing the total TCP program during the first year or two.) Later on, when the process has been well established and people are more experienced, the leadership may rotate among committee members. In the beginning, however, it is important to maintain continuity and establish smooth routines and procedures.

The leader, working with the principal, is responsible for establishing the agenda, setting and announcing goals for the meeting, conducting the meeting, reviewing the minutes before they are duplicated and distributed. He also provides training and evaluation in group process for participants by conducting an end of session critique.

In the early stages of TCP, a consultant may conduct the meetings and demonstrate the action planning process and the facilitator role. When the TCP coordinator is sufficiently trained, the consultant turns over the facilitator role to him.

Agenda

The TCP coordinator prepares a preliminary agenda and reviews it with the principal before the meeting. Agenda items

An active Student Council makes the democratic ideal a reality.

may be submitted to the coordinator by anyone on the committee or in the school. Items are placed on the agenda in order
of priority.

The agenda has three main parts:

> *Announcements:* These short items requiring no dis-
> cussion or action may be follow-up reports to items
> from previous meetings or they may be discrete infor-
> mation items.
>
> *Discussion Items:* These are items for which points of
> view, input, give and take, and feed-back are needed,
> but no immediate action or decision is required. (e.g.
> How is the lunch program working out?)
>
> *Action Items:* These require a decision or action at this
> time. Most action items also require discussion.

Sources for the agenda are:

> The TCP coordinator may review the minutes, or
> Action Planning Worksheet *(see Form 16, p. 341)* of the
> previous meeting and select items to bring up at the
> next meeting as announcement, discussion, or action
> items.
>
> At the beginning of the meeting, anybody who has an
> urgent item that needs to be dealt with immediately
> can request it be put on the agenda for that session.
>
> At the end of each meeting, a list is made of items that
> should be brought up next time.

Meeting Format

Stating objectives: The chairman announces the objectives of
the meeting. Each discussion or action item on the agenda has a

specific objective (for example, brainstorming a list of ideas; setting the date for completion of something; naming persons to write a plan, and so forth). The coordinator should state clearly the purpose of each session, what is to be accomplished, and what is the expected product or result of the meeting. If these are not clear in everyone's mind, the meeting may wander. Members will have a sense of frustration or lack of accomplishment if their expectations for the meeting were unrealistic or differed from the actual objectives. When objectives are clearly stated, it is easier to stick to the point and to evaluate effectiveness at the end of the session.

Adding Agenda Items: The chairman distributes the agenda for the session and asks for any additional items that need action or discussion on that day.

Taking Up Items on the Agenda: Announcements should not become discussion items. Decisions should be clear and arrived at through acceptance and not acquiescence. (Avoid such statements as: "Well, if nobody objects to the decision, we will consider it approved and move on.") At each stage—the idea, planning, implementing or evaluation stage—the next step should be anticipated. Involving other groups should be considered (is this something that should go to the SCAC, PTA, Student Council, Faculty?).

How many groups or people eventually get involved in a TCP Committee decision depends on how important it is and on how many people are significantly affected. The general rule is to provide an opportunity for some level of involvement for as many of those who will be affected by the decision as possible. For example, if the decision had already been made to brighten up the school and the specific plan decided upon was to recruit PTA volunteers to decorate the principal's office, this would not have to go beyond the PTA. A decision to assign each class the responsibility for decorating its own hall territory would go to the Faculty and the Student Council, but not to the SCAC. On the other hand, a decision to shorten the school day on a regular basis to provide planning time for teachers would go to all groups because it affects everyone and would be controversial.

Responsibility for action may take two forms: A committee member may agree to do it himself, or a member may agree to recruit a noncommittee person or task force to do it. (The latter is most common because otherwise the committee members would be overburdened.) The whole committee does the initial brainstorming on objectives or problems, and may assign one of its members to develop a preliminary plan. At the end of a session, the chairman summarizes the major decisions, reviews briefly with the group the actions decided upon, and lists agenda items for the following week.

Minutes: Many meetings end with people having different versions and assumptions about what was and was not agreed upon and who was supposed to do what by when. This inhibits action and follow-through. To avoid this, a special form is used for minute-taking called the Action Planning Worksheet *(see Form 16, p. 341).* It is designed to highlight decisions taken, personnel assigned, deadlines established, and thus makes responsibility and accountability clear.

The minutes of the meeting go to all faculty members and officers of the parent group and are posted in the school. A complete set of minutes in chronological order is also placed in booklets and kept in the faculty room and in the main office.

Each TCP Committee representative reports back the highlights of the meeting to his group and is available to answer any questions that arise from reading the minutes, which have been distributed. All groups are thus kept informed and anyone can contribute to or react to any decision in person or through a representative.

Critique: To evaluate the session, the following questions are asked: How well did we achieve our objectives? What did you like or dislike about the session? How can we improve it? Periodically evaluation of interpersonal relations and individual participation takes place: What did you like or dislike about your own or anybody else's participation? In other words, hold a feedback session about the group behavior.

Potential Problem Areas

Manipulation: Some administrators may attempt to manipulate sessions so that final decisions always reflect their own wishes. There should be complete clarity about who is responsible for which decisions and how they will be made. The principal must unambiguously "say what he means and mean what he says." If the decision is his, he should say so. If it is to be the group's, he should say so and stick to it.

Shared planning-and-decision-making does not divest the principal of all authority. On any given problem, there is a continuum along which the principal may operate: (1) Here is the problem; you make the decision. (2) Here is the problem; present a recommendation and we will make the decision together. (3) Present a recommendation and I will make the decision. (4) Here is my decision; I'd like your reactions before I implement it. (5) Here is my final decision; I expect you to support it.

TCP schools either begin with, or move toward, 1 and 2. Different schools will move toward participatory leadership more rapidly than others depending on the style and personality of the principal and the leadership qualities of other segments of the school community.

Faculty Resistance: One principal stated, "My first year in the school, I told the faculty, 'You are going to make all the decisions. We will govern by consensus.' It took them two years to realize I meant it. They kept pushing things back on me, and I wouldn't accept it. Although they wouldn't say so, they really preferred me to make the decisions. It's less risky." The principal should aggressively promote participation in planning and decision making and reinforce all efforts on the parts of individuals to take initiative in bringing about constructive change.

Tokenism: Nonteaching staff members, parents, and students may become silent members of the committee if overt attempts are not made to pull them into discussions. Meaningful participation does not occur overnight and will require continual attention. Initially, selection of representatives who are likely to speak up is desirable.

Inter-group Involvement: No rigid rules are possible about when any one committee should solicit input from the other groups. The rule of thumb is that controversial decisions, or those that will affect many people in significant ways, deserve additional input and contact with those who will be affected. This requires judgment and experience which develop over time.

Acquiescence versus Acceptance: Limiting time for deliberation on important decisions sometimes is a way of manipulating decisions. Individuals feel they have insufficient information to take a strong position. When this happens and decisions are made by acquiescence rather than acceptance, they may later meet much resistance. On the other hand, when genuine time limitations and short deadlines make unilateral decisions necessary, if it is clearly explained in advance rather than after the fact, it is more likely to be accepted.

Feedback Sessions: Problems are inevitable and it is extremely important not to by-pass the weekly feedback sessions, which act as a self-correcting mechanism to get feelings out, to clear the air, and to resolve differences.

Effectiveness Features

With the active support and participation of the principal, the TCP committee has great potential for effecting positive change and involving all elements of the school community in the process. Participants can become skilled at using action planning methods for group discussions and problem solving and can make highly efficient use of limited time.

At one TCP school, the committee initiated a great number and variety of activities, including: a task force to publish a school newspaper; a school suggestion box; development and implementation of a plan for school-wide hallway displays; recruitment of volunteers for carpeting the auditorium, making special bulletin boards for halls, mounting displays in halls, obtaining furniture and equipment; reorganization of lunch and playground activities; a new report card and reporting system, including evaluation of school and teachers by students and parents; afternoon enrichment clubs for students on shortened school day; and a Junior Great Books Reading Program training course for teachers and parents.

Particularly impressive was how students representing the Student Council were assimilated into the group. Attitudes of proprietorship, of "we-ness," and a sense of having power to influence things developed throughout the school and contributed to increased teamwork and a sense of community. One teacher remarked at a TCP Committee meeting, "This is the first time in my career I have ever felt that the parents and faculty are on the same side and working together."

School Community Advisory Council (SCAC)

In recent years, one of the innovations to involve parents in the local school has been the formation of parent advisory councils (sometimes called school community advisory councils or other similar names). Broadly, these councils promote

Having a stake and a say in the running of your
school is important.

better understanding and rapport among community members, parents, administrators and faculties. They attempt to
provide community support and involvement to improve the
quality of the educational program and to gear that program to
the needs of the particular pupils and community involved. In
some school districts, advisory councils have been mandated
by Board of Education decree (e.g., in Los Angeles since 1971).
In other districts it may be voluntary although strongly encouraged by the Board. In still others, it may represent a grass roots
community effort that is resisted by the Board of Education
and local administrators.

In most districts the advisory nature of the council is
stressed. The principal retains the legal and actual respon-

sibility and authority for decisions. The role of the council may range, at one extreme, from merely being a rubber stamp for the principal, to community control at the other end of the continuum, where the parent council acts in many respects like a local Board of Education and has great power and influence, including the ability to hire the principal and staff.

In many schools, a major problem is a power struggle between faculty and principal on one side, and parents on the other. In TCP schools, an adversary relationship is avoided and a cooperative partnership between parents and school nurtured. In schools where a School Community Advisory Council is already functioning, it is usually this body that makes the decision to adopt TCP in the first place. If it is not already in existence, one of the first steps in implementing TCP should be to organize such a group.

Functions

In TCP schools, the School Community Advisory Council serves primarily as a policy making and planning group, advising the school on ways to improve the educational program and school conditions. These suggestions will be implemented by the various other committees.

The SCAC functions are to:

Define the educational goals and specify criteria to evaluate progress.

Assess educational needs, establish priorities, and advise on the resource needs of the school.

Help evaluate the school and make recommendations for improvements.

Make recommendations about use of budget resources.

Orient and advise school staff about conditions in the community.

Recommend ways for parents to become involved in the instructional experience of the school.

Recommend ways to keep parents and community members informed about the school and mobilize public support for the school.

When

Each school advisory council establishes its own rules for time, place, and frequency of meetings. Meetings are generally held in the evening because it is more convenient for parents. However, meetings may on occasion take place during the day and on weekends, at the convenience of the members.

Who

In Los Angeles, the size of a council varies from as few as 11 to as many as 35. The majority of members are parents of students of the school. A limited number represent the following groups: faculty, nonteaching staff, and nonparent community members. The principal is an *ex-officio* nonvoting member. The council elects its own chairman and other officers. Members may be elected and/or appointed. Parents are elected at an open general meeting by the community; teachers by the faculty; and nonteaching staff by their peers. Committee meetings are public and all parents, teachers, and staff are encouraged to attend.

Rules, By-Laws, and Procedures

The advisory council establishes its own rules and procedures about meetings, number, nomination and election of members and officers, terms of office, and so forth. Every effort is made to arrive at decisions by consensus. Action planning procedures are used in carrying out the work of the council. Generally, the procedures described for the TCP Committee with regard to leadership, agenda planning, meeting format, and critique of meetings apply to the SCAC.

Relations with Total Parent Community

Ordinarily, the council is authorized to make recommendations on behalf of all parents. Important issues are publicized and attempts are made to get a large turnout to meetings to participate in discussion. Efforts are exerted to inform all parents and get an overt reaction to recommendations. For example, at one school, a new time schedule (shortening the pupils' instructional day) was recommended. Personal contact with over 500 parents was made through large meetings, small groups teas, and home visits. All parents had a chance to express their preferences through questionnaires. In less important matters, all parents might be contacted by questionnaires only. Where a change is minor or involves parents or children on a voluntary basis, reactions of the total population may not be sought. However, attempts are made to keep all parents informed.

Councils sometimes get discouraged because of poor attendance at meetings. Although it is desirable to get full participation, it is unrealistic to expect it. Most people are bored by meetings which involve discussion and prefer something providing more immediate results and gratifications. Usually, large attendance occurs only when there is a crisis.

In TCP, direct participation in the classroom community is stressed. Parent teams are organized to accomplish something immediately related to helping their own children (tutoring at home, playing educational games, and so forth). Once a parent team is stabilized, it is encouraged to send a representative to the SCAC meeting to bring back information for team discussion. If a team consists of nine persons, each member might attend one SCAC meeting a year on a roating basis. This would not be a burden on any of the members, while providing them all with a maximum amount of information. Parent teams increase their influence by providing feedback about their reactions and positions to the SCAC (in writing or through their representative attending council meetings). Further, the classroom telephone tree can be used to get important messages out to all parents, some of whom may not be on a parent team or may have missed meetings. In this way, an informal, active electorate can be built up.

Relations with Other Committees

SCAC either makes recommendations that will be carried out by other committees, or approves recommendations initiated by other groups. Proposals by other groups usually require SCAC approval when they involve significant changes in policy or procedures or when they initiate actions or programs that affect most children in the school. For example, a proposal for a new report card that eliminated letter grades and incorporated student and parent evaluation of the teacher and school originated in the TCP Committee, but had to be approved by SCAC because it significantly affected all parents and students. The TCP Committee then formed a task force to develop and implement plans.

Relations with the Principal

The effectiveness of the SCAC will depend to a large degree on the relationship between the parents on the committee and the principal. An adversary relationship can be very harmful to the school. To avoid a power struggle and to develop a cooperative, constructive relationship both the principal and the council members must share certain attitudes and skills.

The principal must be willing to share his authority for decision making with the council. He must provide them with the information they want or need so that they may develop informed opinions and make informed recommendations about school needs. He must take the initiative in helping to provide the necessary training for members. He must not try to impose his legal authority when the council holds views contrary to his own. He must not over-react to hostility of some members and use that as a reason to disregard the council.

Parents are often viewed as threatening, over-powering, or insensitive when they become impatient, aggressive, or outspoken in trying to reach an objective. The principal must be able to accept criticism. Often when parents are impatient it is because they lack information or are frustrated, or sense they are considered threatening. When agreed upon changes are not implemented, council members should be told why promptly. If a council member makes an unreasonable demand or is provocative in language or manner, the principal may have to assert himself strongly. However, it is better to enlist the aid of other council members to deal with the individual, and make it a council problem rather than a personal conflict between the principal and the individual.

On the other hand, there is much the council can do to establish good working relations with the principal. It should recognize that the transition for most administrators from an autocratic system, where they made unilateral decisions, to participatory decision making is not easy. It takes understanding and patience on both sides. Disagreements or unwillingness to follow all council suggestions should not immediately be considered as a renunciation of shared planning-and-decision-making. The council should take a conciliatory stance rather than push for confrontation on every point.

Relations with the School District

Many school districts have given lip service to local autonomy while resisting movement at the local school level for substantial changes. SCAC will have to push continually to enlarge the degree of freedom with which it can operate without excessive district interference or undue red tape. This may require face-to-face presentations to district administrators and members of the Board of Education. For example, after written requests for a shortened daytime schedule at one school had been turned down, personal presentation by a delegation from the SCAC to the Deputy Superintendent resulted in approval.

Potential Problem Areas

The development of parent cliques struggling for power can be very destructive to the school program. Differences of opinion and some conflict among parents, and between parents and principal are inevitable. Feedback mechanisms should be developed and implemented early to prevent and resolve conflict.

Failure to establish priorities can cause the SCAC to devote too much attention to minor problems or issues and not enough to important ones. Early training in action planning methods (first for officers, then for the entire council) is essential.

Membership on the council, especially for officers, requires time to study the needs of the school, to attend meetings, and to work on recommendations and suggestions. Candidates for the council should be willing and able to devote time to its work.

If teacher attendance at SCAC meetings is lacking, parents may make recommendations in a vacuum. The greater the teacher participation, the more the likelihood of a cooperative rather than an adversary relationship developing. In addition to the elected faculty representatives (usually 1 or 2), it is desirable if other teachers attend on a rotating basis. Of course, all teachers are encouraged to attend as many meetings as possible.

Effectiveness Features

An effective SCAC can participate in bringing about significant change in a school. Examples of some accomplishments at one school include: gaining approval for a weekly shortened day to provide planning time for faculty; getting the school off double sessions; acquiring bungalows to avoid overcrowding; establishing a personnel committee involving parents, teachers, and students in hiring new teachers.

Strong leadership is important. The chairman and officers must have the time and desire to work at the job.

The principal should show enthusiasm for parent participation and optimism about what can be accomplished. He should role model openness and directness in his dealings with the council and provide information and training to help it become a knowledgeable and effective group.

An excellent resource book on organizing and operating a School Community Advisory Council has been prepared by the Staff Development Office of the Los Angeles Unified School District, entitled *Handbook for School-Community Advisory Councils,* October 1971.

Personnel Committee

A good school must have good teachers. Interviewing and selecting staff members is especially critical in a TCP school because not only does the faculty member have to be a capable teacher, but he must also believe in TCP concepts. No matter how experienced or capable the teacher is, if he does not support the program, it will be a serious handicap to progress. The creation of an elementary school embodying TCP concepts requires a well-informed and strongly committed staff working together as a team. Staffing must receive a high priority.

In selecting teachers primary consideration is given to acquiring people with highly compatible educational philosophies, who know what they are getting into and strongly desire to be part of such an effort, and who believe in planning and decision making among children, teachers, parents, and administrators. The TCP personnel procedures and policies should make it hard to get in and easy to get out of a TCP school.

When

The committee meets as staff vacancies occur. Prior to an interviewing session, the committee meets to review the agenda and ground rules for the session. After the interview, the committee meets as a whole to discuss, evaluate, and make its selection. The committee meets periodically to evaluate and revise its procedures.

Who

Included in the committee are: Student Council president and one other 5th or 6th grade student; the principal; the faculty chairman; PTA and SCAC parent representatives; nonteaching personnel representatives; and two faculty representatives. Any faculty members or parents who are interested are welcome to attend interviews as nonvoting observers.

Students participate actively and have an important contribution to make. They ask good questions which frequently focus the interview on basic issues. For example, one student asked a teacher candidate, "Are you really interested in children, or do you just want this job for the money?" Another student inquired, "Why would you want a job in an elementary school? Since you have a Masters Degree couldn't you get a better job that paid more?" Another questioned, "How do you feel about discipline? If a kid misbehaves, do you send him to the principal, paddle him or what?" The teacher responded and then asked the student what he thought should be done with a child who misbehaved. The pupil replied, "I don't know, but I'll tell you this, if you're doing good work the teacher will come by once in a while for a second and say 'Nice work, John;' but if you are misbehaving the teacher will spend hours with you." An excellent discussion ensued about how teachers reinforce misbehavior by rewarding the offender with the teacher's attention while ignoring students who are doing well.

Procedures

Recruitment and Screening: The personnel committee develops its own procedures designed to recruit teachers and to provide prospective teachers with enough information to give them a realistic appreciation of the demands and rewards of being a TCP teacher.

The Tutorial Community Program is publicized in school district media and prospective candidates are requested to write for further information. Literature describing TCP is sent to prospective candidates, including a copy of Commitments for Developing a Tutorial Community School-Action by Teachers *(see Form 43, p. 387).*

Candidates who request an interview are invited to attend a TCP orientation screening workshop conducted by parents and school personnel to give prospective teachers first-hand knowledge and experience about major TCP concepts. It also provides the school community the opportunity to become acquainted with the candidates as they experience TCP processes.

Following the orientation workshop, each candidate is interviewed by the Personnel Committee.

The Interview: Candidates may be interviewed individually or in a group. If it is to be a group interview candidates should be so informed in advance. We have found the group interview a highly effective way to screen out applicants who are attracted to the TCP idea without really understanding what is involved. A group interview is in some ways like a feedback session and encourages frank and open communication. Candidates who would feel uncomfortable with a group interview would most likely feel uncomfortable with feedback sessions and with some of the other processes basic to the tutorial community approach. The importance of recruiting staff who are genuinely committed to the TCP ideas and will be thoroughly comfortable with its procedures and methods cannot be overstressed. It is much more humane in the long run to eliminate people who would not be happy with the program before they become actively involved in the training than it would be to replace them later on. No more than five applicants should be interviewed at once. Informal atmosphere is desirable, with coffee and refreshments served during the session. The principal welcomes the candidates. Each applicant introduces himself.

The principal or TCP coordinator makes a brief statement about TCP and the uniqueness of the personnel committee and interview procedures and describes the sequence to be used during the session. Candidates are encouraged to ask questions to fill out their knowledge of the school and its program, especially the goals, philosophy, and methods of TCP. The committee members discuss positive and negative aspects of TCP and underline some of the difficulties and pressures.

The commitments of teachers are read item by item *(see Form 43, p. 387)* and candidates are asked to state their agreement or disagreement and to discuss the strengths or problems they might have in implementing each item. Com-

People must actually have the power to influence the
conditions and quality of living in the learning
community to which they belong.

mittee members may question interviewees closely (especially
about feedback sessions which are somewhat threatening and
controversial). Taking an aggressive approach gives the opportunity to see how a candidate responds to pressure. For
example, one would want to question a candidate further if he
responded to, "How would you feel about receiving strong
criticism from one of your colleagues" with, "Oh, that
wouldn't bother me at all."

Each candidate is asked to state briefly why he wants to be
a part of this program.

Committee members ask questions such as:

> What are some of the things in teaching you feel you
> have done particularly well, or in which you have
> achieved the greatest success? Why?

What are some of the things about teaching you have found difficult to do? Why?

How do you feel about your present position?

What do you feel has been your greatest frustration or disappointment in your present position? Why?

What would you consider your greatest strength?

What do you feel you could most improve upon?

Are there certain things you feel more confident doing than others?

What are some of the things in teaching that motivate you?

Committee members may make evaluative comments about individual responses during the interview or about information in resumes or letters. Applicants have the opportunity to respond.

Evaluation and Selection: Prior to any discussion, each committee member individually and secretly ranks the candidates. Applicants not meeting minimum requirements are not ranked at all. Considerations in making choices include:

Is the applicant enthusiastic about teaching?

Has he had a history of successful teaching experience?

Does he seem to like children?

Are his responses direct and straightforward?

Does he seem to be the kind of teacher that would explore new ways to stimulate learning?

Is he responsible enough to carry out his commitment to TCP concepts?

How well does he accept criticism?

Does he seem enthusistic about TCP concepts?

Does he have successful experience related to TCP concepts?

Does he appear to have the energy necessary to work in a demanding, innovative program?

A frequency distribution of choices is made to see the degree of consensus that exists. Where there are differences, members discuss the reasons for their ranking. Members may revise their rankings if they wish. The group rankings are discussed until a consensus is reached. Candidates are informed about the decisions.

Self-Critique: The committee evaluates its own process. Each member responds to such questions as: What I liked or disliked about the session; suggestions I have for changes. Either in this session or in a separate feedback meeting, members give each other interpersonal comments (What I liked or disliked about my own participation or about someone else's). As a result of the critique or feedback, procedures may be revised.

Potential Problem Areas

Candidates may not be in touch with their deeper feelings and may sound convincing even though they have serious reservations about the program. Candidates should be warned that if they are not fully committed to TCP principles they will only be fooling themselves and will not be happy in the school. The regular staff feedback sessions publicly bring to light poor attitudes and non-support of the program and cause considerable pressure.

At times, expediency may short-circuit or by-pass the

normal process. For example, if there is difficulty in finding a time that all committee members can meet, the principal may hold interviews and make the decisions himself. This may also occur when a position becomes open suddenly and must be filled quickly. In either case, ways should be found to follow the normal procedures, even if not as thoroughly. Back-up representatives from the different groups should be designated so that personnel committee substitutes can fill in without undue delay for those who have schedule conflicts. Otherwise skepticism about the school's commitment to the shared planning-and-decision-making concept may result.

At times, the principal may override the recommendation of the committee and not honor the group's choice. When this happens, it should be done openly and directly and the reasons carefully explained. If a lower rated person is chosen under conditions that are not understood or made public, it will have a detrimental effect on school morale.

Sometimes, to solve personnel problems within the school district, an administrative transfer may be made, assigning a teacher to the school without going through the school's screening and selection procedure. This is contrary to the philosophy of gathering like-minded persons and is not fair to the new teacher or the school.

If the critique process at the end of the committee interview or meeting is slighted because of pressures of time or for other reasons, the opportunity for correction and improvement of procedures and individual participation is lost.

The personnel committee should also evaluate probationary teachers. If the principal does this alone, these teachers may not feel secure enough to speak freely in his presence at faculty feedback sessions.

Effectiveness Features

The participation of students, parents, and teachers in the personnel process helps develop a genuine sense of proprietorship in the school and a feeling of importance among participants. It is also a dramatic and effective demonstration to new teachers of the team approach in a tutorial community school. Right from the initial interview, they get a sense of the value and confidence placed in student and parent opinion and ability. The students' participation is often a revelation about how much we underestimate their capabilities.

Participation in this committee is an excellent learning experience for all members. They crystallize, examine and re-examine their thoughts about the school, TCP program, teaching, and values. They learn to articulate the essence of the program and develop sensitivity and skill in helping others present themselves honestly and in evaluating others. Membership should be rotated so that many persons from each segment of the school community population can benefit from this experience.

Members should report back to their respective groups what is happening on the Personnel Committee. Comments, suggestions, and questions should be encouraged.

Parent Teachers Association

In TCP schools, the Parent Teachers Association (PTA) plays a supportive role. It takes the initiative in obtaining volunteers, materials, and funds for the school and in sponsoring social activities and projects to improve school atmosphere (physical and social). Ideas may originate with the PTA, or may come from another committee which requests the PTA's support.

The PTA is not replaced by SCAC. It is the action arm in the areas mentioned above, just as the TCP Commitee is the action arm in the instructional program and management of the school. PTA representatives serve on TCP and SCAC committees.

In general, the procedures described for the TCP Committee with regard to agenda planning, meeting format, critique of meetings, etc., apply to the PTA. Action planning procedures are used and PTA officers are among those who receive initial training in these techniques.

In a tutorial community school parents are encouraged to take an active role in school affairs not only through membership and participation in the PTA, but also through representation and participation in all other school committees.

Student Council

Adults frequently underestimate the capabilities of children. Having little confidence and low expectations becomes a self-fulfilling prophecy.

Through Student Councils, schools attempt to change the second class citizen status of children. However, these councils can be token organizations with little impact on the school if students take little initiative and merely follow the directions of teachers. The goal in a TCP school is to have an active student council that deals with important issues affecting the school and student concerns.

Function

Upper grade students meet regularly to study the needs and problems of the school, to recommend changes to improve school atmosphere and effectiveness. The council contributes to school development in two ways: by recommending to other school committees ideas and action initiated by the student body, and by reacting to or acting on ideas initiated by other groups (TCP, PTA, SCAC). Council members also represent the student body on two other committees—TCP and Personnel.

The Student Council gives students a sense of ownership in the school. It also provides an opportunity to further develop their skills of leadership, group problem solving, and teamwork. Council members represent the entire student body and attempt to express the feelings and concerns of all their schoolmates.

Who

At the outset, to keep organizational problems relatively simple and uncomplicated, the council may consist of 5th and 6th grade students. The council may have from 8 to 12 members, with one or two representatives elected by their classmates from each 5th and 6th grade class. Later on, 4th grade students may be added to the council. When the council begins to feel secure and to function smoothly, other students from each class are encouraged to observe one or two sessions on a rotating basis until almost all students have had a first hand glimpse of how it operates. Primary teachers can also select 1st, 2nd, and 3rd graders to visit and observe. Eventually, council representatives may come from all grades.

When

Council meetings take place once weekly during school hours. Members are excused from their classes. It is important that meetings are held during school hours, rather than after school, to emphasize that this activity is an integral part of the school program and of students' learning experiences and not an appendage or extracurricular activity. Meetings are generally held from 11:00 A.M. to 12 noon, with members then eating lunch together.

Leadership Training

A faculty sponsor works with the students and conducts initial meetings. In the first few sessions they receive orientation training on the purposes of the student council, on how to conduct a meeting, on how to solve problems in a group, and on action planning concepts. The sessions do not stay theoretical. Almost from the start, students begin to engage in the action planning process by brainstorming school problems and concerns, and by exploring solutions.

After about six weeks, the council elects its own chairman, who then begins to co-chair the meetings with the teacher, and eventually takes over alone. Later, as the group gains experience, it may elect a co-chairman and rotate the chairmanship on a monthly basis. In schools that terminate at 6th grade, one-half of the fifth graders serve for a second year to provide continuity.

A leadership workshop is provided during summer school for students interested in receiving training in group problem solving and for all who may wish to serve on the Student Council in the fall. The critiques at the end of each meeting,

When children are given opportunities for planning and decision making, they grow up able to exercise initiative and independence.

and participation on the TCP and Personnel Committees, provide additional training.

Agenda

The teacher-advisor meets with the student chairman the day before the council meeting to establish the agenda. Sources may be suggestions made by council members at the end of the previous meeting, or minutes of previous meetings (using the Action Planning Worksheet, p. 341.) Also, each class has a suggestion box and may forward suggestions of school-wide significance to the council. In conducting their meetings, the Student Council procedures generally parallel those of the TCP Committee.

Relationship to Other Committees

Student Council proposals usually are presented to the TCP Committee for approval. The TCP Committee may recommend that some of these proposals be presented to the teachers at a Faculty meeting. Representation on the TCP and Personnel Committees is rotated so that by the end of the year most Student Council members have had the experience. Student representatives report back proceedings of the TCP Committee to the council and vice versa.

Relationship to Total Student Body

Activities of the Student Council are publicized in several ways. The council has its own bulletin board in the main school hallway where minutes are regularly posted. The suggestion-of-the-week is posted along with a description of any action taken. Later, a cumulative list of suggestions and actions is posted. A copy of the minutes is sent to each class where teachers may have class read and discuss them. Each council member reports back to his own class highlights of council activities and solicits comments, reactions and suggestions from classmates. Suggestion boxes in each classroom are a source of input to the council. Students visit and observe council meetings. The council can use assembly or class meetings for announcements and presentations.

Potential Problem Areas

Overeagerness to implement a Student Council may result in attempts to have schoolwide elections, and to have representatives from every class from grades 1 to 6 before teachers and students are really ready. It is wise to limit membership in the early stages of council development to a modest number of upper graders. This can be expanded in subsequent years after teachers and students are experienced.

The most popular students are not necessarily the best representatives. Teachers should precede class elections with a discussion of the purpose of the Student Council, what constitutes leadership qualities, and what criteria are useful for electing representatives. This is a good learning exercise in social studies for the class.

The faculty advisor should be careful not to dominate the group but rather to serve as trainer, facilitator, and guide. The teacher-facilitator moves to the background as quickly as possible.

Students must be encouraged to express themselves openly and forcefully. They should not be put down if some of their ideas seem a little far out. They need encouragement from teachers and principal. At the same time, students must be cautioned against the unrealistic expectation that everything they want or suggest will be approved. Otherwise, they will become disappointed, discouraged, and disillusioned.

Teachers must view council participation as an important and valuable learning experience. They must support it and not penalize students by conducting group activities during times scheduled for Council meetings.

Effectiveness Features

When teachers, parents, and the principal value student participation in Student Council and in Personnel and TCP committees, students can make important contributions to the improvement of the school program and atmosphere. Student proposals resulted in reinstatement of a school nutrition program; changes in lunch menus; solutions to problems of waiting on long lines for lunch; planning the graduation program; improving the cleanliness of bathrooms; providing better access to playground equipment; and instituting Friday noon dancing. Students who served on the Student Council indicated that their participation made the year one of the best they had ever experienced in school.

Faculty

Traditionally, faculty meetings are a giant bore. They generally occur after school when teachers are tired, and consist largely of one-way communication with the principal doing all the talking and the faculty listening. The content is mainly announcements of information that could have been posted on bulletin boards.

In TCP schools, faculty meetings become a school senate or forum for deliberation, discussion, and decision. Topics are those of schoolwide importance that require consideration by all teachers. Thorough discussion and approval by the total faculty is generally necessary for all significant changes.

Who

The principal, TCP coordinator, and all faculty members are

regular participants. All parents are invited to attend, especially officers of the PTA and SCAC. The meetings are also open to any nonteaching staff who are free. Teachers encourage parents and student teachers who are helping in their classrooms to attend.

The faculty chairman conducts the meetings. The principal should encourage teachers to speak up and express their views, and to make it their meeting. Of course, he should make sure that issues he feels are important also get discussed.

When

An effective combination appears to be to hold short meetings regularly and schedule an occasional long meeting when important issues and problems require it.

The short meetings may occur before or after school. A 10 to 15 minute break between the end of the meeting and the beginning of class in the morning is important. Shortened school days, on a regular basis, are highly desirable to provide time for teachers to meet.

Agenda

The agenda is prepared by the faculty chairman and the principal. The procedures are the same as for the TCP Committee. Minutes of TCP Committee, SCAC, and prior Faculty Meetings are reviewed as sources of items for the agenda.

Some examples of items that have appeared on the agenda for Faculty meetings are:

Improving racial relations in the school.

The problem of double sessions.

Improving the report card system.

Should we move toward a school-within-a-school set-up?

District rules about time schedules that interfere with planning meetings and staff development.

Should the film program be expanded? Student demonstration of special film making project.

Potential Problem Areas

If the principal dominates the meeting, making up the agenda and conducting the meeting by himself, the interests and concerns of the faculty may not be reflected. If the principal shows hostility toward opinions that differ from his, it has a very inhibiting effect. Collaboration with the faculty chairman insures more relevant and involved meetings. The faculty chairman, who was elected by the teachers and represents them on the TCP Committee, is in close touch with the faculty's thinking and with what's going on in the school.

Lack of pre-planning and careless attention to the agenda causes meetings to be chaotic, boring, or degenerate into gripe sessions. The agenda should not be left to the last minute. A regular time should be set for the faculty chairman and principal to meet. Opportunities for teachers to submit items must be provided.

Expectations about starting time, leaving time, and attendance should be made clear. Meetings should start and end on time.

Rigid adherence to the pre-planned agenda can be detrimental. If an item becomes controversial and is important enough, the chairman should continue the discussion even if other items have to be delayed. On the other hand, it is important to cut off discussion when it is repetitious and a waste of time. These are matters of judgment. The critique at the end of the session provides an opportunity to get feedback on possible errors of judgment.

Working only in large groups is not an effective means of planning and decision making. There is little opportunity for real give and take. Frequently, large group discussions are dominated by a few persons, usually the loudest, most extroverted, or articulate. For most effective participation, small groups should be used whenever possible. The groups can be used for brainstorming, discussing pros and cons, establishing priorities, and developing preliminary plans. They can report back to the total group and check for consensus. If discussion in the large group does not lead to consensus, a small *ad hoc* task force may be assigned to work out a solution and report back to the meeting.

Insufficient time to deal adequately with important questions leaves participants frustrated as they try to deal with a multitude of problems. Realistic limitations must be recognized. Establishing priorities is essential; new projects must be undertaken gradually as others are completed and time and personnel become available.

The specific objective to be accomplished at each session should be stated clearly. The group should evaluate its effectiveness at the end. A meeting may have been very effective in accomplishing a limited goal, and yet participants will feel frustrated or negative if the goal had not been made clear and participants had different expectations.

Although the school may have made much progress in solving problems and improving conditions, people may not be aware of it because the focus is usually on what's wrong now, and of course there are always new problems. It may appear to members who are involved that nothing has changed. Making successes visible is important for group morale. For example, it is worthwhile to post reports on bulletins listing: activities initiated by parent or student teams, new programs (e.g. computer assisted instruction) initiated, comments by visitors, the number of parents volunteering in classrooms, the number of students engaged in tutoring, independent study and on teams.

Effectiveness Features

Inviting visitors to meetings to make brief presentations or to act as resource people is stimulating and adds variety to meetings. For example, a presentation by students on how they operate a computer terminal for computer assisted instruction in math, reading, and writing poetry was fascinating to faculty members.

Seating arrangements which enable all persons to see each other (circles) are more conducive to discussion than auditorium style seating. Fishbowl discussions are effective with large groups. The inner circle discusses an issue for a limited period while the outer circle listens. Then they exchange places and roles.

For longer meetings, a change of setting is desirable. Meeting away from their work environment in teachers' or parents' homes or restaurants, hotels, or conference centers in pleasant locations can be relaxing and stimulating for teachers occasionally.

Through the TCP Committee, Student Council, SCAC and Personnel Committee, the faculty receives tremendous support from parents, students, and nonteaching staff in bringing about change.

Other Committees

Elementary schools are like small communities. They require organization, thought, and support. In addition to the major committees described above, other committees are organized as needed to carry out specific functions, such as: special events, music, library, assemblies, field trips.

Some committees have ongoing work throughout the year (e.g. audiovisual materials and equipment); others may be activated for a once or twice-a-year activity (school-wide testing). Committee assignments are based on teachers' preferences and prior experience. Each year teachers rotate from a high-weighted (much work) to a low-weighted (little work) activity. Assignments should be equitable and, whenever possible, voluntary.

A job description for each committee is prepared indicating goals, tasks, time, materials and training required *(see Form 17, Committee Task Description, p. 342)*. Each new member receives a copy as part of orientation to the committee.

At the end of the year, each committee chairman and members complete an evaluation questionnaire *(see Form 18, Committee Evaluation, p. 342)* indicating time spent in task accomplishments, problems, and suggestions for future about number of members needed, time requirements, materials, and training.

Each committee uses action planning techniques to conduct its work. Committee chairmen report to the faculty chairman and to the principal and work under their guidance.

To make committee functioning most effective, chairmanships should be rotated; individual assignments should not be too long or too onerous; feedback sessions should keep faculty and administration accountable.

ACTION PLANNING

Whether or not a tutorial community school will function effectively in achieving its objectives depends to a large extent on how well the various committees function and on how actively all members of the school community participate in committee work and planning. But people need training and experience in how to work together on committees.

Paired teachers pool their ideas in a teacher resource group.

The Need for Action Planning

Getting two or more persons to engage cooperatively and effectively in careful, systematic planning is more rare than most people imagine. Good planning, although rare, is rarely a waste of time. On the contrary, it usually contributes enormously to work satisfaction and effectiveness. Unfortunately, however, most people are reluctant to devote themselves to committee work because their experiences in working in groups have been unrewarding or frustrating.

Why do groups fail? Why are many inefficient? Why do people hate to go to meetings? Why do most committees have only a handful of people who attend consistently and do most of the work? Why do people complain about not having any influence but, at the same time, stay uninvolved and allow a few individuals to make all the decisions? What makes group problem solving and planning so difficult?

Some typical comments after committee meetings are: "What a bore! What a waste of time! We didn't accomplish a thing! We seem to be forever rehashing the problem without ever getting to the solution! We never get anything done! What was the purpose of the meeting? We never stick to the point!"

Some of the worst meetings I have attended shared certain characteristics. They did not start on time. The chairperson usually delayed starting the meeting until everyone (or certain key persons) got there. Those who had arrived on time became impatient, frustrated, hostile, resentful about wasting their time. Meetings rarely ended at the prescribed time. Indeed, many did not end at all but sort of faded away.

Often the goals are not made explicit. The issue under discussion is vague or ill-defined, hindering effective communication. Little attempt is made to elicit different points of view and suggestions. The group may lock in on the first idea proposed. Tangential or nonrelevant discussion often takes place. Disagreements take up an inordinate amount of time. Too much time is devoted to minor problems and too little to major ones. Little or no attempt is made to analyze, evaluate, or consider ways of improving procedures and interactions among participants. Hidden agendas, interpersonal problems, and lack of a mechanism to deal with them stifle progress.

In view of these inadequacies, it is not surprising that few people are willing to get involved in this process on a continuing basis. Most groups probably operate at about 10-20% efficiency in problem-solving, planning, and decision making.

To eliminate these problems and provide constructive experiences in group planning, all members of the school community receive training in action planning.

Action planning is a systematic approach to planning and decision making. It is the main approach used in tutorial community schools to bring about change and improvement. When used consistently, it contributes to teamwork, feelings of proprietorship and a sense of community among all participants.

Basic Assumptions

More people would be willing to attend and participate in planning meetings if they were more productive.

There are always more problems and things to do than there are time and people available to get them done. Thus, efficiency in planning is necessary. Although "an ounce of prevention is worth a pound of cure," planning is frequently neglected or slighted in organizations because people become impatient, want instant action, and want to see immediate results for their efforts. Most people resist getting involved in systematic planning.

Most groups and committees are highly inefficient in planning, problem solving, and decision making.

Usually little effort is expended in evaluating and improving group process.

Even a poor plan is usually better than no plan because it facilitates the analysis and identification of mistakes, and the revision and improvement of procedures.

The quality of planning and decision making can be greatly improved by training in systematic action planning procedures. The techniques involved in action planning are not complex and can be mastered by most persons.

Major Steps and Procedures

Defining Problems and Goals

The first step in action planning is to identify the problem, question, or objective clearly so that everyone is talking about the same thing and there is genuine agreement that it is a worthwhile topic.

An objective must be described specifically enough so that those planning for its achievement can recognize it and communicate clearly about it. Vaguely stated objectives or problems often cause confusion and a dissipation of efforts. Without a clear definition, there is no sound basis for selecting appropriate methods and developing plans.

For example, one may start with the general goal of "improving human relations in the school," but this will have to be defined more closely. Whom does it involve—teachers, parents, students, staff, administrators? All of them? Relations within or between these groups? What measurable or observable outcomes can we look for: more social contacts within and between groups of students, parents, teachers of different ethnic groups? Fewer fights among students? Reduction of conflicts between parents and teachers? How long will it take to achieve the specific outcomes desired?

A specifically stated objective has to include the answers to such questions. For example, the general goal: "improvement of human relations" may be defined to mean: "developing friendly, courteous, and cooperative relations among children, teachers, and parents, as indicated by a 50% reduction within a six-month period in: fighting among children, number of students sent to the principal for disciplining, and complaints by parents about mistreatment of children at school." Stating the goal explicitly will facilitate evaluation of progress along the way and of ultimate outcomes.

Brainstorming, Getting Ideas Out

Brainstorming is a method that elicits the maximum number of ideas in a minimum amount of time. It also is used to achieve immediate involvement of all participants in the planning process. It loosens up thinking and brings forth more innovative ideas. It has been said that we all use only about 10% of our brain power and even less of our potential creativity. Frequently, only a severely limited number of possible ideas are considered at a planning session. Groups lock in on the first suggestion mentioned, or get involved too early in a lengthy discussion of an idea, or prematurely eliminate a proposal because someone objects to it.

Brainstorming was designed to overcome these difficulties and bring about more creative problem solving. The idea is to spill out and record as many ideas as possible without any discussion, criticism, evaluation, interpretation, clarification, or refinement of language. Time spent in premature discussion inhibits getting ideas out. For example, it often happens that a suggestion is made and someone immediately says, "it won't work because . . ." An hour of discussion may ensue as to why this idea would or would not work. Meanwhile, many other ideas (some potentially far superior to the one under discussion) never see the light of day. Initially, the goal is quantity— getting out many ideas for more careful consideration later.

Brainstorming can be done by an individual or by a group of any size, although generally, a large group is divided into smaller groups of from five to ten persons. One person is appointed as a recorder/moderator to write down every idea in full view of all participants (for example, on a blackboard or large newsprint) and to keep the group moving within the ground rules (no discussion, evaluation, and so forth). The recorder writes down suggestions exactly as stated. (The recorder may also suggest ideas.) No attempt is made to clarify language at this time.

The small group establishes its own working plan. Members speak randomly or in turn. Random participation encourages spontaneity, while taking turns insures total participation.

Participants are instructed not to screen ideas, to think boldly and wildly, to free associate, to give free reign to their imaginations, and not to consider feasibility.

The physical surroundings should be comfortable and pleasant. The group should arrange itself so that each one can see and hear all others and the moderator. A time limit may be set or the activity may be open-ended. In either case, the moderator usually decides when the group has dried up and reached the end of its ideas. He should not be too hasty. Sometimes a group may just be resting between spurts of ideas. The moderator will have to use his judgment as to whether to let the group rest for a while at a low productivity rate, to try to restimulate, or to end the session.

Most of us are fairly timid, traditional and rigid in our thinking. Some warm-up, loosening activities (such as passing an imaginary medicine ball around or hopping in place on one foot) may be desirable to facilitate spontaneity and informality. Then participants are encouraged to make any suggestions; no matter how absurd they may seem. Think big! You can always act small later. Post the brainstorming lists so that everyone can see how many ideas were generated in a short time. Brainstorming is a good way to get total involvement and participation.

For training purposes, periodically evaluate the brainstorming session immediately after it ends. Find out which groups stuck to the ground rules. Compare the procedures of the group that had the least number of ideas with those of the one having the most. Discuss how many people participated within the group and how this could be increased. Discuss how to improve the process in general.

Time is always a problem. A decision must be made about the relative efficiency of the whole group working on something, as opposed to leaving it to a small group or to one or two people. The question of when and how to delegate applies not only to brainstorming but to all other steps in the action planning process.

Refining Ideas

Refining attempts to get the ideas released in the brainstorming session into clear, concise, workable language so that everyone understands what is meant and is talking about the same thing. For example, a suggestion initially listed as "Open forum" may be changed to "Question-answer evening for parents" or "Parent-faculty discussion evening."

The following procedure is recommended: Each idea is read to the group. If a question is raised about its meaning, the statement is rewritten until the meaning is clear to everyone. If one idea is the same or similar to another, they will be combined or one of them eliminated. Items that are too general and cannot be acted upon should also be eliminated. These usually are placed on a separate list for further brainstorming. For example, "Make parents feel comfortable at school" would have to be brainstormed to come up with specific ways of doing this. On the other hand, "Assign child to explain classroom organization to visiting parents" is specific and usable.

Try to avoid the semantic trap—do not bicker over individual words; do not waste time trying to find the most precise words; any word will suffice as long as everyone understands how it is being used. At the conclusion of this step, the product is a concise list of clearly stated suggestions understood by all participants.

Categorizing

To avoid some of the common stumbling blocks which cause frustration, inefficiency, and wasted time and effort, ideas should be categorized by the degree of feasibility, agreement, complexity, and risk involved in each one.

FEASIBILITY AND CONTROL   Groups often waste much time discussing a suggestion which is beyond their power to implement, either by themselves or within a reasonable period of time. For example, a suggestion for improving human relations in the school might be to hire an additional full time principal who would serve as a counselor/facilitator in the area of interpersonal relations and communication. This would not be within the power of a school-community to bring about because it would involve budget factors, Board of Education and perhaps state regulations, and would affect all schools in a district.

Another example of an unfeasible suggestion is that the school principal be a teacher elected for a one-year term by faculty members and parents. The idea may be good and important but it is not something a particular school group could bring about.

Getting caught up in lengthy, involved, although sometimes interesting, discussions of things they cannot do anything about may be a form of unconscious avoidance behavior. It keeps the group from getting on with issues which it can control but which arouse anxieties when further action, commitment, or involvement are discussed.

To avoid discussions which take time away from dealing with things the group could change, the refined ideas are reviewed and those which are not within the group's control are eliminated, or if important, tabled for future reference or discussion. Sometimes an idea which is recognized as desirable but beyond the power of the group to implement may be passed along (without lengthy discussion) to a more appropriate body for further consideration.

AGREEMENT   Groups frequently get hung up discussing and arguing about ideas on which there is disagreement. This is debilitating and counter-productive. Much time is wasted and frequently an impasse reached. Items on which there would be agreement are not made available for discussion and implementation. Also, heated arguments create hostility and a negative atmosphere in which agreement becomes even more difficult. As tangible accomplishments decrease, frustration, pessimism, and negativism increase and a vicious cycle ensues.

To avoid this, during this stage in the action planning process the group should make a quick, cursory check to identify those ideas about which there is agreement. If anyone in the group disagrees with a suggestion, or has reservations, the idea is set aside for further discussion at an appropriate, convenient, and more favorable future time. Building up a backlog of agreement and accomplishment creates a more positive climate. Later on, when the group discusses those ideas over which there is some conflict, the likelihood of eventual agreement or compromise is increased.

COMPLEXITY Working with the list of feasible suggestions upon which there is agreement, the next step is to distinguish between simple ideas which are straightforward and require little effort or resources to implement and complex ideas which require considerable planning and many resources. Two separate lists are prepared. Implementing the simple ideas quickly gives the group a sense of progress and accomplishment and greater motivation and momentum in tackling the more complex ideas. It is similar to taking a test. If you get hung up on a difficult test item about which you are unsure, you may spend so much time on it that you never get to other items which were simple and which you could have answered easily and quickly.

RISK A high risk decision involves considerable resources (time, materials, money, people), or affects many people or a few important persons. If things go wrong, the potential damage is considerable. Low risk is the opposite; not too many resources are involved and even if everything went wrong, the loss would not be great.

We sometimes spend an inordinate amount of time on low risk decisions and inadequate time on high risk decisions. For example, we may spend a week thinking and planning the furniture arrangement in an apartment and make a snap judgment about accepting a new job in another city. Some people agonize over the purchase of a $10 item of clothes, soliciting the opinion of a friend or relative, but agree to serious and extensive surgery without consulting a second doctor. A principal might hire a new teacher after a brief interview without consulting anyone, while agonizing for days and consulting many people over what color to paint his office or whether to serve coffee and tea or soft drinks at the orientation for new teachers.

The next step in action planning is to assign each item on the list of agreed upon, feasible, simple or complex suggestions a preliminary designation of either high risk (H) or low risk (L). These designations are tentative and can be revised subsequently, but are extremely useful in deciding how much time to spend in planning, whether or not to delegate, whether and what kind of consultation and follow-up procedures are needed.

Setting Priorities

Armed with a list of ideas which are feasible, agreed upon, and designated as simple or complex, and as high or low risk, the group is ready for the next step: establishing priorities to determine the order in which things will be implemented.

Setting priorities involves making conscious decisions about what seems to be most important to us. Unless we establish priorities and attempt to stick to them, we may find that much of our time is spent on things of minor importance. A principal may say that his first priority is community relations but spend most of his time on other activities. Many persons and groups are crisis oriented, always putting out fires, responding to pressure, and acting randomly instead of according to a plan. Consciously establishing priorities makes it easier to: allocate time, act rather than react, say "no" to some things and "yes" to others, and evaluate how time and resources are being expended.

The two lists of agreed upon, simple and complex ideas are rank-ordered separately by importance. These priority lists represent the order in which the ideas are to be implemented. Generally, the simple ideas will be implemented first. However, sometimes a complex suggestion will be so important that it takes priority over some or all of the simpler ones.

One way of establishing the priority listing is to ask the question, "If only one of these ideas could be accomplished this year (this month, this week) which should be chosen?" That idea becomes first on the list. Then, "If only one more idea could be accomplished in this period, which would it be?" And so on, until the entire list of simple and complex ideas is rank-ordered by importance.

Once priorities have been established, a time log *(see Form 19, Time Utilization Log, p. 345)* may be kept for a week, or longer, to check on how time is being spent. Each activity is recorded and the time spent on each activity is detailed. It then becomes clear whether most of the time is spent on high priority items. If not, why not?

Testing for Agreement

Testing for agreement goes on at almost every step of the action planning process. However, it is emphasized more at certain important junctures. During the categorizing phase, it is done quickly and briefly. At this point, just prior to beginning detailed planning and prior to implementation, it is much more thorough.

An important distinction must be made between acquiescence and acceptance. Acquiescence is going along with something but not really agreeing. It means your heart is not really in it, that you are saying "yes" with serious unstated reservations. Acceptance is true agreement and implies a commitment to follow through and get things done. People rarely follow through when they have merely acquiesced.

Many decisions in groups get made by default. The leader or strongest person in the group may say, "I think we are all agreed, so let's move on" or, "If there aren't any objections, let's move on." Silence is considered agreement. There may be objections or reservations or questions that do not get voiced for many reasons. People may not want to appear stupid, resistant, or opposed to the majority. There may be fear of conflict, disagreement, or rejection.

Fear of disagreement and conflict is one of the reasons that many discussions remain general, abstract, or superficial. To give the appearance of agreement and smooth over conflict, you often hear the statement, "I think we are really saying the same thing but are using different words," or "I think we are basically in agreement on the main concept, but are saying it differently."

The more general the goal or idea, the easier it is to get agreement. For example, everyone will agree with the general concept: "Respect and honesty are important in dealing with people." Yet if you try to define specific examples of behavior that is respectful or honest, you may find considerable disagreement. Strive for specificity so that it is clear whether there is agreement or disagreement, acquiescence, or acceptance.

When requesting overt expressions of acceptance, be sensitive to verbal and nonverbal behavior which may indicate lack of acceptance despite what a person says. Encourage questions and expressions of reservations or concern. It is better to deal with disagreements openly than to have them come back to haunt you in the form of resistance and subversion during the implementation phase.

Developing Implementation Plans

Plans may be extremely simple and brief or elaborate and detailed, depending on the complexity of the activity and on whether it is a high or low risk venture. Some or all of the following steps may be involved:

1. List all questions for which answers or data are needed. Decide where data can be obtained and gather the information.

2. Identify forces which might block successful implementation of the idea. For example, under "Home visitation by teacher," blocking forces might be: parents working during the day; teacher not living in the community making night visits difficult; teacher fears. For each blocking factor, list possible ways (use brainstorming) of overcoming it and incorporate these into the plans. If anticipated in advance, many potential obstacles can be overcome or avoided.

   Identify forces which might facilitate successful implementation. For each facilitating factor, brainstorm possible ways it can be used to advantage and strengthened.

3. Formulate a plan (specific steps, procedures, materials, schedule) to implement the idea. If possible, develop more than one plan, especially for high risk ideas. Weigh the advantages and disadvantages of each plan and select the one that offers the best opportunity for success.

4. Test the plan for possible flaws by checking with persons who will be involved or affected by it. Often plans look good on paper but fall apart when put into practice. Persons who will have a direct interest can frequently detect weaknesses and problems which can be handled simply during the planning stage, avoiding expensive, time-consuming corrections when discovered in practice.

5. Decide whether the plan is ready to be implemented. At this stage, there should be a final testing

for acceptance of the overall plan and of its major elements.

Assigning Personnel and Target Dates

Any plan is only as good as the persons who will have the responsibility to carry it out. Assignment of personnel is crucial. Primary considerations are: Who is best qualified? Who has the time and is not overloaded? And, who could benefit most from the experience? On high risk items, qualifications should carry the greatest weight. On low risk items, personnel might be assigned for the purposes of gaining training and experience.

Avoid overloading people who seem to be involved in everything because they are competent and dependable, or because they volunteer for everything. However agreeable they may be, these people often get burned out or turn sour. Wherever possible, spread the responsibility. Develop new talent.

The Action Planning Worksheet *(see Form 16, p. 341)* may be used to keep an ongoing record of accountability.

Evaluation and Revision

No matter how well thought out a plan is or how good it looks on paper, in practice some things are certain to go wrong. Continuous evaluation while the project is in progress (known as *process evaluation*) is important to:

Determine if the plan is working, if objectives are being achieved.

Strengthen parts of plan that are working well.

Revise parts of plan that are not working well.

Evaluate and improve the plan through feedback among participants.

Evaluate and improve individual performances and cope with interpersonal problems through feedback.

Each meeting opens with a statement of the meeting's objectives and ends with a critique of the meeting. During the end-of-meeting critique, group members address the following questions: To what extent were the goals achieved? What did you like or dislike about the meeting? What suggestions do you have for improvement?

Periodically, at the end of these meetings, each participant answers the question "What did I like and dislike about my own participation?" and also receives feedback from the other group members about what they liked and disliked about the individual's involvement. The Group Process Questionnaire *(see Form 13, p. 334)* is helpful for discussion, evaluation, and probing of group effectiveness.

Evaluating final results is known as *product evaluation*. Success is measured in terms of the criteria established in the initial objectives. To what extent did the final product meet original expectations? All the steps in the action planning process and implementation phases are reviewed to identify weaknesses and to recommend changes for future action planning.

Flexibility in Procedures

Time constraints, complexity of activity, and level of risk determine how thoroughly the action planning process is applied and how much time is devoted to each step. With practice and experience, the process takes less and less time. In the beginning, it is valuable to go through each step for the practice. To best use time and personnel, decisions should be made as to whether each step in the process is best accomplished by a large group, small group, or one or two persons.

Careful, systematic planning saves time and energy and enormously contributes to individual and group morale and effectiveness. The action planning process has been discussed here mainly as a tool for committee work, but all of the steps in the process are applicable to an individual working alone.

TRAINING IN SHARED PLANNING-AND-DECISION-MAKING

Although we live in a democratic society which encourages a great deal of individual freedom, most of us have little experience in planning and organizing the social organizations and policies under which we are governed. Many of us tend to avoid the responsibility of making decisions. We are used, or resigned, to allowing other people to plan and manage our lives since we are ill prepared and disinclined to plan our own individually or in groups.

In the tutorial community school, it is important that every member become an active planner and decision maker. An essential part of the program, therefore, is training all personnel in these vital skills.

Initial training is designed to: introduce personnel to the major concepts of shared planning-and-decision-making; discuss goals, procedures, and gound rules; and give participants an opportunity to raise questions and to voice their concerns and reservations. Participants should develop realistic expectations, an idea of their own responsibilities, and a positive attitude and a sense of excitement about sharing in planning activities.

Later training develops knowledge and skill in team building, leadership and action planning. Key personnel are involved at first, and subsequently, this training is provided for all members of major committees and for the total faculty, and for as many parents and nonteaching staff as possible.

Orientation Seminar

Orientation seminars involve readings, film presentations, questions and answers, discussion, and role playing.

The seminar facilitator should be an experienced educator who is knowledgeable about TCP (a teacher or principal from the target school or another school, or a staff person from the district office) and has experience in the theory and practice of shared planning. An outside consultant with expertise in organizational development may also be used.

At the seminar, the facilitator presents the rationale underlying shared planning, the general goals, and a brief overview of procedures. A discussion is held on how shared planning can lead to personal and organizational growth and improvement and to a heightened sense of ownership. Participants list all the questions they have about shared planning and they are discussed. The TCP film may be shown, or quotes from various scenes in the film may be used as a point of departure to discuss the significance of shared planning in a self-renewing program.

Examples of quotes which may be used:

PRINCIPAL: They told me, 'you say one thing but do another!' And I had to change my role.

PRINCIPAL: It's the first time I saw teachers speaking to each other honestly and saying things that had consequences for each other and that's what I call professionalism with a capital 'P.'

PARENT: You have to have everyone involved or the program won't work.

STUDENT: (to prospective teacher) How come if you have a master's degree you want to teach in an elementary school? Couldn't you get a better job?

PARENT: As parents become more involved, the school is going to be held more accountable.

Team Building and Leadership Training

In order for people to develop their ability to work constructively in groups, and at the same time to exercise initiative and leadership, they have to develop certain sensitivities about themselves, their impact on others, and the impact of others on them. The individual behaves differently when he is alone and when he is in a group. People have to learn how to work together in groups and make maximum use of individual talents and knowledge.

Group Development Exercises

Numerous training exercises have been developed which contribute to an individual's understanding of group process and make him aware of his own strengths and weaknesses in working with others.

The *NASA Exercise*** is a good initial group development exercise. It is a simulated experience which postulates that a group of people are stranded on the moon and have to make decisions that affect their ability to survive. *(See Form 20, NASA Exercise, p. 346.)*

---

* This is one of numerous group problem solving exercises available for such training. See Pfeiffer, J.W. and J.E. Jones, *A Handbook of Structured Experiences for Human Relations Training*, Vols. 1-4, La Jolla, Calif.; University Associates Publisher, Inc., 1969, 1970, 1971, 1973.

This exercise in group decision making enables participants to compare the results of individual decision making with group decision making, and to analyze the interpersonal behavior and communication among group members. The discussion following the exercise focuses on exchanging feedback about each person's attitudes, feelings, behavior, and contributions as a member of the group, and on the group's ability to utilize adequately the knowledge and talents of its members. The exercise generally demonstrates the superiority of group over individual planning and also points out obstacles to group effectiveness.

The FIRO exercises, like the NASA exercise, are excellent for group development analysis. Fundamental Interpersonal Relations Orientation (FIRO) is a theory about group development proposed by William Schutz.[*] He postulated that group development deals sequentially with three main issues: inclusion (interaction with the group); control (responsibility and influence); and affection (love or emotional closeness). *(See Form 21, Group Development, p. 352.)*

The exercises consist of structured activities that were developed to illustrate in concrete behavioral ways each of these concepts. Inclusion is demonstrated by choosing up sides for a debate, control by Indian thumb wrestling, and affection by strength bombardment. *(See Form 22, Exercises Demonstrating FIRO B Concepts, p. 354, for explanation and directions for these exercises.)*

Training of Administration

The modern school is a complex organization requiring skilled leaders. The principal as the chief administrator-managerfacilitator in the school has a crucial role to play in developing

---

[*] Schutz, William, *The Interpersonal World,* Palo Alto, California: Science and Behavior Books, 1966.

shared planning-and-decision-making. He must be able to model the desired behavior and also help train others in the significant processes. The principal should receive special training in the theory and practice of organizational development so that he may intervene effectively to improve the group processes in his school.

Opportunities for such training include one and two-day and two to three-week workshops, and ongoing courses lasting several months. The training may be offered by the staff development section of the school district itself, by local colleges and universities, or by such organizations as the National Training Laboratories (NTL).

IN CONCLUSION

Shared planning-and-decision-making are crucial processes for a tutorial community school. A person's sense of community develops in direct proportion to his sense of control of his own destiny and of his ability to influence the forces of change about him. This is no less true for a student than a teacher or parent. All segments of the population must be informed about the school's philosophy, program, problems, needs, and successes. Everyone must be involved and feel part of the total picture. Everyone must see the relationship between his role and the rest of the school, and feel tied to the other people as they work cooperatively toward improvement.

A visitor to a TCP school once asked what the ultimate TCP school would look like. The answer was that there is no such thing as a definitive TCP school. Part of the essence of TCP is the constant process of empirical evaluation, revision, change. That's what makes a TCP school a self-correcting, self-renewing organization. Although certain concepts will always be a part of any TCP school (mutual learning and teaching, mutual ownership through shared planning-and-decision-making, mutual concern and accountability through continuous open, frank feedback, and parent involvement), the forms and methods by which these concepts are realized vary greatly. TCP will be different at different times in each school, and it will take different forms at different schools.

The organizational structure and approach described in this chapter were developed at several TCP schools through experimentation and trial and error. They appeared to meet the needs for mutual ownership at a given time. Although TCP schools elsewhere might develop quite different organizational forms and procedures for their own community, they would have in common shared planning-and-decision-making among students, teachers, parents, and administrators.

4 PARENT INVOLVEMENT

Expanding the Learning Community: Parents as Active Members of the School Community.

INTRODUCTION: HUMANIZING PARENT-TEACHER-SCHOOL RELATIONSHIPS

"The teachers are loose! The teachers are loose! How come the teachers are loose in town?" These were the outbursts of incredulous youngsters who were witnessing the astonishing scene of teachers walking in the streets of their neighborhood and knocking on doors to visit parents in their homes. These teachers were making home visits as part of a summer TCP activity. Children came by the project office to find out what was happening. They were not used to seeing teachers on the streets in their neighborhoods, let alone in their homes.

These children did not really view teachers as people. To them, a teacher was someone who stood at the blackboard with chalk in his hand and yelled directions at them. They had no view of a teacher as someone's mother, daughter or favorite aunt, a person who ate and slept and cried and laughed and went to the bathroom and was once a kid who sat in classrooms and squirmed like them.

Teachers were not people, but stereotypes. Children frequently referred to them by the appellation "teacher" rather than by name. Learning was impersonal. Parents and children related to teachers as strangers, and sometimes as adversaries, rather than as friends and collaborators.

When teachers began visiting parents in their homes, not only did something start to happen to parents; something happened to teachers, too. Teachers were surprised and delighted at how warmly they were received and found not only that they had something to offer the parents, but that they could learn from parents, too. As one teacher remarked, "We shared anecdotes and stories about our children and when I told the parent some problems I was having with my older son, she gave me some excellent advice. I left with a real warm feeling."

When teachers see children in their home, they start looking at them as total human beings. And when children know their parents and teachers know each other, they feel good and they begin to look at teachers differently. Learning becomes more personal, more human.

Achieving positive changes in how parents feel about the teacher and the school may actually be the best way to improve children's learning. If the parent treats learning as important, talks about school with respect and warmth, pays attention to, and shows interest in what the child does in school and praises his efforts to learn, this may do more for learning than any efforts to improve teaching materials or techniques. The reverse is true, too. If parents are not interested in or are hostile toward the school and their children know this, the best efforts may be of little avail.

Yet little energy or time is normally expended in creating a healthy parent-teacher-school relationship. Teachers regard parents as mostly apathetic and unresponsive. Parents regard the school as mostly uninviting and hostile, a place where they are talked down to and where they are summoned only when a child misbehaves. Parents feel like outsiders in the school and teachers feel like outsiders in the community. To change all this requires giving parent involvement a high priority, making it part of the teacher's job, and providing the necessary time. The payoff can be enormous.

UNDERLYING CONCEPTS

Quality education requires school staff, students, and community members to work together harmoniously and cooperatively in an atmosphere of mutual trust and respect. Education becomes more personal, meaningful, and relevant as parents and teachers have more frequent positive contacts.

The educational enterprise is benefited by taking the school into the community and the community into the school.

People grow, learn, and contribute best in an environment where they feel they have some control over their own destiny.

Most parents are vitally concerned with their children's welfare and education. Parent apathy may be due to the fact that the school has not created the necessary or desirable conditions for good relations with parents. Given the proper conditions, they will get involved in the school.

GENERAL GOALS

The aim is to develop a learning community where children, parents, teachers, nonteaching staff, and administrators share responsibility, concern, pride, and satisfaction in a cooperative effort to improve the learning of all. Improvement is sought in the following four major areas:

Information Flow

School personnel must be kept aware of community problems, needs, significant events, services and agencies, and of the out-of-school life of children.

Community persons must be kept informed about the

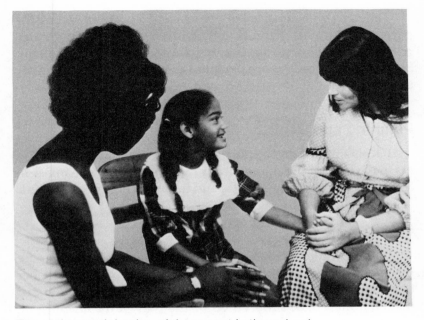

The active participation of the parent in the school
may be the most significant factor in improving
teaching and learning.

school program, and about the growth and development of
individual children.

Both school and community persons need to be informed
about new educational ideas, concepts, and programs.

Interpersonal Relations

Teachers and parents need to get to know each other better
as people rather than as stereotypes, need to feel more comfortable with each other, and need to communicate more easily
and directly with one another. Then, fears that parents and
teachers have of each other will be diminished or eliminated.

Teachers will gain greater respect and a positive feeling for parents and pupils. Parents and children will develop greater respect and a more positive feeling for teachers and the school. School will become more personal and enjoyable for teachers and children.

Planning and Decision Making

Parents must have opportunities to participate with teachers in evaluating the school program, in suggesting changes, in reacting to proposed changes, and in preparing specific plans.

Service

Opportunities need to be extended to parents to participate directly in school activities: to help in classrooms as teacher aides and tutors; to help in the school with development of teaching materials, supervision of the play yard, lunchroom, library. Parents can learn to tutor their own children at home with training from teachers.

Teachers can draw on the special knowledge, skills, and talents parents possess. Teachers can become knowledgeable about community services and agencies and can assist parents and families in using community resources.

As parent participation in school increases, parents will become more responsive to communications from school.

Parent assistance will increase children's interest in school and improve learning.

Discipline problems will decrease.

PRACTICAL CONSIDERATIONS

The teacher and principal should take the initiative in creating and maintaining positive contacts between home and school.

At the same time, parents must be encouraged by the PTA and School Advisory Council not to sit back and wait but also to take initiative to create positive contacts on their own. There is no single approach that will work for all teachers and all parents. A variety of methods and procedures should be tried. Because many parents work during the day, ways will have to be found to involve them in the evening or on weekends.

Parent participation, day or evening, does not necessarily have to be at the school. There are many things parents can do in their own homes to keep informed, to be in touch with the teacher, to be of service to the school, and to help their children.

Teachers, too, are not only busy with their full-time jobs and with teaching preparations, but also have their own out-of-school lives. Ways to make contacts must be found that are relatively simple and not overly time consuming. The school must find ways to support and reward teachers for these efforts.

It is unrealistic to expect large numbers of people to get involved in schoolwide planning or service activities. It is more realistic to expect that parents will become involved in activities which offer immediate benefit to their own children. Teachers are also more likely to put in extra time and effort in activities that directly pay off in terms of greater support from parents or cooperation from children.

To develop a "classroom community" there must be peer helping relationships and parent involvement. A core group of a few parents can work closely with the teacher to organize an information network (telephone tree) involving all parents. Gradually parent teams are formed and parents tutor their own children at home; meet regularly to share experiences and develop new ideas; and recruit and train other parents and help them become a team.

GRADUAL PROGRESSION OR PHASING

Like the tutoring program, the parent involvement program proceeds in phases, moving from simple to more complex activities in carefully designed, sequential steps. This gradual progression enables parents to have increasingly meaningful contacts and involvements with teachers and the school.

Each activity is independent and has its own value. Teachers will exercise personal preference in choosing activities. Many activities may be conducted simultaneously, and some will cut across phases. However, the parent involvement plan will work most smoothly and successfully if teachers engage in as many of the activities suggested here as possible during each phase.

Phases I, II and III focus on the individual teacher's relationship to the parents of his children. The notion is developed of the classroom community where parents work with the teacher and, are resources for each other on parent teams.

Phase IV focuses on schoolwide involvement of parents and on school-parent relations in general. Phase IV activities go on simultaneously with the activities of the other phases. (Form 23, Sequence of Steps in Implementing the Parent Involvement Program, p. 360, shows the steps within all four phases.)

Phase I: Laying the Foundation for Positive Teacher-Parent Relations

The foundation for productive and constructive parent-teacher relations begins with getting acquainted and establishing channels for back-and-forth communication. The emphasis is on positive, friendly, and informative contacts.

In the initial contact the teacher conveys his accessibility through a message that says essentially: "Hello, welcome to our class. I would like to tell you a little about myself and what I am going to try to achieve with your child this year. I would like to get to know you better and work with you toward that end. I would appreciate your suggestions and assistance."

This contact is followed up by a series of others. Some of the activities are one time occurrences, while others are repeated as needed or are regular events.

Children can and should play an important role in securing greater parent participation in classroom and school programs. They should have some understanding of the purpose of the various contacts and proposed activities. Indeed, the children ideally will have participated in their formulation.

1. Teacher's Introductory Note to Parents

The teacher sends a note to the parents of each child in his class to introduce himself, extend a welcome to the classroom, and express a desire to work with the parents for the benefit of the children. *(See Form 24, Introductory Note to Parents, p. 362.)*

Notes are generally sent at the end of the first week of school. Additional introductory notes are sent throughout the year when new children enter the class.

It is very important to involve children in parent contacts. However, children must be prepared for this. The content and purpose of messages sent to parents should be discussed with the children; children should be given specific assignments to get a response; and the teacher should follow up by discussing the results with the class. *(See Form 25, Involving Children in Involving Parents, p. 363.)*

Before children have had this kind of training it is probably better to mail the very first notes home to parents to assure their delivery. However, training children to participate in parent involvement should take place very early in the school year. When this is done, children understand the new school philosophy and become responsible participants. Subsequent notes to parents may then be entrusted to children to be hand delivered.

2. Paired Teachers' Introductory Note to Parents

The teachers whose classrooms are paired for tutoring write a joint note to the parents of each child in both classes. They mention briefly the philosophy of a TCP school and the nature of the cooperative effort in which the classes are to be involved, and they invite the parents to a social at which the program will be explained and discussed. *(See Form 26, Sample Paired Teachers' Introductory Note to Parents, p. 364.)*

These notes should be sent after the beginning class reorganization has taken place, usually during the second or third week of school. These notes may be sent home with the children. The children should be involved in such a way as to insure maximum response from parents. *(See Form 25, Involving Children in Involving Parents, p. 363.)*

3. Initial Teacher Telephone Contact

The teacher calls each family to say hello and make personal contact. He usually says that he is calling to say hello personally. He indicates he is pleased to have the child in his class and tries to make a specific positive statement about the child. He encourages the parents to visit the classroom and invites them to a get acquainted evening at the school.

These calls are usually made within the first month of the school year. The teacher tries to limit each call to about three minutes.

Traditionally, parents receive calls from teachers only when a child misbehaves or is in trouble. By contrast, this call helps lay the foundation for positive, supportive teacher-parent relationships.

A "joint-evening" with paired teachers and their
parents demonstrates the concept of cooperative
learning and teaching.

4. Regular Telephone Contacts

To maintain positive rapport, the teacher regularly telephones
the parents of each child. The teacher may provide information about the child (especially praiseworthy), or the school, or
may seek information from the parent.

   If possible, these calls should be made to each parent as
often as once every six to ten weeks. At a minimum, they
should be made twice per semester. Teachers have found this
activity manageable if they limit calls to ten calls per week and
to three minutes duration. In this way, within a four-week
period most parents in a class can be contacted if the teacher
spends about one hour per week on the phone. To maximize
the probability of parents being at home, the teacher can set up

a regular schedule and notify the parents in advance.

An alternative plan is for the teacher to establish telephone receiving hours and have parents initiate the calls. The teacher can send a note home to parents indicating the night and time he is available to receive calls. The calls may still be limited to approximately three minutes.

Some teachers prefer to give out their phone numbers and encourage parents to call when they have any problems and can't get to school to talk about them. *(See Form 27, Sample Teacher Note About Telephone Contact, p. 365.)*

Teachers report that parents are surprised and delighted to hear from them. Students are also delighted, especially if they answer the phone and get to talk to the teacher. The payoff in improved parent and child attitudes is well worth the extra time. *(See Form 28, Teacher Report on Telephoning Parents, p. 366.)* Subsequently, if teachers have to call about a problem, parents are receptive and cooperative.

Teachers should be allowed to charge the school for phone calls made to parents from home. Otherwise, the cost may be a factor in keeping teachers from engaging in this activity.

5. Paired Teacher and Parent Get Acquainted Activity

The paired teachers invite the parents of both classes to meet informally at school for an evening of discussion and refreshments. Holding a "joint-evening" demonstrates the concept of cooperative learning and teaching. Approximately two hours should be reserved for the meeting. The meeting enables parents to become better acquainted with each other and with the teachers. They see the classrooms, learn about the school program and about how they can become involved.

This meeting should take place early in the semester, by the third or fourth week, but after most parents have been contacted by telephone. The initial telephone contact may be used to invite parents. The teachers should then follow up with a

written invitation. *(See Form 29, Sample Paired Teachers'
Invitation to Get Acquainted Evening, p. 367.)* The teachers
should get the children involved in motivating parents to
attend. *(See Form 25, Involving Children in Involving Parents,
p. 363.)* Request a response to the invitation. Send notes to
parents who did not attend the meeting. *(See Form 30, Sample
Follow-Up Note, p. 368.)*

After introductions, the teachers talk briefly about the
philosophy of a TCP school, emphasizing the concept of the
helping relationship. If possible, show the TCP film and elicit
questions and discussion. Have appropriate "handouts" available to give to the parents ("About TCP" booklet, statement of
goals, description of parent involvement activities). Discuss
plans for the semester and goals for children. Describe how the
two classes will work together.

After a coffee and refreshment break, each teacher should
meet separately with his students' parents. Describe how
parents can become involved and the benefits to the children.
*(See Form 31, Suggested Activities for Parent Involvement, p.
369.)*

Teachers (individually or in pairs) may want to schedule a
coffee and donut breakfast meeting at school for parents who
are unable to attend the evening session. This might last one
hour, and should be scheduled early enough so working parents can get to their jobs on time. Some teachers may want to
hold regular breakfast meetings throughout the year.

6. Parent Telephone Tree

A telephone tree enables the teacher to communicate information effectively and rapidly to all parents in the classroom with
minimum burden. The telephone tree also can be used to
obtain information from parents.

As early as possible in the semester, after classes have
stabilized, the telephone tree should be initiated. This should

occur by the third or fourth week, as soon after the parent get acquainted meeting as possible.

The teacher recruits one parent as telephone tree chairman. The chairman compiles a class list with name of each child, parents' names and telephone numbers.

To break up the task of having innumerable calls to make, the chairman and teacher recruit six parent telephone coordinators. Four or five parents are assigned to each coordinator. When the teacher has a message to communicate to all parents, he tells the chairman the essential content to be passed on, the deadlines for doing so, and whether a response from parents is necessary. The chairmen passes on the information to the six coordinators, who in turn call the four or five persons for whom they have responsibility. If the chairman cannot reach one of the coordinators, he or the teacher makes the calls to that branch of the tree.

The teacher sends a note to all parents describing the system and the reasons for it and asks for their cooperation. The chairman or teacher meet periodically with the six coordinators to make necessary revisions and improvements. (For an example of the use to which the telephone tree may be put, *see Form 32, Use of Telephone Tree to Obtain Material for Classroom Project, p. 370.*)

Although the initial use is for the teacher to pass on and obtain information from parents, the tree could later be linked to parent involvement teams. For example, when a member of a parent team attends a School Community Advisory Council meeting or other committee activity, the tree can be used to pass on highlights of the meeting to all parents on the team.

7. Parent Classroom Coordinator

The teacher recruits one or two parents to help involve parents in classroom projects. This should be done early in the school year.

The parent classroom coordinator becomes knowledgeable about the total program; helps recruit parents for jobs and activities; and assists in organizing parent teams.

The parent coordinator is introduced and his role is described to all parents at meetings or through written communication. Parents are encouraged to use this person as a resource and contact for keeping informed and getting involved.

The parent classroom coordinator works closely with the telephone chairman.

8. Student and Class Progress Notes

A brief note is sent to parents informing them of some of the things the class or the child is into recently. It may include a short statement on how the child is doing. Notes should be sent monthly.

The teacher and the class discuss what they have been doing that parents might be interested in knowing about. They list these assignments, projects, activities, or events on the board, and discuss what is special about any of the activities listed. The teacher or the children then write a brief note (maximum one page) describing the chosen activities. Younger children can dictate letters to older tutors. The teacher can also add a postscript to make some comment about the individual child, or may send a separate note commenting on some positive aspect of the child's behavior. (*See Forms 33, 34, 35, Sample Notes to Parents, pp. 371-373.*)

9. Examples of Student Work Sent Home

A completed assignment, project, art work, composition, or test paper may be sent home so that parents can see examples of their child's work. This should be done regularly, once monthly at the minimum.

In class discussion, children talk about what they want to take home. Children are asked to report back some response from parents (reactions, comments, questions).

10. Student Thank You Notes to Parents

When parents assist in the classroom or help with special activities, students write thank you notes. These should be written whenever appropriate, usually immediately after the parent's participation ends (or while it is going on if assistance continues over a substantial period).

Younger students write notes with guidance of teachers, special helpers within class, or tutor. If the child has difficulty writing, he can dictate the note to a helper.

11. Written Feedback From Parents

Every ten weeks, as part of the regular reporting period, a report card goes home for each child. On the student report card, room is provided for the parents to give written feedback to teachers about their feelings, thoughts, opinions, and questions about the school and classroom program, and about their child's achievement.

The reasons for parent feedback and its importance are thoroughly discussed with the children just before they take their report cards home. It should be stressed that the purpose of reporting progress and getting feedback is to improve learning conditions.

Parents may make suggestions. They may express positive or negative reactions. The data from all parents is compiled and summarized and each teacher uses this information to make constructive change. Each teacher follows up promptly on parent questions in writing or by phone.

Teachers may share with each other suggestions from parents which seem worthwhile. Where appropriate, they attempt to implement them in their own class. Data are supplied to the School Community Advisory Council, and a summary of parent comments is distributed to all parents through the school newsletter or by special bulletin.

Phase II: Expanded Parent-Teacher Contacts

Phase II activities are designed to deepen the parents' knowledge about the class program and the teachers' understanding of the child and the community. Information is exchanged in greater depth. Personal contacts continue to build a positive, cooperative relationship between teacher and parent and between school and home.

1. School Visitation

During the third, fourth and fifth months of the school year, two to four parents are invited each week to visit the classroom until all parents have visited. Generally, the teacher designates two hours per day, one or two days per week as parent visiting time. The teacher sends a note home to parents explaining the importance of personally observing the learning situation to get a first hand feel for what goes on. A sign-up sheet is provided on which parents can reserve a date or indicate days they are available. Or the teacher may invite parents for specific times and make adjustments as needed.

The teacher may wish to prepare a brief memorandum as a guide to parents. It might describe classroom philosophy and procedures, and indicate what parents should look for during their visit. *(See Form 36, Guidelines For Visiting Parents, p. 373.)*

A child greets parents as they arrive and acts as a guide during the visit. The child may show parents points of special interest elsewhere in the school (hallway displays, resource center, special projects).

At the end of the visit, the teacher reserves some time to discuss the parent's observations and to answer questions. The class engages in independent activity or learning teams at this time.

Parents are free to, and encouraged to, drop in and visit the classroom at all times. However, an open invitation may not be taken seriously. The formal program is an attempt to be sure that all parents come at least once or twice.

2. Parent-Student-Teacher Conference

At least twice yearly (usually in the middle of each semester), the teacher meets with each student and his parent in a three-way conference to discuss the student's progress and to exchange honest feedback. The purpose is to improve instruction and learning conditions, *not* to compare and rank-order students. This face-to-face conference should enable all persons (1) to gain clear understanding of the amount and quality of the student's learning progress, and (2) to identify how each of the three parties can contribute toward improving student learning. Continuous self-evaluation and the importance of deeply involving a learner in his own evaluation are stressed.

In the course of the conference between teacher, parent, student, the following should occur:

1. Each evaluates his own efforts to achieve goals previously established.

2. Each receives feedback from the other two about his efforts.

3. Each makes suggestions for the future.

4. Goals and commitments for next period are established.

A summary of comments of participants should be recorded. *(See Form 44, Evaluation of Factors Contributing to Student Progress, p. 391.)* These may then be compared from one conference to the next. A contract about future goals should be agreed upon by all of the participants. *(See Form 45, Parent-Child Teacher Contract to Improve Instructional Climate, p. 397.)*

3. Home Visitation

At least once a year, beginning as early in the year as feasible, the teacher tries to visit the parents of each child in their home.

Teacher visits may take different forms:

> The teacher might accompany a different child home each day after school and chat informally with the parent.

> The teacher could visit neighboring parents during the lunch period. (The details—eating in advance, bringing a box lunch, parent preparing lunch—would be worked out in whatever way is most comfortable.)

> Teachers could send notes home suggesting days and times he could come and requesting parents to indicate the best times for them. The appointments could also be made by telephone. Early evening appears to be the best time for visits. Both parents are more likely to be available.

> If teachers get their new class lists before the summer, home visits just prior to the start of school or at other times during the summer are an excellent way to initiate teacher-parent contact.

Generally, the TCP coordinator, or the principal or consultant should conduct orientation and training for teachers prior to home visits, especially if teachers will be visiting ethnic groups predominantly different from their own. Initial anxiety can be alleviated by sharing experiences with other teachers who have had positive home visits, and by discussion with one or two parents from the community. Parents can anticipate community reactions and attitudes and provide information about the community.

Parents are usually pleased to have teachers extend themselves and meet them on their home grounds. Children are delighted to see teachers in their home and neighborhood. The teachers see new dimensions of the child and get a feel for his home environment. Initial fears and reticence by teachers turn to enthusiasm when they are warmly received by parents and children, and as teachers see the positive effects on the children's attitudes.

Home visits are time consuming. If this activity is to receive the priority it merits, teachers will need support through released time, salary point credit, or monetary compensation.

4. Class Social Evening

Each class hosts a special evening of discussion, student presentation, and socializing for parents at least once a year, toward the end of the first semester or beginning of the second semester, or an evening or Saturday morning. Saturday morning has several advantages. There is higher probability of having both parents attend, and children and teachers do not have to go to school the next day, nor do parents have to work.

Using action planning methods, the teacher involves the children in deciding the content of the get together and in planning its implementation. One part of the program may be an open discussion involving parents, children, and teacher on topics, problems, issues, or questions of concern and interest (aspects of TCP, or special topics such as discipline, physical education, lunch program, field trips).

A second part of the evening may be a student presentation chosen by the teachers and students. It could be a demonstration of a TCP activity, such as a student feedback session, tutoring, a learning team activity, a shared planning meeting, or it could be a dramatic or singing presentation. Refreshments and informal conversation are part of the evening.

Phase III: Parent Assistance, Parent Teams

Phase III extends the concept of the classroom as a community. Parents become involved not only with their own children, but with all the children in the class. Parents become resources for each other and for the school, working with children both at home and in the classroom programs. Parents work closely with one another in teams to combine their talent, skills, ideas. The school still takes the initiative in organizing these activities, but also encourages parental initiative.

When recruiting parents for volunteer activities, the teacher should recognize that frequently persons do not become involved because of fears (of the unknown, of being inadequate, of becoming overcommitted). It is helpful if the teacher specifies the nature of the activity, the skill needed, training provided, and the amount of time required. Try to keep the time required to a minimum. Once involved, if parents find it rewarding, they will usually volunteer to give more time.

1. Parent Home Tutoring, Involvement Teams

Parents from the same classroom form small teams to share in several experiences: preparing for and conducting tutoring of their own children at home; working on ways to assist teachers to improve the classroom program; serving as resources for each other; and socializing together. Through the teams, parents keep informed about and are able to influence school development and change.

The concept of parent teams is introduced at the first Class Get Acquainted meeting. The teacher recruits a core group of five to seven volunteers to be trained to tutor their own children at home. If a sufficient number of volunteers for one team do not come forward, a special meeting can be held to explain the idea and recruit parents. The parent teams meet regularly (weekly or semimonthly) under the guidance of the teacher (or a parent coordinator) to share experiences, revise plans and procedures, plan tutoring activities, and receive appropriate training.

Once the tutoring is functioning smoothly, the initial team recruits other parents and helps them become a tutoring team. This process continues until all parents of the class are organized into teams.

The team usually begins tutoring with a reading or reading related activity. Tutoring sessions with a child at home should be relaxed and enjoyable for both parent and child. They should be conducted two to three times weekly and kept short initially, 15 to 20 minutes. It is better to stop while enthusiasm is high rather than risk overdoing it. If the session has been fun and rewarding, time and frequency will gradually increase.

A team can also serve as an information network. Team members can rotate attendance at important committee meetings and bring back information to the group. Thereby no one person is overburdened, yet all can stay informed. Teams can discuss important issues facing the school and have team members represent their views at subsequent meetings. When a meeting is important enough, all can attend.

The team members serve as resources for each other, exchanging experiences and suggestions in a wide range of topics related to child rearing. Parents can assist each other in such practical ways as baby sitting to free each other for different activities; sharing materials and equipment; and tutoring each other's children in areas where they have different skills and expertise.

The team can also serve as a resource to the school by undertaking various projects to improve the school atmosphere, conditions, and relationships.

Many teachers will want to give the training of parent teams a high priority because the potential benefits are so great. The teacher should personally recruit and start teams. It cannot be delegated to parent assistants. In the early stages the teacher should attend the evening or Saturday morning team meetings. Later, a parent coordinator (a volunteer or paid assistant to teacher) can take over. Eventually the team gains enough momentum to continue without the presence of the teacher or coordinator.

The following excerpts from teachers' reports describe the content, procedures, and effects of some parent team meetings.

The parents received training in a variety of activities, from making and using educational games to reading stories. During the week, they would work with their children at home. At the next team meeting, they would evaluate and share experiences. Thus, the team meetings consisted of discussions of tutoring activities, problems, and suggestions for resolving some of these problems. New activities were offered after satisfactory completion of previous tasks. Choice of activities was available. The parents reached agreement by consensus. The parents as a team decided what subject area or skill they wished to work on; then each decided which particular activity would be used.

Refreshments were served and a considerable amount of socializing took place. The group started to become friends. Discussions went beyond tutoring, and parents shared experiences and concerns they had about a range of topics from amount and

*kind of TV watching, to eating problems, bedtime
hours, and so on.*

*The reactions and effects on teachers, parents,
and children were very positive. The teachers' and
parents' involvement in the process and with each
other grew steadily. Apathy and fear turned to
strong positive feelings.*

One teacher commented, "The first few meetings I dread-
ed because I was tired and didn't look forward to going back to
school in the evening. I accepted because I thought it was
important and would benefit the children. After the fourth
meeting, my attitude changed. Instead of dreading coming
back to school, I actually looked forward to it.

"This feeling, I know through talking with the parents, was
felt by them also. When parents couldn't make the meetings,
they would call or send a note. After each meeting, going
home, I would always have a feeling of elation—that I had
done something important—but most of all that the school
meetings could be fun and still accomplish something. The
meetings gave me an opportunity to compliment children
whose parents previously had only heard from teachers about
poor behavior. We would discuss openly particular needs and
problems, and I gained greater understanding of the child
through knowledge of the home situation."

Parents gained insights into themselves and the school. One
parent who had been highly critical and demanding of the
teachers, realized that she was doing very little for her own
child and nothing for the school. One father attended the
meetings faithfully, even though he was a fanatic sports fan
and occasionally had to miss a big sports event on television.

Social relationships formed. Parents would get together to
go to the movies, have coffee together, and so forth. A social
outing with children from the paired classes and their parents

was a big success. Two teams continued activities during the summer, including having a picnic at the beach with their children (this was without the teacher).

Also, the helping relationship began to spread. Sometimes, parents would exchange children. After one parent worked with another's child, they would discuss the activity together. Genuine concern for the other person's child developed.

Parents commented that they told their children that the teacher was their friend and wanted the children to cooperate in every way. Chidren seemed delighted with the relationship between parent and teacher. They would remind parents and teacher of meeting nights. Positive changes in classroom behavior and attitudes were strongly noticeable in some "problem children" whose parents were involved in the program.

On the whole, the teachers felt the rewards for their effort were great. It made their teaching easier and more enjoyable and led to teacher, child, and parent working closely together.

2. Classroom Advisory Council (Core Group)

Soon after the teacher has had sufficient contact with most parents of her class, the teacher, with the aid of the parent classroom coordinator, recruits three to six parents to work closely on improving the classroom learning environment. The core group or Class Advisory Council may be made up of one representative from each parent team. The teacher, parent team members, children, or other parents can pass on to the core group topics for discusion (e.g. testing, discipline, materials). The council may recommend action to the teacher and recruit a parent team to carry it out (e.g. make materials, train other parents, develop enrichment club plan). Students are brought into discussions by parents as desirable.

Meetings may take place regularly or as needed at the discretion of the teacher and core group members.

With the support of such a group, the teacher can expand

the scope of the classroom program. He can call on parents to organize, plan, and assist with field trips, social events, and with making special materials. The group also becomes an important source in bringing to the teacher knowledge about community resources that can enhance the children's learning.

3. Parents Assisting in Classroom

Parents can assist teachers in the classroom in numerous ways: tutoring, supervising student activities, grading papers, making materials, sharing talents, teaching games, and storytelling. This program can begin as soon as the teacher is able to make concrete plans for using and training volunteers.

Two different sets of plans for parent volunteers are needed. One is for the parent who assists regularly over a period of time (e.g. once weekly for a semester). The second plan is for parents who drop in when they have free time but not on a regular basis.

All parent volunteers receive orientation and training from the teacher, another parent, or the coordinator. Uncomplicated activities are selected initially to simplify training.

Recruiting of parent volunteers is done through get acquainted meetings, use of the telephone tree, newsletter announcements. The teacher establishes the goal of how many parents can be used regularly and works with the classroom coordinator and core group to achieve this goal.

The teacher must think through the need for volunteers and exactly how they are to be used. Otherwise, they get in the way and become a burden. Parents become frustrated if they wind up doing meaningless busy work or if they are not clear about what they are supposed to do or of the value of what they are doing.

Parents should be treated as colleagues, included in feedback sessions, and encouraged to make observations and suggestions to the teacher. There should be a genuine sense of teamwork.

Parent teams can be an excellent source for maintaining a consistent, reliable, and efficient corps of volunteers in the classroom. If members of a team take turns volunteering for periods of time, they can keep each other informed and train one another.

4. Parents Assisting With Trips

Parents are recruited to assist teachers in planning and accompanying the class on trips throughout the school year. Trips may be walking trips within the community (e.g. to a branch library) or by bus to more distant places. A schedule of bus trips may be sent home and parents encouraged to sign up in advance to assist. *(See Form 37, Sample Note on Field Trips, p. 376.)*

Teachers are encouraged to consider the entire community as the classroom. An excellent resource for exploring the learning potential of the community is *Yellow Pages of Learning Resources* published by the Group for Environmental Education, Inc. It describes and analyzes the learning possibilities available in visits to organizations and persons in a city, including the airport, bakery, banks, department stores, accountants, architects, telephone companies, television stations. Teachers frequently begin by exploring the local neighborhood and then branch out to the rest of the city.

5. Parents Assisting at Home

Parents can be of service to the classroom by working at home on tasks specified by the teacher such as: making materials (tutor kits), devising learning games, grading papers, obtaining information, drawing up plans. The teacher may provide explicit written instructions to aid parents in accomplishing tasks at home.

Many parents work and cannot help out in the classroom or school but would welcome an opportunity to assist at home. As teachers begin to use this resource, the list of possible parent contributions will grow.

6. Parent Initiated Social

Once per semester a social event is planned, organized, and conducted by the parents of the paired classrooms. It may be a picnic, classroom party, or other social affair. The parent classroom coordinators of both classes work with the class-room advisory councils or parent teams to plan this event for the teachers, children and parents of both classes. The parents take full responsibility for the planning and implementation of this event.

Phase IV: Parent Involvement Schoolwide

In previous phases, a major thrust of parent involvement was to develop a close relationship between the parent and the teacher, and among the parents of children in the same or paired classrooms. Simultaneous with this thrust, an attempt is made to develop a sense of community and school spirit that goes beyond the individual classroom.

In Phase IV, school activities are designed to keep parents informed about the total school program, events, problems, and needs; to increase parent contact with the school; and to enlist their participation and service in schoolwide activities.

1. Principal's Opening Welcome Note

During the first week of the school year the principal sends each family a note welcoming parents and children to their school for the new year. Also included is a general description and overview of the TCP philosophy and methods. Parents are invited to participate actively in developing the finest learning community possible and they are encouraged to keep informed, contribute criticism, ideas, and service, and have fun in the process.

2. Welcoming New Families

On the first day of school, an orientation and social get together is held for kindergarten parents and other families new to the school. Parents (PTA and first grade parents) organize it and provide refreshments. Teachers are available to support parent organizers in giving information and answering questions.

3. School Information Booklet

The school prepares and makes available to parents an information booklet that includes things that would give parents an understanding of the school and facilitate their knowing what is expected of them and their children. It tells where to go for specific information about TCP philosophy, the school program, materials, school schedule, staff responsibilites, scheduled events, and includes the year's calendar. The booklet may be prepared by a parent committee with the assistance of school staff.

4. Know Your Faculty/Staff Booklet

A booklet (with photos) of all faculty members, significant staff positions, and parent organization officers, accompanied by brief biographical data including school responsibilities may be prepared by a school committee and distributed to all families and staff early in the school year.

In a three-way conference, the parent, student and teacher discuss the student's progress and exchange honest feedback about what each can contribute to improve learning.

5. School Newsletter

A monthly newsletter, prepared by parents with supervision by a teacher, is sent to all families and staff. Its goal is to keep everyone informed about happenings of general interest, and to promote team spirit and a feeling of community. Content may include: schedules for meetings; highlights of meetings; a principal's report; report on tutoring program; want ads; calendar of coming events; personnel changes; good citizens of the week report; student and parent suggestions; special activities or achievements of individual students or classes; interesting anecdotes and humor; classroom practices, experiments, or innovations of special note.

Teachers can have their classes contribute to the newsletter by regularly setting aside time for students to write a few paragraphs on noteworthy events. Each class can decide which contributions to submit to the school newsletter. The remaining articles can be used for the class newsletter. Another source for items for the newsletter would be the minutes (Action Planning Worksheet) of the various committees.

6. Community News Bulletin Board

A bulletin board in the school's main building, near the main office, is maintained by the School Community Advisory Council to promote community interest and involvement. Items may include: announcements of school and community events; parent activities, achievements, suggestions, and feedback; photos of parent officers; special announcements; and want ads for parent volunteers.

7. Principal's Open Forum

Regularly (weekly, semimonthly), in the evening, the principal hosts an informal get together open to all parents. The school is made more accessible by providing a scheduled, after school time when parents can drop in to chat informally and become acquainted with school personnel and give and obtain information. A general invitation is sent to all parents to attend the principal's informal conversations. Students are involved in getting the message out, as is the parent telephone tree.

The atmosphere for these sessions is informal. Parents can drop in and stay for as long as they want. The group sits in a circle. Over coffee and refreshments, the principal encourages parents to ask questions, express concerns, raise issues, and make suggestions or observations. The emphasis is on listening to parents nondefensively and nonjudgmentally, on providing information where appropriate, and on engaging in the give and take of good discussion on a variety of topics. This informal conversation is an opportunity for principal and staff to model for parents the process of active listening and willingness to receive criticism. It develops rapport between school and parents so that parents feel more comfortable in the school and become actively supportive of the school program. Teacher pairs may take turns with principal in hosting the meetings.

It is not expected that large numbers of parents will attend at first. However, if done regularly, word will get out and more and more parents will drop by.

The meetings should not be cancelled except in the case of an emergency. Otherwise parents lose confidence in the school's reliability and stop coming. If the principal cannot attend, he should have someone take his place to host it.

8. Attendance at Committee Meetings

All school meetings and organizations are open to parent participation, either as active participants or as observers. Schedules of meetings (PTA, SCAC, TCP, Personnel, Faculty, Student Council, grade level chairmen, paired teachers, social, curriculum, library, and so forth) are published repeatedly in the school newsletter and displayed on school and community bulletin boards. The notion of an open school is promoted by encouraging parents to attend any or all meetings of their choice.

9. Community Nights

To promote a community or family atmosphere, at least one evening or Saturday each semester a social activity is planned for parents, faculty, and staff. Different parent teams can take charge and sponsor the event. Suggested activities include:

> *Family Night Pot Luck Supper:* Parents and teachers prepare and donate food. Each donor brings a different dish. Meal could have a theme (ethnic dishes). A prize is given for the most popular dish of the evening. A committee plans fun activities.

> *School Picnic:* Parents sponsor a school picnic for faculty, parents, children, staff at a local park. Food, games, fun activities are planned by a parent committee.

> *Film Showing:* A film is rented and a small admission fee is charged. Profits can go to the PTA. The admission charge for students is bringing one parent. The film is followed by refreshments and socializing.

> *Parent and Child Sports Night:* An evening or Saturday built around an Olympic type sports activity. Competition would include individual and group sports involving children and parents.

> *Arts and Crafts Fair:* A get together combining display of students' arts and crafts projects. Students in each class exhibit their work on art projects (flat work, mobiles, painting, ceramics, papier-mache, and so forth) individually, in pairs, or in small groups. Refreshments are served.

> *Book Fair:* Parents accumulate books from personal collections. A sale is held at school at low prices with the proceeds going to PTA or school improvement

funds. Refreshments are served and opportunities for informal conversation with faculty members and parent organization officers are provided.

10. Suggestion Box

A parent suggestion box is placed in the main hallway or office under the community bulletin board. Children write notes to their parents explaining it and asking parents to use it. Parent suggestions, and implementation of these, should be regularly publicized in the newsletter and on bulletin boards.

11. Hallway Displays

Each class has a hallway territory assigned to it to display individual or group work of any kind (writing, art, photos with captions, magazine or newspaper articles). Parents are encouraged to contribute displays of their own that will be used in the hallway area assigned to their child's class. *(See Form 38, Invitation to Contribute to Hallway Displays, p. 378.)*

12. Invite a Teacher to Dinner or Lunch

On nights when teachers have to remain or return to school for meetings, parents may invite them to their homes for dinner. SCAC and PTA officers may start this and then encourage parents from each teacher's class to do the same. Invitations can be handled through the parent classroom coordinator and parent teams. Children are thrilled to have teachers at home for a meal.

Parent teams may take turns inviting teachers to have lunch with the entire team at one team member's home.

Potential Problem Areas

Unrealistic expectations about parents' responses to or participation in an activity is a common blocking factor. We must get away from the "numbers game." The building of parental involvement is slow. Large meetings, mass announcements, the shotgun approach will not work to overcome the apathy stemming from poor school experiences, fear, and lack of time.

We must expect to start with small numbers and not become discouraged when only a few parents turn out to a class meeting. If those few have a satisfying experience, it will build from there. Growth must come through person-to-person, one-to-one word of mouth. A parent who has had an experience that was beneficial to himself or his child influences a neighbor to become involved. Each one recruits one. Success breeds success.

Although everyone's time is limited, people always find time to do what is important or enjoyable. Getting started is the most difficult thing. The teacher's early input is extremely important. Later, parents can carry the ball. Start with simple things and limited demands on parent time. Try to get maximum payoff for minimum investment. Once people get involved and enjoy something, they will put more time in on their own. It is better to underwhelm rather than overwhelm them. Leave them wanting more.

Teachers sometimes think they are expected to implement an entire new program immediately. The plan for parent involvement was developed out of teachers' experiences over time. It takes a number of years to effectively implement all phases of it. Some teachers may be able to move faster than others. The teachers who are not progressing so fast must not feel like failures or feel under pressure. For a variety of reasons teachers will move ahead at different rates.

New activities for parental involvement should be tried out by one or two teachers first, rather than involving the time and energy of all teachers in something that may not work or may have little payoff. Once a teacher has had a successful experience, it is easier for others to see the benefits.

Speed is not the goal. The important thing is to create a

positive atmosphere and to enjoy the process every step of the way.

IN CONCLUSION

Time and effort spent by teachers in obtaining parent involvement will pay off in better rapport with children, improved atmosphere in class, reduction of energy draining friction with problem children or parents. Gaining parent assistance makes the teacher's job less frustrating and more interesting and enjoyable. However, these benefits do not occur overnight. They require that the school make parent involvement a high priority and build it into the teacher's job.

Encouragement from the principal, and practical support in terms of release time or a shortened school day, salary point credit, funds for extras, and added clerical help, are important.

Although the emphasis in this chapter has been on teacher and school initiative in improving parent-teacher and school-community relations, parents (both individually and under the leadership of parent advisory councils) should reach out on their own and give support to teachers. Many of the activities described can be initiated or requested by parents.

Sandra Haggerty, in an article published in the *Los Angeles Times*,* has some important comments about parent initiative:

> *How can we parents on an individual basis help to improve our schools? Involvement! Go to the schools, cooperate with teachers and administrators, attend PTA meetings. Talk and listen to your child about his school experiences. Let the teachers and administrators know you and your concerns. Con-*

---

* Haggerty, Sandra, "Back to School," *Los Angeles Times*, Part II, page 7, Sept. 3, 1973.

front incidents of racism openly and constructively. Help your children with their homework, and encourage older brothers and sisters to help younger children in your home and in the neighborhood. "Each one teach one" is a valuable concept.

Turn off that television at an early hour to see that your children get adequate rest for school the next day. Make sure the children eat breakfast, either at home or at the free breakfast school program. Encourage excitement and a positive attitude about learning.

As parents, we can make a significant difference in our public schools. We have the power, if executed, to make our school system one of excellence for ALL our children.

5 TASK-ORIENTED FEEDBACK

Developing a Caring and Self-Correcting School

INTRODUCTION: OPEN COMMUNICATION

It was a few weeks before the end of the school year. The sixth grade teanhers had been rehearsing and drilling their students daily for over a week in preparation for graduation ceremonies. They were practicing a song for the third time and the students were restless, fidgety, and talkative. One of the teachers read the riot act to them, "If you don't stop talking and settle down and behave yourselves, you won't have a graduation at all! I'm not sure you deserve it anyway! One more word out of any of you and that's it!" One of the sixth graders raised his hand and asked, "Can I say something?" Before the teacher could respond, young Anthony blurted out, "I'm sick and tired of hearing you say this is our graduation. *You* picked the songs. *You* chose the dances. *You* wrote the speeches. *You* decided everything and you call it our graduation. It's your graduation and I don't care if you do call it off!" Other students joined in, "Yeah, Anthony's right." "Right on, Anthony!" "Why can't we pick our own songs and dances?" The confrontation continued for a few moments with another teacher and other students joining in, and then the class was dismissed.

This incident took place during the first year of TCP at a

232

school where not all the teachers were wholehearted volunteers. Apparently some of the pupils had absorbed the TCP philosophy and some of the teachers had not.

At a teacher feedback session that afternoon, the incident was discussed. Different points of view were expressed. Ultimately the teachers agreed to allow the students to select two songs and one dance of their own for the graduation. The important thing in this situation was that the teachers did listen, did examine their own behavior critically, and were flexible enough to make changes even at the last minute. Significantly, it was the existence of the feedback mechanism that provided the opportunity for this to occur.

Underlying Concepts

Growth does not occur in a vacuum. Just as the student needs feedback from the teacher on how he is doing, so does the teacher need feedback to gain in self-awareness and to improve performance. Building school spirit and a sense of community requires the adults to role model the behavior they expect and desire from the children. Teachers cannot talk effectively to children about teamwork, sharing, and cooperation if they don't share or cooperate with each other. They cannot talk effectively to children about lateness if they are late to class and to meetings. They cannot talk effectively to children about neatness, cleanliness, and putting things away if they have cluttered desks and messy storage cabinets. They cannot talk effectively to children about independence and responsibility if they behave autocratically. They cannot talk effectively to the children about learning through correction if they will not accept correction. They cannot talk effectively to children about self-expression if they are not open to ideas.

The main problems in schools are not technical problems, but people problems. Good educational practices have been around for a long time. The reason many have failed or have not lasted is because the people problems could not be worked out. We have the technical potential to solve most problems of materials, time, space, curriculum, finances, and methods. Our major difficulty lies in our inability to communicate with each other, to get along, to solve problems together, to have the patience to stay with things long enough to work them out, to resist discouragement, competitiveness, and pettiness. Frequently, we do not attempt to communicate or solve problems until it is too late. We wait until there is a crisis or an explosion.

A feedback session is an occasion to share both positive and negative feelings about things which seem to be facilitating or hindering achievement of school goals.

Hal Bennett* points out that people, not subjects, should be the main focus of education. As he has said, the hardest thing of all appears to be to focus attention on people—on students, teachers, parents, administrators, and staff. We need to stop treating the behavior, thoughts, and feelings of individuals as interruptions in the school day and to regard them as the main business of the school. We need to place as much value on people as on curriculum; the people business *is* the curriculum. When people focus on people and a sense of community develops, the academic problems will no longer appear overwhelming.

Social growth is perhaps the most neglected aspect of the school curriculum. Growth in self-understanding, in human relations and in open communication among students, teachers, administrators, and parents is as important as, and closely related to, academic achievement.

Improving human relations is not a one-shot deal, something you achieve and then have for all time, but is rather a continuous ongoing process. Growth occurs best in an atmosphere which encourages and provides explicit, regular occasions for open, direct, and frank expression of thoughts and feelings.

The feedback session attempts to provide such an atmosphere. It is an occasion to share honestly both positive and negative feelings about things which seem to be facilitating or hindering achievement of school goals. It is an opportunity to get to know oneself better and to understand the effects of one's actions on other people. It is an occasion for making contact and getting to know other people better, for develop-

---

* Bennett, Hal, "An Immodest Proposal," *Open Space Teacher Center*, Vol. 2, no. 5, June, 1973.

ing familiarity out of which grow the trust and confidence necessary for teamwork and a sense of community. It is a time when people can share problems and ask for and offer help, suggestions, and points of view. It is an exercise in self-government where all decisions and actions can be questioned, including those of the principal, and everyone is accountable to everyone else and everyone's voice is equal.

Instituting feedback sessions as an integral part of school life is a unique undertaking in American education. It is an attempt to create an atmosphere where people are not threatened by differences and conflict, where conflict is viewed as a means to bring about desired and creative change. It is an attempt to develop a caring and self-correcting school through mutual concern and accountability.

Change, because it usually introduces turbulence into the life of an individual or institution, is often threatening. Significant change does not occur without some fear, anxiety, and difficulty. Feedback sessions, when introduced into a school, generally involve some discomfort and turbulence.

Given the knowledge explosion and the rapid rate of change in society, school problems change rapidly. Today's solutions may be tomorrow's problems. Under these circumstances, it is important to create and maintain an educational program or learning community which is flexible, adaptive, and open to self-correction and change. One of the best guarantees of maintaining this capability for self-renewal is by providing formally for regular feedback sessions among all who share responsibility for the success of the school—principal, teachers, support staff, parents, students.

Feedback sessions examine feelings and behavior only insofar as they relate to school situations and problems. The sessions are neither designed to solve personal problems nor to provide group therapy, but rather to improve human interrelationships for the benefit of the school functioning.

Successful feedback sessions are based on voluntary participation.

General Goals

Some of the long range outcomes expected from these group experiences are described by Carl Rogers in *Freedom to Learn: A View of What Education Might Become,* Columbus, Ohio, Charles E. Merrill, 1969. The following list has been extrapolated from Rogers.

The School and All its Participants:

Will feel more free to express both positive and negative feelings, and to listen to others.

Will work toward gaining realistic relationships by expressing feelings instead of burying them until they are explosive.

Will be more likely to work out interpersonal frictions and problems, rather than dealing with such issues in a disciplinary or punitive manner.

Will be more able to accept feedback, both positive and negative, and to use it for constructive insight.

Will enjoy greater trust of student initiatives by teachers, parents, and others and of teacher initiatives by the principal.

Will attempt more experimentation and risk taking with less fear of failure.

Will experience greater teamwork and cooperative relations and less jealousy and competition.

Will communicate more clearly with superiors, peers, and subordinates because communications will be oriented toward an openly declared purpose and not toward covert self-protection.

Will have fewer children sent to the principal for

disciplinary action, because most problems will be solved in classrooms.

Will place greater emphasis on changing behavior through positive reinforcement rather than through fear, threats, and punishment.

Will use the resources of all its members.

Each segment of the school community population should experience the following additional outcomes:

The Student:

Will have more energy to devote to learning because he will have less fear of evaluation and punishment.

Will discover he has a responsibility for his own learning as he becomes more of a participant in the group learning process.

Will feel free to take off on exciting avenues of learning, with assurance that his teacher will understand.

Will find that both his awe of authority and his rebellion against authority will diminish as he discovers teachers and administrators to be fallible human beings relating in imperfect ways to students.

Will find that the learning process enables him to grapple directly and personally with the problem of the meaning of his life.

The Teacher:

Will be more ready to accept the innovative, challenging, "troublesome," creative ideas which emerge in students, rather than reacting to these as threats and insisting on conformity.

Will tend to pay as much attention to his relationship with his students as to the content of the course.

Will develop a more egalitarian atmosphere in the classroom, conducive to spontaneity, to creative thinking, and to independent and self-directed work.

The Administrator:

Will be less protective of his own constructs and beliefs, and hence able to listen more accurately to others.

Will find it easier and less threatening to accept innovative ideas.

Will be more person-oriented and democratic in staff or faculty meetings and will draw more widely and deeply on the resource potential of his faculty and staff.

Focus, in a feedback session, is on the here and now, on things that are going on and affecting members currently.

The Parent:

> Will feel more comfortable and free to visit the school and to inquire about his child's progress.

> Will be better able to accept negative feedback about his child from teachers or administrators, without becoming overly defensive or overly punitive toward the child, and with greater ability to use the feedback to help the child.

> Will be more free to offer criticism or praise to teachers, administrators, and other parents as a way to improve school conditions.

> Will be better able to listen to his child, especially to the expressions of his feelings.

Gradual Progression or Phasing

Instituting feedback as a schoolwide procedure requires extensive training and experience for all personnel. As with other major aspects of TCP, the task-oriented feedback program is developd gradually in several phases. The plan is to move from simple to more complex activities to assure the probability of success at each step of the way. The program will begin with a limited number of key personnel and gradually extend to other members of the school community. Eventually, all persons connected with a TCP school regularly participate in two types of feedback sessions: (1) horizontal groups made up primarily of peers and (2) vertical groups which cut across the various populations (teachers, students, parents, administrative and nonteaching staff).

The background, experience, skill, and motivation of the principal, teachers, and parents dictate the pace and sequence. There will be numerous occasions, because of local conditions, where the sequence will be different from that outlined here, and where activities from different phases will occur simultaneously. (For the complete Sequence of Steps in Implementing a Feedback Program, *see Form 39, p. 378.*)

DESCRIPTION AND CONDUCT OF FEEDBACK SESSIONS

A small group of from ten to fifteen persons is seated informally in a circle and talk to each other as honestly as they can. The sessions are unstructured. There is no agenda and anyone can talk about anything. There is, however, a requirement that the exchange focus on things that appear to be either blocking or enhancing achievement of school goals. This is why it is called *task-oriented* feedback. Participants feel free to disclose problems and request and offer help. This is a broad mandate and can cover a multitude of areas. For example, somone conceivably might discuss a personal problem he was having at home if he felt it affected his performance and effectiveness in school and wanted to bring it up. However, the emphasis would not be on trying to provide advice on the home situation, but on the consequences at school and how they might be handled.

Focus is on the here and now, on things that are going on and affecting members currently.

Ground Rules

Establishing a self-correcting, caring learning community through feedback sessions requires that participants accept new norms to guide their behavior in these sessions. The ground rules are thoroughly discussed at orientation and training workshops prior to the initial feedback session. Discussion includes problems which may block adherence to the ground rules. The group then essentially formulates a contract in which everyone has permission to suspend the normal rules of polite society and agrees to strive to achieve the following new behavior patterns:

Share your school-related concerns, problems and feelings with others rather than maintaining secrecy.

Ask for help and don't view this as a sign of weakness.

Take responsibility for your own feelings and actions rather than blaming others.

Respond to people's overt behavior, and not to what you think their motivations may be.

Confront colleagues with criticism which you previously would have repressed or expressed by indirect acts such as unfriendliness, lack of cooperation, gossip, procrastination.

Trust your feelings and get them out spontaneously without trying to screen them or put them in the best light. Take the risk of expressing feelings and thoughts while they are still tentative, without being sure of their correctness, appropriateness, or validity. Don't try to evaluate whether something is worth bringing up. If it's on your mind, bring it up. The feedback session is a place to take chances, explore, try things out, clear the air, get things off your mind, and make room for new thoughts and feelings.

Make your position known. Do not hide behind questions or ambiguous references. Speak your mind. Say what you mean and mean what you say. Be direct. Don't beat around the bush.

Don't be afraid to express strong feelings or emotions or to use strong language. Do not screen to try to make things sound nicer. State your feelings and thoughts as they are, in whatever language comes out or feels comfortable.

Present yourself spontaneously, as you are, without trying to maintain some image of how you would like to be perceived.

Face conflict and differences openly and directly; do not try to smooth over problems. Don't try to water down or avoid conflict or confrontation. Have trust that when difficulties are brought to light, the talent and goodwill are there to work them out. When conflicts are repressed, they don't go away but become explosive and eventually come out in more disruptive ways.

View criticism as an act of friendship and concern, not hostility. When someone's comments cause you discomfort or bad feelings, express them at the time; don't hold grudges. Try to appreciate another person's comments as an expression of interest in you, whether or not you agree with or accept the feedback. If bad feelings persist outside the session, bring them back to the group for discussion.

Don't be afraid to give positive feedback. Sometimes groups dwell on the negative, and individuals fear that if they say something nice their motives may be suspect.

Don't expect to leave every session feeling great. Learning, especially when it involves learning about our own mistakes or shortcomings, can be uncomfortable. Some of the most valuable learning experiences come from sessions where you are upset.

Don't expect to find magic solutions at any one session or to solve problems quickly. Feedback sessions are not problem solving sessions *per se*. They deal with the things that cause problems and get in the way of solving them and are an ongoing process. A by-product of the feedback sessions is that it becomes easier to work together in other settings, thus preventing problems and facilitating finding solutions to those that do arise.

Samples from Sessions

The following excerpts from teacher feedback sessions that took place in different TCP schools illustrate the rules and procedures. Anyone can say anything he wants, or not say anything at all, but one must accept the consequences of one's behavior. For example, one consequence may be that someone will express annoyance at a member's silence. Frequently the deeper implications that have a bearing on one's effectiveness in the classroom are not immediately apparent at the outset of a dialogue but come to light as the issue is explored.

Learning to listen to and accept valid feedback, both positive and negative, is the basis for constructive insights which can lead to the elimination of self-defeating behavior.

Sample 1

SANDRA: Your silence really bothers me. You never say anything.

ELLEN: Just because I don't say much doesn't mean I'm not involved. I'm very involved and am learning a lot.

LAURA: That's great! You may be getting something, but you're not contributing. We don't get anything from you.

LOIS: I think you have a lot of hostility that you're not expressing.

SANDRA: I just would like to get to know you better and can't when you don't speak.

ELLEN: Well, I don't think anyone should have to talk. I'll talk when I have something to say or when I'm ready.

SANDRA: Do your kids have that option? How do you feel about your pupils who don't participate or won't answer you? I've seen you. You get very upset with them.

LOIS: I have the feeling you don't communicate any better with your kids than you do with us.

LINDA: I resent the implications. Just because she doesn't talk here doesn't mean she doesn't communicate with her kids.

SANDRA: Why are you so jumpy? Why are you defending her? Can't we talk about it?

BONNIE: Why are you so quiet, Ellen? What are you afraid of?

ELLEN: I don't know. Maybe I'm afraid I'll say the wrong thing or someone will get mad at me or find out some of my weaknesses as a teacher.

BONNIE: Maybe that's what we do to the kids. They don't feel it's safe to say anything or to say what they are really feeling.

In a sense, the feedback session is a mechanism for trying out various points of view. It's an opportunity for self-exploration and self-actualization. In the above interaction, Ellen's silence in the group may or may not have reflected the level of her communication with kids. The important thing was that someone thought there might be a relationship and could suggest it and let the person and the group explore it. In other words, the feedback session is a *learning laboratory* in human

relations that can help participants better understand themselves and how their feelings and actions affect others, and
vice-versa. It can help them function better, both independently and together. In peer relations, concern, contact and

In a feedback session, parents learn it's okay to
criticize the teacher and that the teacher cares.

accountability are valued, and people are not ignored, written off, or just tolerated.

Sample 2

JOYCE: Julie, what's going on with you? You're usually the most cheerful, cooperative person in the school. But this week you've looked down in the dumps, and would hardly say hello to anyone.

SYLVIA: Yeah, I asked to borrow something from you, and you almost snapped my head off. That's not like you. What's with you, Julie?

Sample 3

DONNA: Mary, why were you late to today's session? We always seem to be waiting for you.

MARY: I had to stop in the office and call a parent.

DONNA: You always have some dumb excuse.

MARY: What's so dumb about that? Anyway, I was only 15 minutes late. What's the big deal? We never get started on time anyway.

DONNA: Your attitude really disgusts me. You're always complaining about the kids' manners and about them not following through on things. But you're always late. You don't show any consideration. You don't even excuse yourself.

Sample 4

JEAN: Barbara, I thought you did a fantastic job of handling that fight in the lunch room. I just wanted you to know I admired the way you did that.

SARAH: What did she do?

JEAN: Why don't you tell everyone, Barbara.

BARBARA: It wasn't anything.

ANN: You seem embarrassed. Do compliments bother you? You're really great with the kids. Why don't you share what you do with us?

BARBARA: Sure. It's just that I don't think I'm that good or that the lunch thing was a big deal.

The feedback session is not for problem-solving. Although problems may be aired and solutions suggested, the details would not be worked out in this setting but rather in some committee meeting. The focus here is on the originating teacher's feelings, what he does about them, how he possibly contributes to the problem, and what others did to cause the breakdown of the system. Unless these things are dealt with, a new system probably would not fare any better. No systems are people proof.

Nor is the feedback session a therapy group. Nobody is trying to cure anyone of anything. There is no deep delving into the psyche to ferret out psychological antecedents to personality quirks. The focus is on behavior and its consequences. Teachers confront each other and hold each other directly accountable rather than complaining behind each others' backs.

Sample 5

JEAN: Marge, what happened yesterday? How come the tutors from your class didn't show up?

MARGE: The class was very noisy and disruptive and I was punishing them.

JEAN: That makes me angry. Why didn't you let me know? My kids were waiting.

MARGE: I'm sorry, I should have let you know. But I really don't like the schedule we worked out for the tutoring.

JEAN: Well, we can discuss the schedule at our resource group meeting tomorrow. But why use the tutoring as punishment when we are trying to get this program started? As a matter of fact, I've been wondering whether you really support the tutoring program. You've only observed the kids tutoring once and aren't holding feedback sessions with them regularly.

The feedback session also serves as a self-governing mechanism where decisions and actions of all persons can be questioned, including those of the principal. For many teachers, giving feedback to the principal is a major breakthrough in trusting the process and taking a risk.

Sample 6

JUDY: I feel very uncomfortable saying this, Carl, but I have to get it out. I know you are going to be angry with me for bringing it up, but I am really furious with you.

CARL: Well, what is it?

JUDY: I'm getting there. You really made me feel terrible yesterday in your office. I didn't mind your criticizing me. And I agreed with some of your points. But why did you start threatening me and say you were going to write things down and keep a record? I used to think we were on the same side. Now I feel that you are out to get me. I was so upset I couldn't sleep at all last night.

CARL: Judy, I do resent your bringing it up. I think you are using the group to put pressure on me and gain sympathy. All I did was give you honest feedback on my observations on what is happening in your class. That's part of my job. I was trying to give you some helpful advice.

RITA: Wait a minute, Carl. Why shouldn't she bring it up here if that's the way she feels? Isn't that one of the things this group is for?

SANDY: I wasn't there, Carl, and I don't know exactly what took place, but I don't think you realize how you come over sometimes. I've gotten some of your friendly advice at times and have felt you were trying to put me down rather than give me a hand. And I really resent your criticizing Judy for bringing it up here. Why are you so defensive?

CARL: Yeah, I'll have to look at that. I'm sorry. I think it's good that you brought it up. I guess I'm still struggling with not wanting my actions questioned.

ELLEN: Weren't you just plain angry with Judy because her class seems to be going downhill and didn't you just want to give her hell rather than be helpful?

CARL: I didn't think so at the time, but maybe it's so.

ANITA: How are you feeling, Judy?

JUDY: Well, I feel better for having brought it up. But I still don't think I have Carl's support.

Sample 7

KAREN: I came into your office Monday all excited about showing you some of the great letters my kids had written home to their parents and all you could say was, "You can't send them home on school stationery. You shouldn't have done that." I could have killed you. The kids had felt so important writing on stationery with the school letterhead.

CARL: I told you it's against regulations. Anything on school stationery must go out under my signature. If you had asked me first I would have told you and you wouldn't have had to disappoint the kids.

WILMA: Oh, shit! I don't know why you couldn't have made an exception. But even if you could not, you handled it badly. I was in your office and was appalled. You showed no sensitivity for Karen's feelings. At least if you had read the letters, complimented her on the idea, and showed some concern or regret for having to stop it. But all you did was quote the rule and show some chagrin. That was really cold, Carl.

Giving positive feedback to the principal can also be difficult at times.

Sample 8

MICHELLE: I want to say something. I wasn't going to because I was afraid I would be misunderstood. I wanted to say something nice about Carl, but I was afraid people would think I was taking sides in his dispute with Nina and that I was against Nina, which isn't true. It actually had nothing to do with that situation. I just wanted to thank Carl for the support he gave me last week with a problem I had with a student and a very difficult parent. I really appreciated it.

Because sessions are unstructured and without an agenda, the content and emotional tone of any given session are unpredictable. They depend on the mood of the participants, what is going on in the school, and what individuals have on their minds at a given time. There is not necessarily continuity of content from one session to another, although some themes may persist for a time. The early stages are marked by considerable caution and reserve, especially toward the principal. Teachers test how far they can go in challenging authority and in bringing up controversial issues. As the principal and a few teachers begin to take risks, the climate of caution changes and individuals start to talk about things which were held back earlier.

Practical Arrangements

Time, Place, Setting

Feedback sessions do not begin until training of personnel involved has taken place. Once started, sessions should occur regularly, at least once weekly for approximately two hours. At different schools, groups have met right after school or evenings, but ideally, time should be built into the school day. Some schools have done this by shortening the pupils' day. Local control to experiment with different time schedules is important.

A change of atmosphere from school is desirable if possible (sessions can be held in the home of a teacher who lives near the school). When the sessions are held at the school, a comfortable, aesthetically pleasing setting is nice. The teachers' lounge, or the library, or possibly a classroom can be set up for this purpose. Some simple refreshments contribute to a positive ambiance.

If a weekend feedback session is held, a comfortable hotel or conference center away from the immediate vicinity of school and home should be sought. Separation from the familiar environment and cares of daily life provides greater freedom and facilitates a higher level of openness and good socializing experiences.

Size and Composition of Group

The group should be small enough for everyone to participate. In large groups, some people hide and get lost, especially the shy person. The group should be large enough to provide diversity and different points of view. Ten to thirteen is a good size, with fifteen the maximum and eight a minimum.

Obviously, there is no right or ideal number. Each school should experiment to ascertain what is most comfortable and productive for it. Groups can be reconstituted periodically, and the entire group can be brought together regularly (monthly, quarterly) to keep everyone in contact, maintain a sense of the whole, and avoid any tendency toward polarization between groups.

In addition to the faculty, administrator, and supervisory staff, others who may be included are officers of parent groups, interested parents, community leaders, office manager, head custodian, counselor, nurse, cafeteria manager. Initially, the group contains teachers and principal. The others are added gradually. Eventually, all nonteaching staff and many parents will be involved in separate groups, with some cross-fertilization.

A feedback group may be made up of four to eight sets of paired teachers. The principal would alternate, each week attending another group session.

Flexibility is maintained. Anyone may request to be in a

group with some other specific person in any given week if he has something to discuss with that person. Except for such requests, the groups can remain relatively stable for a period of time (4 to 8 weeks). Then they can be reorganized. Reassigning the pairs insures that everyone will have sustained extended contact with everyone else. Experimentation with groupings is important. If groups get bogged down, changes should be tried to keep them vital, and viable.

When the total group gets together regularly, the format of an unstructured town hall meeting may be used and the question "How well are we doing together?" may be raised. Or a fishbowl arrangement can be used, with 10 to 15 participants in an inner circle and the others in an outer circle as observers. Two chairs are left empty in the inner circle. Any observer who feels the urge can take a seat and participate. After a designated period of time, the people in the two circles can exchange places.

The Role of the Facilitator

People who work together tend to build up over time a set of "implicit contracts" by which individuals tacitly agree to avoid confronting many of the real issues that face them as members of a team. An outside, trained facilitator is valuable at the beginning to help the group confront these "contracts," to open them for examination and for change. Most schools should have a trained facilitator, on a regular basis, during the beginning phases of the program. He can help to insure that the ground rules and guidelines for the proper conduct of feedback sessions become established as norms. Once the norm of inquiry is established and the ground rules for feedback are accepted by the group, work colleagues can monitor, evaluate, and modify their own functioning without a trained facilitator.

The ultimate goal of TCP schools is to develop self-directed groups which function effectively without a trained facilitator. This is consistent with the basic notion of TCP as a learning community where people are resources for each other. As TCP develops teachers take turns in co-facilitating feedback sessions.

A distinction should be made between a leader and the leadership function. Any member may perform the leadership function. In different sessions different leaders emerge. The word facilitator is used rather than leader to convey a specific function that is performed among co-equals, rather than a dominant-dependent relationship. Since the designated function rotates, and all teachers receive the experience, it emphasizes the facilitator rather than the leader role.

The functions of the facilitator-participant in the feedback sessions are to:

Start and end the session.

Serve as a model of active participation by being personally involved, taking risks, and sharing feelings.

Encourage all participants to assume responsibility and initiative for all aspects of group participation.

Be aware of silent members and attempt to draw them in.

See to it that one person does not monopolize the session.

Conduct the post-session critique.

Some Effects of Feedback

As a result of feedback sessions, teachers become more self-critical and less afraid to talk about mistakes, problems, or shortcomings, as illustrated in the following teacher comment: "What a mess I made of trying to individualize instruction all at once. I've had complete chaos for a week and have gone back to a structured approach which I don't like at all."

Another teacher sent up the following distress signal, "Who can help me? I've got this ego battle going with this boy, and it's driving me crazy."

And still another teacher observed, "When kids came in the morning before 9:00 A.M. I let them in the room, but made them sit still and quietly on the floor so as not to disturb me. Suddenly I began to wonder. What am I teaching these kids—that learning only begins at 9:00 A.M.?"

Insights are gained. For example, one teacher received much sympathy from her colleagues after talking about how disgusted, saddened, and upset she was that a child stole $25 from her purse. Another teacher had the following insight: "It just dawned upon me that when a child comes up to me distraught and says, 'Mrs. Jones, someone took 15¢ from my lunch pail,' I frequently will pass it off, because I am busy and have lots of things on my mind, with a 'we'll talk about it later,' or 'be more careful next time.' I just realized that the 15¢ may be just as important to the student as the $25 is to Margo. I may not be able to do anything about it, but I could at least be a little more empathic. I might put my arm around her and say, 'I'm really sorry about that, Mary.'"

Another teacher made this remark, "It's interesting, we make demands on kids for perfection and self-discipline that we cannot attain ourselves. I'm always after them about keeping their desks and areas clean. My desk is usually messier than theirs."

Resolutions to change are made. A teacher disclosed, "For years I've had a tendency for needling and sarcasm. In fact, I've been a master at it, frequently hurting people. Recently I have caught myself on several occasions and stopped it, and I honestly feel a lot better."

After a weekend training session a principal stated, "I had a conversation with two college students that was more honest and personal than I had ever had with my own sons. A teacher asked me if it was too late to do it with my sons now and suggested I would have to face possible rejection if I tried now, and I replied that I guess I'll just have to risk that."

TRAINING IN TASK-ORIENTED FEEDBACK

In order to develop open and honest communication there must be mutual trust and confidence, and people must be willing to open up and take risks. Much preparation is needed before the regular ongoing feedback sessions are started in the school. Seminars and workshops are conducted for the various segments of the school population: administrators, teachers, parents, key personnel group. The training activities include readings (see works by Egan, Rogers, Simon, Solomon in Bibliography), film presentations, discussion, role playing, feedback sessions, weekend group experiences.

Ultimately all groups will receive feedback training, but generally the first group to undergo such training is the key personnel, those who have influence in the school and serve as role models to others: the principal, faculty chairman, TCP coordinator, Teachers' Association representative, chairman of SCAC and PTA. The various school populations will receive training in greater or lesser depth depending on prior experience, need and interest, but the activities described here are generally experienced by all personnel in the sequence presented. Post-session critiques are an essential ingredient of all training and feedback sessions.

Orientation Seminars

Seminars introduce the major concepts of feedback; goals, procedures, and ground rules are discussed; participants have an opportunity to raise questions, especially about their concerns, anxieties, and reservations. The purpose is to have them develop realistic expectations, form an idea of their own responsibilities, and begin the feedback sessions with a positive set and sense of excitement.

During the early training stages, a trained facilitator is generally employed. The seminar facilitator may be an experienced school person (a teacher or principal from the target school or another school, or a staff person from the district office) who is knowledgeable about TCP and has experince in the theory and practice of feedback sessions. If an outside consultant with expertise in the group process is used, he should be assisted by a teacher who can talk from personal experience in the classroom.

Film Discussion

The TCP documentary film, "Tomorrow We'll See What Happens," may be shown and some of the issues raised in the film discussed. For example:

> Personal risks involved in making changes.

> How to tackle interpersonal factors that interfere with dealing with school problems.

> What interferes with going directly to the person whose actions bothered you.

> The fear of dealing with people in authority.

> The difference between exercising authority and exercising influence.

> Is honesty the best policy?

Johari Window

The Johari Window framework is presented to illustrate how self-disclosure and feedback lead to personal and organizational growth and improvement, and to suggest that feedback can prevent problems from festering and stagnation from setting in. (For a description of the concept, *see Form 40, p. 380*. Directions for the exercise designed to assess one's "window" or level of self-disclosure are presented in *Form 41, p. 384.*)

Discussion of Ground Rules

The ground rules for feedback are read. Questions and reactions to each ground rule are elicited. Discussion of the meaning, significance and difficulties of carrying out the ground rules is entertained.

Structured Exercises in Communication

The exercises below are conducted in pairs or small groups to give participants gradual experience in open communication and feedback. A discussion is held following the exercises.

1. Each person in the small group mentions one thing he likes and one thing he dislikes about himself as a teacher. The group then reacts to what has been said.

2. Each person writes down ten attributes (positive or negative) that he thinks characterize him as a teacher (e.g., too serious; lose patience easily; become very nervous with visitors in room; can communicate my joy of learning to children). The group divides into pairs. The pairs exchange lists and each person reacts to each attribute on the other person's list (asks for clarification or an example of behavior that demonstrates the quality listed, agrees or disagrees, or raises doubts and questions).

3. The group divides into pairs. Each person gives the other some positive or negative feedback not given previously (e.g., A parent told me you are her favorite teacher in the school. A child said you have no sense of humor.)

4. Participants are organized into triads and each person takes a role as Problem Definer, Helper, or Observer. The Problem Definer presents a prob-

Feedback sessions provide students with explicit opportunities to openly and frankly express and understand their feelings about themselves and about their relationships with others.

lem and the Helper draws him out through questions designed to clarify the problem. At the conclusion of the interaction, the Observer feeds back his observations about the facilitating and blocking aspects of the Problem Definer's and the Helper's behavior. This is followed by a brief discussion and evaluation of the interaction by all three. The triad members exchange roles and the exercise is repeated with a new problem. This is done once more so that all participants have played all roles. *(See Form 42, The Helping Trios Exercise, p. 386.)*

Demonstration Feedback Session

Ten to fifteen people are asked to volunteer to participate in a short (15 to 30 minutes) feedback session. They may discuss anything—their reactions to the seminar activities, to each other, to the facilitator, to teaching in general, to their school, etc.

They sit in an inner circle. The rest of the group sits around them in an outer circle and observes. Two empty seats are provided in the inner circle for outer circle members to join in at will. When these two extra seats are occupied, any individual in the outer circle can tap someone in the inner circle on the shoulder to replace him in the feedback session. After a half hour, all inner circle persons exchange places with outer circle members.

A discussion is held about the demonstration feedback session with the entire group.

Advanced Workshop

Following the orientation seminars, some of the school personnel receive further training. The workshop includes didactic presentations and structured exercises which involve participants with each other in problem solving, team building, and group leadership activities and offer considerable opportunity for exchanging feedback.

Review of Prior Training

The group is invited to make comments and raise questions about the experiences they have had so far and to express their reactions and concerns about TCP and the feedback process. The facilitator might ask participants to talk about the problems they think they might have as members of regular feedback sessions with colleagues and with students.

FIRO B Exercises and NASA Exercises

These exercises were discussed in Chapter III in relation to their use in training personnel in shared planning-and-decision-making. They are also very useful in training people for the feedback process.

The structured exercises *(see Form 22, p. 354)*, Choosing Up Sides for a Debate, Thumb Wrestling, and Strength Bombardment, illustrate the operation of FIRO B concepts of inclusion, control and affection factors in interpersonal relations *(see Form 21, p. 352)*.

The NASA Exercise *(Form 20, p. 346)* in group versus individual decision making is used in the feedback training workshop to focus on the interpersonal behavior and communication of group members with each other.

Micro-Lab Feedback Sessions

The group engages in a series of short feedback sessions, each one followed by discussion and a critique of the process.

Content may deal with the behavior and interactions of participants during the workshop or anything else. Each micro session generally lasts 10 to 30 minutes, at the discretion of the facilitator. Prior to the sessions, the participants read and discuss briefly Guidelines for Improving Feedback Sessions *(see p. 266)*. Following each micro-session, the group discusses how well the Guidelines were implemented, and what they liked or disliked about the session and about their own participation.

Weekend Workshop

It is helpful if some of the staff members (especially key personnel) have participated in a stranger group experience. A stranger group is one where the participants do not know each other and will probably not see each other again after the workshop. This experience, held away from the home environment, is usually less threatening and more conducive to participants' opening up and becoming actively and personally involved. In a weekend encounter experience, participants are free from home and work responsibilities, free from having to maintain an image in front of colleagues or friends, free from the usual stimuli and distractions, and they have enough time to get a good feel for the process.

These small group experiences come under many different names: encounter, laboratory training, senitivity training, human interaction laboratory, T-group, intensive small group experience, communications workshop, human relations group, human potential, group dynamics, feedback workshop. In TCP, we prefer the term feedback because it describes the process functionally. Whatever the name, the school experience is not group therapy. The purpose is not to solve individual emotional or psychological problems. The main purpose is to encourage more open communication by better understanding one's feelings and reactions and how they affect and are affected by other people.

Many human potential centers and universities offer weekend encounter experiences. However, these are not all of equal value. Before making a final decision, investigate the reputation of the sponsoring organization through reliable, known people who have participated in their activities. Where possible, the project coordinator should attend in person, prior to arranging for other staff members to attend.

The following institutions are among those that offer training in human relations:

> The National Training Laboratories (NTL) offer laboratory training workshops throughout the year in different parts of the country. Some are especially geared for educators.

> The Esalen Institute offers these experiences (also geared especially for educators) throughout the year in California.

> The Synanon Foundation offers opportunities for participation in the Synanon Game.

> The Center for the Study of the Person (CSP) has an active weekend program throughout the summer at La Jolla, California.

> The Association for Humanistic Psychology, 325 Ninth Street, San Francisco, California 94103, will provide information about organizations and growth centers offering training experiences throughout the country.

Administrator Training in Feedback

The principal plays a crucial role in implementing the

feedback program in a school. He must role model the desired behavior and create an atmosphere of mutual trust, confidence and risk taking. He has the major responsibility for breaking down the boss-employee relationship between himself and the teachers so that they will feel free to speak directly and critically. Before beginning feedback sessions with the faculty, to build his confidence, security and skill, the principal should receive training and experience with the feedback process over and above the training undergone by all other personnel.

A gradual approach is necessary here as with other TCP aspects. Before regular interpersonal feedback sessions are initiated at a schoool, it would be a good idea for the principal to initiate a limited interaction with one other person, preferably someone with special responsibility in the school (such as the faculty chairman, TCP coordinator, or office manager) with whom he has a relatively good relationship (low threat level). They would meet weekly to give each other feedback, following the suggestions in "Guidelines for Improving Feedback Sessions" *(p. 266)*. Both the principal and the other person would come prepared to ask for and give direct feedback (positive and negative), raise any problems, issues, questions, concerns or doubts on his mind, and evaluate the quality of their interaction.

Depending on the principal's prior experience and his anxiety or confidence level, he may wish to start regular feedback sessions with more than one person (a small cross-section of key persons, grade level chairmen, committee chairmen). This would put the principal and a small core group in a better position subsequently to role model the desired feedback behavior for the entire school staff.

Visits to other schools where the principal can sit in on a faculty feedback session and possibly co-facilitate with the principal of that school are helpful. A regular feedback session with other principals who share similar problems and know each other in ways that teachers do not is also an excellent experience. A principal's resource group, similar to teachers' resource groups, provides an opportunity for mutual support among principals.

GUIDELINES FOR IMPROVING FEEDBACK SESSIONS

In order for all participants to reap the full benefits of feedback sessions, practice and experience in actual sessions are important and necessary, but not always sufficient. Even after much experience in groups, some people persist in silence, avoidance behavior, overintellectualization, holding back, smoothing things over, excessive defensiveness, screening be-

Through feedback, one learns to take responsibility for one's own actions instead of blaming others.

fore speaking. These behaviors may also characterize the group as a whole. Frequently the group may be unaware of persistent practices that may be self-defeating. In addition to increased experience, improvement requires thoughtful analysis, evaluation, and practice. It means becoming conscious about the group process and one's own participation and performance. It means defining what constitutes a good session and a poor one; what makes you feel good or bad; what was a learning experience and what wasn't. It means trying to work out methods and conditions which support positive aspects.

Improvement in group or individual performance is uneven and fluctuating. It is a dynamic process requiring continuous evaluation and revision.

What the Individual Can Do

The movement toward greater openness and trust and confidence in the feedback process and in each other typically is slow. The desire for honest, frank, direct relations as a means of personal and organizational self-correction and growth exists side by side with the fear of it. Progress will take place through individual efforts to improve the process. Each individual has the power to raise the level of effectiveness of each feedback session, for himself and for others by coming to sessions prepared to do four things:

1. Ask for Personal Feedback from Others

Ask the group as a whole, "What did I do this week that caused you to have either positive or negative feelings?"

The same question can be asked of an individual (e.g., tutoring partner, principal, TCP coordinator, reading consultant, parent coordinator, other teacher, etc. When addressing the question to an individual make it more specific:

> "John, how did you feel about my part in the feedback session with your kids?"

> "Mary, when we had our planning meeting on Wednesday, I had the feeling you were uneasy about something. Did I say something that bothered you?"

> "Edna, were you uncomfortable with the noise level in my room yesterday?"

2. Give Personal Feedback to Others

Before the session ask yourself about your reactions to each person in the group, "Do I have any positive or negative feedback to give this person?" Make mental notes. In the session address the individual. Where possible be specific, but it's all right to make general observations too.

Specific:

> "I didn't like your rigidity in not wanting to change our meeting time."

> "You did a lousy job in the tutor feedback session. You did all the talking and didn't give the kids a chance to say anything."

> "Why can't you get the supplies ordered on time? It's a simple task and your procrastination is irritating."

> "I thought you did a fantastic job of training the new group of tutors."

General:

> "You seem troubled this week. You don't look good. Is something bothering you?"

"I think your attitude is turning the kids off to tutoring."

"You have been a pleasure to work with all week."

Remember, in these sessions you don't have to be sure of yourself to make a comment. You don't have to be right or to have proof. This is the place to get out feelings, thoughts, assumptions even if they are only tentatively formed or half-developed. It is a place where you take chances, try things out. The important thing is to get things that are on your mind into the open, to clear the air, to make room for new thoughts and feelings.

3. Receive Feedback with an Open Mind

Listen non-defensively to what the person giving the feedback has to say. Hear him out and try to really understand what is being expressed. If you don't understand, ask for clarification, ask him to be specific. For example, if someone says, "You don't seem to give a damn about what's happening this week," you might reply, "I don't know what you mean; can you give me an example." If someone says, "Nothing is going right in my class this week," ask for examples of things that are going wrong.

The feedback sessions should be viewed as a learning opportunity. They should be used to exchange information and points of view. The information can be used by you to make changes or it can be discarded. If negative feedback bothers you even though you think it's untrue, you should ask yourself why you are upset. Perhaps there is a grain of truth in the comment. Perhaps you are afraid of looking bad in the eyes of others. Even if the feedback is inaccurate or false, it is better to have it out in the open. You can check on what you might be doing to cause this false impression. You might supply the other person with information to correct his view. In any case,

Don't expect to leave every feedback session feeling great. Learning, especially when it involves learning about our own mistakes or shortcomings, can be uncomfortable.

the air is cleared and the person giving the feedback will not hold on to bad feelings only to express them in other ways. If the feedback is true, it might cause you some discomfort. But it should help you change your behavior to correct the situation.

4. Bring Up Problems Or Issues

Think about questions or problems you have. They can be directly related to you or to the school in general. Don't try to evaluate if they're worth talking about. If it's on your mind, bring it up. The group will tell you if they want to discuss it. Here are some examples:

> "I can't seem to do a thing with my class this week. My math program seems to be floundering."

> "John Jones is driving me crazy."

> "I think we should do something about the yard."

> "I'm concerned with how we arrive at decisions."

5. Cultivate Positive Attitudes

Giving and receiving feedback must be undertaken with a positive attitude. If you are honest and sincere, in the long run you will be respected for your opinions, even if the receiver experiences some initial discomfort or appears upset with you. If you are the receiver of negative feedback, don't hold grudges. Show appreciation for someone's comments, whether or not you agree or accept them.

Don't be a spectator. You'll get out of a session what you put into it. Don't screen. When in doubt, speak up. No matter how inconsequential your input may seem to you, others can learn from it.

Do not have unrealistic expectations for each session. All

differences are not resolved in one session. Remember, you are engaged in an ongoing process.

Post-Session Critique

The post-feedback-session critique is an important mechanism for improving the feedback process.

Procedure

At the conclusion of each regular one-to-two-hour feedback session, all persons participate in a brief (15-30 minutes) evaluation and discussion of the session. Periodically (every 4 to 6 weeks), the critique time may be extended (45 minutes to one hour).

Each person rates the feedback session as a whole and his own participation in it on a five point scale (excellent, good, fair, poor, very poor). He also selects one thing he liked and one thing he disliked about the session as a whole and about his own performance. Sometimes this is done entirely orally. However, taking 2 to 3 minutes to write down one's evaluation has the advantage of giving each person the opportunity to formulate his own thoughts and position without being influenced by what others say.

Each person presents his evaluation to the group, without comments from the others. After all have spoken, the group discusses the reactions. The discussion is unstructured and may go in various directions, perhaps focusing on the pattern of responses, or identifying specific factors that helped or hindered open communication, or discussing specific individual reactions.

Participants are encouraged to keep weekly logs on their feedback performance. In addition to rating the session and commenting on the one thing liked and disliked about self and session, they include such items as: Things I wanted to say and didn't, or should have said and was afraid to. Was I specific and direct or vague and general? Did I try to speak to everyone? How well did I listen when someone talked to me? How defensive was I? Things I would like to do next time to improve my participation.

Key Personnel

Following the critique at the end of the feedback session, key personnel and any other participants who volunteer, may meet for another 30 to 45 minutes of more intensive evaluation. The question explored in greater depth is: What factors contributed to, or detracted from, group effectiveness? Examples are: the room was too warm; people came late and we didn't start on time; Mary asked Barbara to be specific when she was complaining about teachers not following through on their responsibilities; Ann pointed out that we are avoiding discussing directly with the principal an issue that was being gossiped about constantly in the lunch room; so-and-so talked too much and dominated the group and no one did anything about it.

The key personnel critique can be tape recorded and later listened to by teachers who could not attend the session. Tapes can also be used for discussion at training seminars and workshops.

Benefits of Critique

Most critique sessions have proved to be interesting and enjoyable experiences. Participants have indicated that their general understanding of the feedback process improved as did their feedback performance. Other interesting by-products occur. People who were silent during the session frequently speak up and participate during the critique. It appears to be less threatening and helps them break the ice.

Sometimes inhibitions break down. People who hold back

from saying something to someone during the session sometimes say it during the discussion. It usually comes out as "What I didn't like about my participation was that I didn't tell John that I was upset with him." This sometimes leads to subsequent participation by people who had never done so previously.

People sometimes acquire information and insights about the feedback process or about themselves. For example, someone who was bored by the session, while listening to another person who was enthusiastic may realize what he missed and may recognize that you get out of a session what you put into it.

Sometimes the openness of communication, breadth of participation, and degree of involvement in the critique exceeds that of the particular feedback session itself.

STUDENT FEEDBACK

An essential element in a TCP school is that students are among those who participate in feedback.

Students regularly gather with their teacher to give their impressions and reactions to school life and to discuss what seems to be helping or hindering the achievement of school goals. Special problems are talked about. Often the teacher himself receives criticism.

Feedback sessions energize the classroom community. All students, along with tutors and teachers, have an opportunity to get everything out in the open. If there is conflict, if it goes poorly for a learner, if someone is being overlooked, these things can be said in plain language.

Change can be mutually instituted rather than unilaterally administered. Problems of discipline are resolved by the group instead of by an adult authority. By demonstrating the adult's willingness to accept criticism, feedback sessions further cultivate a sense of trust, and liberate fresh and innovative ideas.

Sessions can be tied into the academic curriculum by using themes that emerge from the children's discussions as a basis for writing assignments; for reading; or for further research and investigations by individuals or teams.

Underlying Concepts and Goals

Learning involves both feelings and intellect. Much lip service is given to the importance of emotional growth and to the idea that a student's feelings about himself and others and about his educational experiences have an important effect on his cognitive achievement. In practice, however, the emphasis in school is almost uniquely on developing cognitive skills. Teachers generally feel better equipped, and more comfortable, and are better trained to handle academic content.

Students must be provided explicit opportunities to express and understand their feelings about themselves and about their relationships with others. Some children who are shy and withdrawn in academic activities start to open up and get involved during feedback.

Although much is said about improving communication between students and teacher, the school's hierarchical structure (teachers viewed by the students as authority figures and administrators viewed in the same way by teachers) fosters a climate of defensiveness which inhibits the development of positive caring relationships. The student-teacher relationship will not improve, and the affective domain will continue to be neglected, unless time and procedures for dealing directly with these areas are built into the curriculum.

Repressed feelings often become explosive. When conflicts and bad feelings are talked out, they are less likely to be acted out in antisocial behavior.

Student feedback establishes norms of openness, directness, and honesty in classroom communications. It provides students with the opportunities to express both positive and negative feelings and to learn that having negative feelings or "bad thoughts" does not make them "bad" persons.

Student feedback sessions provide information to the teacher about student feelings, which may be useful in assessing need for changes in classroom procedures and behavior.

Gradual Progression or Phasing

The teacher's preparation to conduct feedback sessions with children begins with his direct participation in adult sessions. When teachers become more open and direct with each other, it is easier for them to open up with children. The teacher who is in touch with his own feelings and is able to express them openly and naturally when he wants to, can listen sensitively to the expression of another's feelings. He is also in a better position to role model the kind of behavior and participation desired from the children.

At any point where the teacher feels comfortable with the adult feedback process, he can decide to begin feedback sessions with children. He then proceeds gradually from limited feedback in the first stage to in-depth discussions at advanced stages.

Description and Conduct of Sessions

Before he conducts the first student feedback session, the teacher orients the students to the rationale, ground rules and procedures.

Ground Rules

Ground rules are few, but strongly adhered to: sit in a circle, no fighting, one person talks at a time. Children do not raise hands or ask the teacher for permission to talk. Initially, the teacher deals with nonobservance of the ground rules by calling the offender's attention to the behavior and giving him feedback about the effect of his behavior on the group. Gradually, the children themselves take on this responsibility. Persistent disregard of ground rules becomes a focus for group concern and discussion, and thus encourages the violator to learn better self-management.

Beginning Feedback

The teacher meets regularly with the whole class to have the children tell how they felt about school that day or that week.

The teacher usually starts the session by asking, "Did you have a good or bad day today? What made it that way for you? What did *I* do today that you liked? What did *I* do that you disliked?"

The session lasts about 15 or 20 minutes, preferably at the end of the day. The sessions may be held several times a week. It is not a problem-solving session. The activity is limited to the teacher's encouraging the children to express themselves and to listen to each other without evaluating or interpreting. The children learn that it's okay to have and to express negative feelings and to criticize the teacher. They learn that the teacher cares about what they have to say.

Advanced Student Feedback

When the teacher feels satisfied with the limited feedback sessions, he may move into the more advanced stage. These sessions emphasize student-student interaction. The teacher functions as a facilitator of the communication process. The students give each other and the teacher feedback about those things they see anyone doing that facilitate or hinder achievement of school goals or the enjoyment of school life.

PROCEDURES   The advanced feedback sessions should be held at least once a week for about 45 to 60 minutes. The class is divided into two groups. While one group engages in the feedback session, the second group may be involved in silent reading or some other quiet activity which does not interfere. A student may request to switch groups for a session if there is someone he wishes to speak to in the other group. Occasionally, the teacher will hold the session with the entire class, especially if there is a major issue to be discussed. Sometimes the paired teachers will co-facilitate the session. This is especially desirable in the beginning because it takes some of the pressure off the individual teacher and provides another adult point of view.

As participant/facilitators, the teachers engage in giving and receiving honest feedback with students. Co-facilitating teachers are encouraged to be spontaneous and to feel free to agree or disagree with each other. In this way, they come across to the children as real people and not as stereotypes.

Brief post-session critique sessions (5 to 10 minutes) paralleling the adult critiques are helpful in improving the process.

In the later stages of the advanced phase, the teacher transfers the facilitator role to the students. Two students act as co-facilitators for each session. This function rotates so that all students eventually gain experience in the facilitator role. The teacher helps train students by giving them a pre-session orientation and post-session critique.

Spontaneous feedback sessions may be held whenever needed, involving the whole class or some sub-group (tutors, tutees, a learning team, a committee, or some students having a conflict). The feedback sessions may cut across two or more classes (tutors and tutees from paired classes, a schoolwide committee, 6th graders involved in graduation planning, and so forth).

Persons who want to visit should get the permission of the

children and teacher. They should sit in the circle and participate, and be encouraged to express themselves spontaneously. They might begin by briefly telling who they are and why they are there.

SAMPLES FROM ADVANCED SESSIONS   Because the feedback session is the arena for open communication, a wide range of topics is discussed. However, as with the adult sessions, the point of departure is task-oriented. How are we doing together in trying to achieve our goals and enjoy school life?

Some examples from actual sessions follow.

1. *Tutoring Problem* (6th Grade Tutors). Having different students present things from their own perspectives can be very helpful.

BOBBY (John's tutor):	John doesn't want to learn. He fools around and doesn't pay attention. I'm fed up with him.
TEACHER:	What do you think we should do?
BOBBY:	I'd like to crack him in the mouth.
TEACHER:	Anyone else have any suggestions?
CARL:	Make him stand in the corner during tutoring.
LOU:	That's no good. He's causing trouble all day. Send him to the principal to be paddled.
MIKE:	I don't think he's so bad just because he doesn't want to learn. It just ain't interesting for him. I like him.
TEACHER:	What do you think should be done, Mike?

MIKE:	I think he needs a friend. Somebody has to be friendly with him first.
BOBBY:	I tried. You can't be friends with him.
MIKE:	How about if I tried? Why don't we trade tutees?
BOBBY:	Great stuff!
TEACHER:	What do the rest of you think of that?
CARL AND LOU:	Right on! Good idea!It's worth a try!

2. *Crying* (3rd Grade Class).

MARTY:	I don't like Jean because she cries in class.
TEACHER:	What's wrong with crying?
MARTY:	Only sissies and girls cry. Boys don't cry.
EDWARD:	I feel like crying sometimes.
TEACHER:	When is that?
EDWARD:	When my mommy or daddy yells at me.
TEACHER:	Why *don't* you cry then?
EDWARD:	Sometimes I do, but then I feel bad because I get called a baby. Boys aren't supposed to cry.
TEACHER:	Do you all agree with that?
JACK:	I think boys cry on the inside and girls cry on the outside.

3. *Friendship* (2nd Graders).

HAROLD:	I hate school. I'm going to run away from home and never come back.

PETE: Where will you go?

HAROLD: To Africa.

BARRY: How will you get there?

HAROLD: I'll steal a car and drive there.

JAY: A car can't go across an ocean. You'll drown.

HAROLD: Well, I'll get there some way.

RICHIE: What's bugging you, anyway? Why do you want to run away?

HAROLD: Cause nobody likes me. I ain't got no friends.

PETE: I like you. I'll be your friend.

HAROLD: Gee, would ya really!

4. *Criticizing Teacher* (First Grade Class).

GEORGE: I don't like when you yell at us.

TEACHER: If you did what you're supposed to, I wouldn't have to yell at you.

STEVE: But it isn't fair.

TEACHER: What's not fair?

STEVE: One kid does something wrong, and you punish all of us. It isn't fair. It makes me mad.

Training Teachers for Student Feedback

Before initiating student feedback sessions, teachers generally participate in orientation seminars (two of approximately two hours each). These seminars include a discussion of the purpose and procedures of beginning student feedback,

Feedback makes people the main business of the
school.

with emphasis on the teacher's role as listening to and reflect-
ing students' feelings without evaluating or interpreting them.
Teachers usually have considerable difficulty refraining from
defending or explaining their behavior when children criticize
or express negative feelings about them.

The seminar leader (an experienced teacher, the TCP
coordinator, principal or consultant) demonstrates the function of the feedback facilitator and the teachers role play as
students. Then each teacher in turn conducts a beginning
feedback session, with the other teachers taking the part of the
students. Each role playing session is followed by a critique.
The processes of role playing, critique and discussion of
session are repeated so that each teacher has conducted several
sessions and gained some skill and confidence.

Further training in conducting student feedback sessions
may consist of the following activities: observation of an
experienced teacher in action; co-facilitation with an experi-

enced teacher followed by a critique; sharing experiences with paired teachers; having an experienced person observe an actual session and comment afterwards; tape recording a session with children and playing it back for self-evaluation, or for students to evaluate; these tapes can also be played at teacher resource group meetings for comments by other teachers.

POTENTIAL PROBLEM AREAS

It is inevitable that problems will arise in relation to both adult and student feedback sessions since it is a very new concept and procedure for most educational institutions. These are some of the problems encountered in conducting feedback in target TCP schools.

Student Feedback

Unrealistic Expectations

Teachers sometimes are impatient when students don't speak up readily. They should realize the process is gradual and progress is uneven. It takes time for students to develop trust and to realize it is okay to talk honestly about their feelings in school.

Another problem that teachers have is that they expect that the new school program will yield immediate results and improvements and are disappointed when this doesn't happen.

Overemphasis on Teacher-Child Interaction

In the beginning, children tend to address all comments to the teacher. Teachers may slip into this teacher-child interaction.

They should consciously encourage direct child-child interaction (Why don't you say that to John?). Also, the teacher can emphasize at the beginning of the session, "Talk to each other unless you have feelings to express about something I've done."

Teacher Domination of Pupil Sessions

Teachers often moralize and teach a lesson rather than allowing the give and take of honest expression of feelings. They may intervene too much and dominate. Teachers should periodically tape record their sessions and listen for this. Co-facilitators should watch for this and give each other feedback.

Handling Conflict

Teachers sometimes are uncomfortable with conflict among children and want to resolve and smooth over problems. They may attempt to talk children out of their feelings ("You don't really feel that way, do you? You're really not angry with Robert.") At teacher resource group meetings teachers should discuss situations that made them uncomfortable so that they may gain alternative ways of handling them.

Sensitive Material

When children bring up sensitive material about their personal lives or family members, teachers sometimes are unsure how to handle it. There is no simple answer. Most of the time it is not necessary that the teacher do anything at all. If the child has felt comfortable enough and free enough to talk about a home problem it does not mean that the teacher has to follow it through to find a solution. Unburdening himself may be enough for the child at this point. If the teacher feels it will be helpful, he may discuss the situation at paired teacher or resource group meetings and see what others do when similar material comes up.

Adult Feedback

Obtaining Full Participation

Some persons maintain a low profile and do not participate much because of fear, shyness, or apathy. The more verbal, aggressive people (sometimes the least sensitive) may dominate the sessions. If this continues indefinitely, the strong get stronger and the weak weaker. There are several ways to combat this. One is to limit the size of the group. Another way is to start by having each person state one thing that bothers him at school and one thing he feels positive about. No comments are made until everyone has spoken. Then the normal group interaction takes place; but now there is considerable input to involve everyone.

Also, the facilitator, or any member, can attempt to bring someone in directly by asking, "I wonder what you think about that, Mary," or by describing how a member's silence makes him feel.

Handling Positive Feedback

Positive feedback is difficult for some people to accept. It makes them feel uncomfortable. Sometimes people prefer not to acknowledge success and competence because it makes them feel that people will expect more of them. Also, some members may feel that saying good things is Pollyannaish. They fear that making positive statements may be misconstrued as trying to ingratiate oneself or obligate people. Especially when sessions become mainly negative, the group should be reminded that it's okay to talk positively. An occasional session might begin with each person taking thirty seconds to think and/or tell about something someone did that was positive.

Gossip and Confidentiality

Although some gossip is natural and harmless, some can be harmful and destructive. The feedback sessions offer opportunities for clarification and airing of rumors and gossip which may have become distorted and disruptive.

Telling people things in confidence about other people can be destructive. The person being talked about has no chance to hear the criticism and do something about it if it is true, or present his side if it is not true. The person hearing it may consciously or unconsciously form some opinion about the individual which may affect his behavior toward that person. The principal, TCP coordinator, and others in responsible positions often find themselves in the position of being the recipient of confidential information. A good ground rule is "no confidences about other people." The best place to bring up such information is in the feedback sessions themselves.

Some people are concerned that they may be quoted outside of the group to individuals who are not participants (to community members, teachers at other schools, district administrators, parents, or others). The usual understanding is that the material stays in the group among the group members.

Public vs. Private Discussion of Problems

When specifically asked about a problem, sometimes individuals say they plan to work it out privately and don't see any need to bring it up in the group. This is often a form of avoidance behavior. It is desirable to bring things up in the group because it gives the individuals involved the objective points of view of people who are not ego-involved in the problem. It also gives the group an opportunity to learn from the problem.

Planning vs. Feedback

In the feedback sessions, feelings, problems, issues, and conflicts get aired, but usually are not resolved. They get resolved over a series of sessions or at meetings outside of these sessions. Individuals who need immediate closure on everything will sometimes try to change the session into a developmental or planning meeting to work out all the details of a problem. The group has constantly to be aware when it is digressing and getting caught up in minutiae, or in details that are more appropriately left to committee meetings.

Reluctant Participation

Those who do not believe in the feedback process should not be required to participate. These sessions go counter to many of the accepted mores and values of teachers. If participation is half-hearted, much time will be spent trying to convince people of the value of the process, sessions will be unproductive, and the morale of the faculty will be adversely affected.

Parallel Structure

Because everyone is equal in the feedback session, and everyone is accountable to everyone else, teachers sometimes forget that outside the session different individuals have varying responsibilities to make decisions. Members need to understand this parallel structure. Although there is shared planning-and-decision-making, one person usually has the ultimate responsibility for making final decision about some things. The others have to follow through on these decisions.

However, in the feedback sessions these decisions can be challenged. Group feedback is the self-correcting mechanism used to change incorrect decisions or to prevent their recurrence.

Administrator as Positive Role Model

Teachers may have a difficult time believing they can say negative things to the "boss" without repercussions. Some may resist bringing up things that bother them, although they continue to discuss these behind his back. Sometimes the principal unconsciously contributes to this attitude.

Irregular attendance by the principal and frequent interruptions (leaving the session before it is over or to answer telephone calls, or attend to visitors) are detrimental to group morale. The group will feel that he gives the importance of feedback mere lip service. They will also feel frustrated if they have something specific to discuss with him and he is not there.

The principal must, by word and action, reinforce the importance of feedback and the notion that everyone in the group is equal and that anyone can say anything with impunity. He must positively reinforce teachers who are candid and direct with him, even though he may not accept or agree with what they say. His own directness and candor will trigger theirs.

As the authority figure, much hostility may be directed toward the principal at the outset. He may become the scapegoat, rightly or wrongly, for all the school's problems. Excessive defensiveness, denial, anger, or avoidance by him will prolong this initial period. Even when he makes changes, some individuals may remain skeptical or question his motives. The principal must try not to become discouraged. Gradually, the group will start dealing with each other and the principal will become just another participant and fallible human being. He can set a positive constructive tone by his ability to praise and accept praise, offer help and ask for it, criticize and accept criticism.

IN CONCLUSION

If one aspect of TCP were to be singled out as most important, it would probably be the task-oriented feedback program. It is the glue that holds everything together and the lubricant that keeps programs from becoming frozen. It is the system's principal self-correction and self-renewing mechanism. It makes people the main business of the school.

The introduction of feedback sessions requires significant changes in the attitudes and behavior of people and cannot occur without some anxiety and discomfort. Consequently, feedback has been the most controversial and difficult aspect of TCP to implement. A feedback program cannot be successful unless the participants believe in it and want to make it work. Voluntary participation is vital.

Gradual development of the task-oriented feedback program is important. All participants receive orientation and training prior to participation in actual school feedback sessions. Ongoing evaluation and modification are an important part of program improvement.

Feedback sessions begin with key personnel. Once this core group gains experience, they help facilitate the involvement of other teachers and children.

Although the groups eventually become self-directed, a trained facilitator is desirable during the early stages of the program. He should act as a participant and should work his way out of the program at the earliest possible time.

Feedback sessions should be incorporated into the regular school day for maximum integration into the entire school program.

6 IMPLEMENTATION STRATEGY

Utilizing the Tutorial Community Program in Whole or in Part

MAIN APPROACHES TO TCP

The concepts and methods that constitute the essence of the Tutorial Community Program will be of interest to anyone who would like to develop a new kind of learning community or improve the present system by utilizing human resources in new and creative ways. The ideas presented in this book may be used in different ways. They may be used for the total redesign of a school, or as a resource for adopting selected TCP features to improve specific aspects of any school program.

In this chapter different ways of implementing TCP are presented. Also described are the essential conditions and procedures involved, the advantages and disadvantages, the recommended sequence in implementation, the problems involved, potential solutions, and resources needed.

There is no single best way that all children learn. Teachers teach in different ways and children learn by a variety of methods throughout this country and throughout the world. Given unity, consistency, desire, and competence, any method can work.

Most schools today are characterized by heterogeneity.

The principal's philosophy of education may differ from the teachers'; one teacher's approach may differ from another's; the parents' philosophy may differ from the principal's or teachers'. With every teacher the student comes in contact with in the same school, he may face different, and often conflicting, philosophies, methods, expectations, and standards.

Any approach to learning, from the most traditional to the most progressive, can be more successful and effective if all the people involved believe in it, want to make it work, cooperate, and maintain consistency and enthusiasm. But where a staff lacks a common philosophy, common goals and methods, there is no teamwork and no sense of community. Individuals often work at cross-purposes and compete rather than cooperate. They may relate to each other as adversaries rather than as team members. This dilutes the educational effort, reduces effectiveness, and inhibits constructive change. Under such conditions teachers, administrators, pupils, and parents are generally dissatisfied. They feel powerless to do anything except perhaps blame each other and complain about the central administration, the establishment.

Providing a choice between different kinds of schools appears to be one answer to the dilemma of improving modern education. An important book on this subject is Mario Fantini's *Public Schools of Choice.* * How would this work? A single school district might have numerous well-defined, clearly different models of education, including the traditional 3 R's, behavior modification, open-structure, Summerhill, vocational, Montessori, TCP, and others. Each school would be staffed by a principal and teachers with compatible philosophies of education and a strong commitment to the particular model. Each school would be populated by children whose parents believed in that model.

---

* Fantini, Mario D., *Public Schools of Choice: A Plan for the Reform of American Education*, New York, Simon and Schuster, 1973.

In this situation, whatever the school model, the energy usually wasted in disagreements, conflict, resistance and apathy could be turned into developing a powerful and exciting learning environment. All schools would have a greater capacity for high achievement, self-correction, and renewal. *Each school (representing a different model) would have a better chance to achieve its own objectives.* Each school would look to itself for the source and solution of problems. Some models might eventually prove more effective and more popular than others. Some might eventually disappear altogether.

This is the rationale underlying the alternative school movement and voucher plan proposals. Many parents who were dissatisfied with the lack of choice within the public school system turned to private schools, or set up their own free schools. In recent years, alternative schools have appeared within the public school system. Many of these have floundered, raising doubts about the viability of alternative public schools. However, examination indicates that a major difficulty has been the lack of a well-defined, clearly formulated model. The founders did not like what existed and knew what they were against, but they did not know exactly what they were for. They often had hazy, vague notions about what they wanted to do. Many lacked the necessary management and interpersonal skills to set up a new organization. Even where a program is well defined, carefully thought out, and agreed to by everyone, implementing it requires considerable time, effort, and know-how. Many initiators of new school programs either underestimated this or were not able to attract the right persons.

The distinction between developing a model and implementing it should be recognized. Development involves describing the model in general terms, e.g. humanistic education, behavior modification, or free school. Implementation requires the formulation of plans for carrying out the desired model. Detailed procedures are specified; materials are procured that reflect the philosophy and procedures; qualifications for staff and training needed are defined; personnel and financial requirements can be estimated.

When one is implementing a well defined model, better results can be expected earlier. Recruiting is facilitated because people have a better idea of what they are getting into. Training of personnel is facilitated because requirements are clear and materials are available.

In developing TCP in the pilot schools in Los Angeles many problems and difficulties were encountered—conflicts between teachers and parents who were committed to the program and those who were opposed or luke-warm, lack of strong administrative leadership at the school level, bureaucratic red-tape interfering with using time, space and personnel flexibly, lack of strong support and positive reinforcement from central administration, lack of continuity in leadership. Details on these problems and other research and development difficulties are presented in TCP annual progress reports *(see Bibliography, Newmark and Melaragno, p. 407)*.

This book will give new schools going into TCP the benefits of a well-defined model. Hopefully, other schools should not require the kind of time and energy to get the program off the ground that the first model did. However, some problems may still be encountered. To avoid these pitfalls, this chapter is designed to spell out some of the factors that contribute to the successful implementation of TCP, whichever approach is adopted.

Approaches to implementing TCP are:

Total Adoption:

1. *Alternative School Model:* A new, alternative school adopts the total program and employs a staff of like-minded persons to implement it.

2. *Intact School Model:* An intact, traditional school decides to adopt the total program and gradually implements it, beginning with the least complex aspects and replacing noncommitted staff over time.

3. *School-Within-a-School Model:* An intact school creates a school-within-a-school. Parents, students, and teachers have a choice between the traditional part of the school and the part in which TCP is being implemented.

Partial Adoption:

1. Intact and alternative schools adopt one or two major aspects of TCP (tutoring, shared planning-and-decision-making, feedback, parent involvement) on a schoolwide basis.

2. Individual teachers in intact or alternative schools adopt selected TCP concepts, ideas or procedures for their own classrooms.

TOTAL ADOPTION

Necessary Conditions

Some of the implementation factors will be different depending on which particular TCP model a school has decided to adopt. However, when a school has chosen to implement the Tutorial Community Program *as a whole* there are certain conditions which will be necessary whether the alternative school model, the intact school model, or the school-within-a-school model is followed. Newmark's equation "like-minded persons + authority to act = accountability and potential for constructive change" defines the principal ingredients of a successful TCP school.

1. Committed Administration

To establish the proper climate for change, the school administration must believe strongly in the major TCP concepts and must actively participate in program activities. Staff members must be supported and encouraged as they attempt to change. When decisions are made, the goal of developing a Tutorial Community School must receive highest priority. The principal must furnish active leadership in role-modeling the behavior desired from the staff. He must subscribe to the commitments for a principal of a TCP school. *(See Form 43, p. 387.)*

An equally strong commitment is necessary at the central office, or Superintendent of Schools level. *(See Form 43, page 387.)* If the central office approves the program with limited knowledge and without clear understanding of the specific support required, the program will meet serious obstacles along the way.

2. Committed Teachers

The staff should consist of like-minded persons with a humanistic philosophy of education. Recruitment of personnel is designed to secure teachers who understand the nature of the program, believe in it strongly, are willing to invest time and energy to make it succeed, and are participating in the program by choice. They must be willing to make substantial changes in their traditional methods and procedures. They must subscribe to the commitments for a TCP teacher. *(See Form 43, p. 387.)*

3. Community Involvement

Parents must understand the TCP approach, believe in it, and want their children to be in the school. This is especially important for creating a learning community based on close interaction and cooperation among children, teachers, parents, and administrators.

4. Shared Authority

One of the main objectives of TCP is to develop a learning community where everyone feels a proprietary interest in what goes on. For this to occur, members must have power to influence the conditions and quality of living in the learning community to which they belong. The local school must have the authority to institute mechanisms and procedures that insure genuine, and not superficial, inclusion of students, parents, and staff members in planning and decision-making.

5. Local Autonomy

If a school is to be innovative, responsive to local needs, and self-renewing, there must be maximum freedom and flexibility to try new things and to change. The experimental approach, or the evaluation-revision strategy, is seriously handicapped if the factors that need to be manipulated are severely limited and are out of the control of the local practitioners. The local school must have the freedom to change most things without undue red tape and delays. Only with autonomy can there be valid accountability for results. Accountability without authority is futile.

Alternative School Model

When this model is adopted, the school is starting from

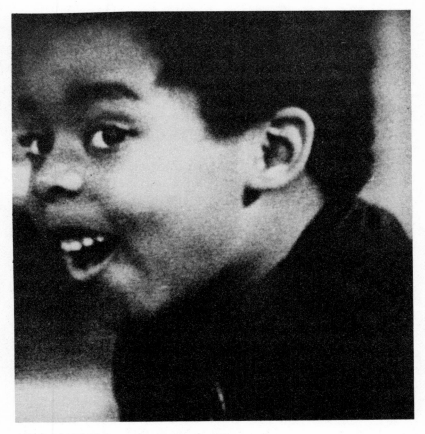

This school belongs to you and me.

scratch to build the ideal school-community. The idea to initiate a new school based on TCP concepts may have originated with a committee of parents and/or teachers and/or administrators who submitted their proposal to the Central Board and gained approval to go ahead. A site is designated and the recruitment of personnel is begun.

Selecting TCP Participants

A person will be needed to coordinate, supervise, and organize initial recruiting efforts. A temporary principal or coordinator is designated for this purpose. Public announcements are made in district media and local news media describing the nature and purpose of the proposed school and requesting interested personnel (parents, teachers, supervisors, support staff) to submit applications.

The coordinator (or temporary principal) and a committee of parents and teachers constitute a Personnel Committee to screen and select applicants. The majority of parents, teaching staff, the permanent principal, and the support staff are selected in that order. The initial parents help select subsequent ones. The parents and initial teachers select subsequent teachers.

A requirement for acceptance of children in the school should be participation of parents in orientation seminars and their endorsement of the commitments for parents. *(See Form 43, p. 387.)*

Implementing the Program

In the alternative school model, phase one of each of the four major TCP areas are implemented simultaneously from the outset. Shared planning-and-decision-making are instituted from the start. The Personnel Committee recruits, screens, and selects new parents and teachers. Feedback sessions begin almost immediately as part of the critique at the end of group committee meetings. Shortly thereafter, regular weekly teacher feedback sessions are initiated.

The first stage of tutoring (with paired classrooms in reading) begins simultaneously with the first stage of parent involvement (contacts with parents via letters, telephone, and social get-together).

Intact School Model

A traditional school typically does not have a well-defined educational model that is distinctive. Its approach is usually eclectic. Its staff generally represents many different educational philosophies, values, and practices. When such a school decides to adopt the total TCP program, it does not do so all at once. Existing conditions and personnel are gradually converted to the TCP model. Over a considerable period of time the school will become a community of like-minded people dedicated to fostering self-learning and mutual learning through cooperative teaching, planning and decision making.

Initiating the TCP Idea

The notion of adopting the TCP model and developing it over time may arise from the district office, which then seeks a willing principal and community. Or it may come from the principal, or from a parent or teacher group of a school. Whatever its inception, all three (principal, district, parents) must agree if it is to suceed.

The teachers are informed that the school is adopting TCP, that classroom implementation will begin with volunteers only, and that the other teachers will have one or two years in which to become more familiar with the program and to become involved if they wish. If their decision is not to get involved, they would be expected to transfer without prejudice to other schools as rapidly as appropriate transfers can be arranged. They would be gradually replaced by teachers who volunteer for the school because they identify with the goals and philosophy of TCP. Eventually the entire staff would be made up of persons who fully and enthusiastically support the program. All teachers, of course, are given the opportunity to transfer immediately. Teachers' organizations should be brought into discussions in the beginning to avoid later conflict over transfers.

Implementing the Program

In the intact situation, it will take a long time before all four major TCP concepts pervade the entire school. Whereas the alternative school implements the initial stages in all areas simultaneously right from the start, the intact school starts with tutoring only.

It is advisable to start with no more than four to six teachers (2 or 3 pairs), even if more volunteer. If there are a few effective, smooth-running classrooms rather than ten struggling ones, it is more likely to evoke a positive response from the other teachers (especially those who are on the fence).

One intact school that adopted TCP started with the principal and two teachers. All the teachers in the school were given opportunities to observe the tutoring once it was operating smoothly in the two classes. During the summer six teachers volunteered for training. Thus, in the second year eight teachers were involved in cross-age tutoring. By the third year, all 20 teachers were involved. For a basically conservative school this represented a remarkable change.

After Phase I of the tutoring is progressing satisfactorily, beginning activities in each of the other major areas are undertaken. Each TCP concept is gradually extended to the entire school in a gradual progression from basic to more advanced stages.

Need for Administrative Support

The problems of introducing TCP into intact schools are numerous. People in these schools are not necessarily extremely dissatisfied with what they or the school are doing. They feel no great need for change. Even if they volunteer for the program, they are prone to become discouraged easily when the inevitable difficulties occur. The commitment and enthusiasm in the alternative school where teachers sought out the program are not present in the intact school, where the program was brought to or imposed on some of the teachers and parents. Volunteering to participate in the program often represents acquiescence rather than true acceptance. The volunteer may have many unstated reservations. He may have been influenced by fear of disapproval from the principal or parents, or may not have wanted to appear to be against progress or change. He may have been motivated by a desire to stay at the school for convenience, or may have feared changing to another school. Some may have thought the new program would not last long anyway. Others may not have fully realized what they were getting into.

Under these conditions many innovative programs last only as long as the chief advocates and change agents are present, and disappear soon after their departure. The critical mass of committed people necessary to continuously develop, improve and sustain the innovation is lacking. Resistance, distractions, and conflicts generated by those who did not volunteer initially and are basically opposed to the program can debilitate volunteers and those on the fence. Cliques and factions can easily develop in the school.

Despite these difficulties, a determined principal with a few experienced, committed teachers and with parental support can succeed over a number of years in developing a fairly successful TCP model. However, there must be unequivocal support by the district and an agreement to transfer nonparticipating teachers at the earliest possible time.

School-Within-a-School Model

In this model, two distinct and separate programs coexist within one school. One is TCP and the other may be a traditional or any other program. Approximately half the teachers and pupils are involved in each program.

This model may be initiated by a principal by design, or because he cannot get full support from parents or staff to implement a total TCP program in an intact school.

302   THIS SCHOOL BELONGS TO YOU & ME

This program has several advantages. It provides a choice for parents, students and teachers without necessitating their moving out of their neighborhood. Also, if a child (or a teacher) is not responding to one program he may change without having to leave the school.

But this model also presents some problems. There is the possibility that competition and conflict will arise between the staffs of the two programs, especially over school resources. The principal will be watched closely for signs of favoritism and may frequently be accused of it by one or the other group of teachers and/or parents. It takes a skillful principal to convince people that he is operating impartially.

To minimize possible areas of conflict, the two programs should be separated in every way possible—pupils, classroom space, yard space, budgets, and materials and equipment. All resources should be assigned in proportion to the number of teachers and children in each program. Every attempt is made to develop a positive cooperative relationship between the programs rather than a competitive, adversary relationship which would hurt both programs.

The procedures described for gradually developing TCP within an intact school apply to the school-within-a-school situation.

PARTIAL ADOPTION

Many individual teachers and schools may be interested in trying a few features of TCP without plunging into the total program. They may select a single discrete activity in one major area (for example, the telephone tree activity in the area of parent involvement). Or they may opt for the systematic development of one entire concept (parent involvement, feedback, tutoring), or one subarea such as intraclass tutoring, student learning teams, classroom self-management, or interest centers. TCP offers a rich source of ideas for improving any school or upgrading and enlivening the classroom of any teacher.

Each chapter of this book may be used independently of the others for people who are interested in one particular aspect. The rationale and procedures are clearly defined in each chapter.

When individual teachers who become aware of TCP (through school district seminars or workshops or reading) adopt all or some of the features in their individual classrooms and are supported by the school principal or district superintendent, their success can influence other teachers. Eventually this may lead to schoolwide adoption of a feature or facet of TCP.

RESOURCES NEEDED TO IMPLEMENT TCP

The time, personnel, materials and cost factors of developing an effective tutorial community program depend on the experience and commitment of the personnel, the size of the school, the rate at which it wishes to proceed, and the scope of the program to be implemented.

Time Factors

The lack of time to plan, develop, and implement change is a major obstacle to the development of TCP in a school. Teachers need time to receive training, to plan and develop new ideas, to train others, to share experiences, to prepare materials, to resolve differences, to solve problems, and to meet with parents. Teachers have done these things voluntarily on their own time, before school, at recess, during lunch, after school, and on evenings and weekends. Such arrangements are not satisfactory. A crowded, frenetic schedule eventually frustrates and wears down the teachers and leaves them with little energy for the children.

Attempts to reduce the total amount of time pupils spend in school in order to provide teachers with pupil-free planning and development time have met with resistance. Yet there is no evidence that increasing the instructional time results in higher achievement. As a matter of fact, one school district in Maine, which went to a four-day instructional week, reported gains in learning.* One pupil-free day a week would give teachers time for activities designed to improve the quality of education, and I believe that this could significantly stimulate learning and improve the total school atmosphere in ways we can hardly imagine. If the break came in the middle of the week it might result in students and teachers being fresher, more alive, excited, patient, and interested in their work all week long. What is important is not the *amount* of time spent in class with students, but the *quality*, or how the time is used. The paradox is: less instructional time can mean better education.

Time is a precious commodity. It is one of the most important variables we have the possibility of manipulating. We should not allow ourselves to become slaves to rigid, inflexible, and anachronistic schedules that work to our disadvantage. The five-day week and two-day weekend, with everyone working about the same hours, results in overcrowded freeways, stores and recreational facilities. Recently there have been limited attempts in industry to break this cycle, with some firms trying a schedule of four ten-hour work days, and three-day weekends. Some companies are scheduling three days off during the week rather than on weekends.

Bold experiments with the creative use of time have been conducted by the Synanon Foundation in California over the past ten years. Its employees work on what is called a cube schedule (symbolizing that a day has many sides and all of its twenty-four hours can be used). Experimenting with longer

---

* Brewster, A. J., "Less School—Better Learning" (mimeo paper), Maine School Administrative District (SAD) No. 3, Unity, Maine, April, 1972.

sustained periods of work, followed by more frequent vacations (e.g. ten days of work of ten hours each followed by ten days off), Synanon has found that people work and play more effectively. They can accomplish more as there is less loss of momentum caused by frequent starting and stopping. The extended vacation time offers numerous possibilities for enriching their lives.

Educational institutions especially should be receptive to, even leaders in, experimentation that might lead to more creative and satisfying use of human resources. TCP schools wishing to experiment with time will have to overcome several obstacles. Parents will have to be shown that "less means more"—that less instructional time can mean more learning. It should be made clear that only the pupils' time in school is shortened, not the teachers'!

Conservative attitudes among district officials may be a problem. Difficulties arise from strict adherence to state or local board rules and regulations about minimum instructional time and how that time must be distributed over a week.

Practical problems usually include deciding what to do with the children on their day or extra time off if parents are working and are not at home. Arrangements can be made to have a sports program at the school, supervised by college students or YMCA personnel, or to provide enrichment club activities sponsored by parents who may supervise or instruct in a variety of interests, hobbies and activities.

If innovative programs are to be successful, and local autonomy and accountability are to have genuine meaning, time is one of the most important variables the local school must be able to control.

Personnel

TCP is a cost-effective program. It does not require special material, equipment, facilities, or personnel. It emphasizes and is based on the creative use of human resources. It taps into and tries to exploit, develop, and maximize the latent, unexplored talent that is there in any school in the teachers, children, and parents.

Nevertheless, as with any new program, there is an initial period of orientation, training, and trial and error, when consultant assistance is needed to support the regular staff. This assistance is temporary, and is to be withdrawn as early as possible, leaving the system to function on its own resources.

During the first two years of the program, it is desirable to have a full or part time coordinator. This person is needed to train and support faculty and parents in developing all aspects of the program. He takes care of the myriad details, maintains an overview of the total program, acts as a liaison among teachers, parents, and administration, is available to troubleshoot as difficulties and problems arise, and serves generally as a catalytic and unifying force.

Consultant help is also desirable during the first two years in providing orientation and training, especially in feedback and shared planning-and-decision-making.

In parent involvement, a parent assistant to work part time with the coordinator during the first year to assist in getting the program off the ground would be helpful.

How critical are the full-time coordinator and consultant help? They are desirable, but not absolutely essential. Without them, the program must start smaller and progress more slowly. Most schools can work out their own tutoring and parent involvement programs. The two areas where a consultant is most needed are in shared planning-and-decision-making and in task-oriented feedback. Consultant assistance and in-service training workshops may be available at no cost to the school through a district staff development branch.

Materials

TCP is essentially curriculum free. It is not limited to any specific type of content or teaching method. Rather, it is a new approach to planning and carrying out instruction that can be applied to almost any content. This does not mean that curriculum and curriculum change are not considered important. TCP has built-in procedures that stimulate and facilitate curriculum change. In the continuous dialogue of feedback sessions, obsolete, ineffective or inappropriate content, materials and methods come under criticism. At regular meetings of resource groups teachers share ideas and materials. As teachers function as resources for each other, new ideas and materials are introduced and disseminated within the school. As TCP develops, greater use is made of the natural materials and resources that exist in every community.

For special materials that may be used in relation to each of the four major TCP areas see Selected Bibliography *(p. 407)*.

Costs

The costs to implement and maintain a TCP program are minimal and optional. If funds are available, they would be useful in three areas: additional personnel, staff development, materials. Personnel needed would be a full-time or part-time TCP coordinator, and a part-time parent assistant in parent involvement. (A very rough estimate would be $20,000 the first year and $10,000 the second.)

Staff development requires consultant services to conduct orientation seminars and supervise training in tutoring, shared planning-and-decision-making and feedback. Costs should provide for approximately 25 to 50 consultant days per year at $100 to $200 per day.

The costs for materials are minor and should not exceed about $1,500. They involve supplying all personnel with manuals and readings on TCP and related topics. The TCP film, "Tomorrow We'll See What Happens," may be purchased for $200 (or it may be rented for about $30 for two days).

DISSEMINATION OF TCP THROUGH INTERSCHOOL COOPERATION

Implementing new programs requires that people put forth extra time and effort. When efforts are spread sequentially over several schools, each succeeding school should be able to profit from the others' mistakes and positive experiences. An experienced school is in an excellent position to assist a school interested in starting TCP.

Sister School Relationship

One proposed strategy for expanding tutorial community concepts to other schools is for an experienced school to assist another school in implementing the model. This assistance may be rendered in any of the following ways:

1. Key personnel in the newly involved school (administrators, officers of the parent advisory council, faculty chairman, the TCP coordinator, and teaching and nonteaching staff representatives) are formed into a group to assume leadership for initiating and maintaining change. Assistance in getting started is given this group by key personnel at the experienced TCP school. The key personnel group in the new school have responsibility for planning, implementation, evaluation, and modification of TCP.

2. Two experienced teachers from the experienced model school (one upper grade and one primary grade) exchange positions with two teachers (at the same grade levels) in the newly involved school. The TCP school teachers conduct orientation workshops for the entire staff of the new school and work closely with at least two of its teachers. At the end of the year, the teachers return to their original schools. There are now four teachers with TCP experience at the new school. Following the same procedure there would be 12

teachers with TCP experience at the new school at the end of two years.

3.   The principal and officers of the advisory council of the experienced school meet together and work closely with their counterparts in the new school to train them in leadership.

League of TCP Schools

Representatives (parents, teachers, and administrators) from different TCP schools may meet periodically to share ideas, experiences, and materials. They form a league of schools to serve as resources for each other and for the further spread of TCP concepts to other schools. Mutually agreeable transfers of teachers are encouraged to promote a better fit between teachers and schools.

Non-TCP schools could make requests to the league for "sister school status," or for limited assistance. Schools beginning a limited program on their own would be provided with materials and with opportunities to attend workshops, seminars, and meetings of league schools. They would have opportunities to observe tutorial community schools in action.

The proposed dissemination strategy is a rifle rather than a shotgun approach. Dissemination of the TCP concept through interschool cooperation is like intraschool tutoring: as much benefit accrues to the helping school as to the one being helped. The goal is to develop self-renewing institutions, through expanding self-reliance and helping relationships, where the joy of learning and of helping is pervasive.

IN CONCLUSION

We have discussed at some length the different possibilities for implementing TCP. The important thing to keep in mind is that the process of change is as important and beneficial as the end product. In the course of the early faltering steps in recruiting, training and implementation of the various TCP concepts, tremendous inner change is going on. Teachers are rethinking their roles; students are developing new self concepts; parents are beginning to share in an area of vital concern to them; a community with new and vital interpersonal interactions is being born, a school is really becoming involved in the business of learning. Mistakes, problems and conflicts are all grist for the mill, the means for learning, experimenting, growing. Each step along the way has its rewards and gratifications. One does not have to wait for the entire process to be complete before reaping benefits. They are there in the very process of instituting the idea or program.

This chapter, as well as the other chapters in this book, presented detailed information and suggestions for implementing the TCP concepts and activities. The most beneficial results for all children and adults are to be derived when the entire TCP program is adopted by a whole school. However, the TCP concepts and strategies can stand up separately, each in its own right. The four major aspects of TCP—tutoring, parent involvement, shared planning-and-decision-making, and feedback—offer exciting new possibilities to all teachers in all schools. However interrelated these concepts and methods may be, each has its own validity and offers excellent means for classroom or school reform. Teachers or schools that are not yet ready, for whatever reasons, to adopt the TCP program on a grand scale are urged and encouraged to try out whatever bits and segments of it have strong appeal to them. The very process of experimenting with some of these ideas and activities can revitalize teaching and learning. One small step may lead to another, and a whole new concept of what a school and learning can be is there waiting to be realized.

APPENDIX

FORM 1
BASIC TUTORING PROGRAM

Overall Tutoring Design

Teachers are paired for tutoring as follows:

Pairings are based on similar teaching philosophy/ styles.

Minimum of two years' difference in grade levels.

Receiving teacher/class: Grades K, 1, 2.

Sending teacher/class: Grades 4, 5, 6.

Classrooms are located close or adjacent to one another.

Pre-service teacher training includes a tutoring workshop designed to develop necessary knowledge and skills to implement program.

Tutor training gives upper graders the general and specific

training necessary to begin tutoring younger students.

Teachers observe tutoring in own classrooms and provide on-the-spot assistance as necessary.

Teacher-tutor feedback session (at least once weekly) evaluates progress, gives feedback, explores suggestions for improvements.

Paired teachers planning meeting (minimum one hour weekly) evaluates and plans changes in tutoring program.

Teacher Resource Group (four to six teacher pairs) meets for purposes of mutual sharing and assistance at least monthly.

Intraclass tutoring (tutoring within a classroom) usually begins after intergrade program is running smoothly. Major elements are the same as intergrade.

Specific Arrangements

CONTENT: Usually begins with reading; later branches to all areas of curriculum.

TIME ALLOTTED: Three to five days per week; approximately 30 minutes per day. One day for training; one to three days for tutoring; one day for feedback.

NUMBER OF TUTORS: Start small (five to ten tutors); add others gradually until whole class involved.

SELECTION: Observe children during paired classes socialization activity. Maximize probability of success; select those who would appear to be most ready and capable (not always highest achievers).

MATERIALS: Basic readers, basic TCP tutoring kit, learning games. (Usually located in receiving teacher's room.)

LOCATION: At first, tutoring takes place in receiving room; when all children in both classes are involved, tutoring takes place in both rooms (half of the tutors and tutees in each room).

NUMBER OF TUTEES PER TUTOR: Initially one tutor is assigned to one learner for one-to-one tutoring. Later a tutor may work with several children together.

TUTOR RESPONSIBILITIES: Maintain a friendly, supportive atmosphere; assist learner with specific learning tasks; keep records of progress; provide teacher with feedback, and receive feedback from teacher and other tutors.

TUTOR MORALE/EFFECTIVENESS: Maintained at high level through: tutor badges; weekly tutor meetings; party; knowing what is expected; training to gain proficiency in task; visible evidence of learner's progress; daily encouragement and positive reinforcement from teachers; praise before class; pictures of tutor and learner posted and taken home; sharing and colleague relationship established by teacher.

FORM 2
SEQUENCE OF STEPS IN DEVELOPING TUTORING, SELF-LEARNING PROGRAM

Phase I: Basic Intergrade and Interclass Tutoring Program

1. Teacher Orientation (total faculty).
2. Teacher Training Workshop (part of faculty).
3. Paired Teacher Planning Sessions.
4. Tutor Training (part of class).
5. Tutoring, Paired Classes (part of each class).
6. Teacher Observation of Tutoring.
7. Teacher-Tutor Feedback Sessions.

8. Teacher Resource Group.

9. Intraclass Tutoring.

10. Expansion to Entire Class and to Additional Classes.

Phase II: Advanced Tutoring Program

11. Expansion of Curriculum Areas and Types of Activities.

12. More Frequent and Longer Contacts Between Paired Classes.

13. Increased Student Choices and Initiative.

14. Tutoring Relations With More Than One Class.

15. Expansion of Cooperative Teaching.

16. Interschool Tutoring Program.

Phase III: Learning Teams

17. Intraclass Learning Teams.

18. Tutor Teams.

19. Student-Initiated Curriculum Teams.

Phase IV: Self-Learning/Individualization

20. Teacher-Initiated Interest Centers.

21. Student-Initiated Interest Centers.

22. Independent Study (selected students).

23. Independent Study (all students).

24. Sharing Interest Centers Across Classes.

25. Class Human Resources Directory.

26. School Human Resources Directory.

27. Family Grouping.

28. The Community as a Classroom.

FORM 3
TUTOR TRAINING CHECKLIST

To the left of each item, enter the date when the activity started or was completed.

Tutor Training—General

_____ 1. TCP overview.

_____ 2. Tutor-learner socialization.

_____ 3. Difficulties children have learning.

_____ 4. Ways to help younger children feel important and successful.

_____ 5. Understanding role of tutor.

_____ 6. Interview project.

_____ 7. Analysis of data from interview.

_____ 8. Tutors' observation of younger students.

_____ 9. Preparing the younger class to receive help.

Tutor Training—Specific

_____ 1. Introduction to the receiving classroom.

_____ 2. Training with tutor reading kit.

_____ 3. Tutor feedback session.

The following teacher activities take place regularly. Next to each item enter the scheduled time for the activity.

_____ 1. Observation of each tutor.

_____ 2. Teacher-tutor feedback.

_____ 3. Paired teachers' meeting.

_____ 4. Teacher Resource Group meeting.

FORM 4
DEMONSTRATION LESSON IN SWAHILI

Goals

1. To demonstrate some of the problems and shortcomings of group instruction.

2. To demonstrate the need to individualize instruction.

3. To demonstrate the value of peer tutoring for both the learner and the tutor.

General Procedures

1. Leader teaches the group a five-minute oral lesson in Swahili (learner attempts to master 5 to 8 conversational phrases).

2. Leader tests group and demonstrates range of achievement among learners (some have mastered almost all

phrases, others almost none). The leader asks the students what problems they had with the lesson, what they thought were the causes of the problems, what feelings they experienced during the lesson, and how they felt when others seemed to learn faster.

3. Leader discusses spread of achievement and implications for moving ahead as a group. (If teacher goes too slow, the fast learners get bored; if too fast, the slow learners get further behind and are discouraged.) Stresses that people learn in different ways and at different paces. Fast learners are not necessarily better learners or more intelligent.

4. Leader discusses need to individualize instruction and difficulty of doing this with one teacher and 30 children to a class. Peer tutoring is discussed as a method of accomplishing individualization.

5. Each student is given the task of preparing a plan to tutor another student on a one-to-one basis in Swahili. They are given a paper with the Swahili phrases to work from and about 10 minutes to plan their lesson.

6. Student-student, one-to-one tutoring takes place. (Learners are brought in from another class.)

7. Leader discusses the tutoring, asking the following questions:

    What were your goals?
    How well did you achieve them?
    What methods did you use and why?
    What would you change and why?
    What did you learn about teaching?

8. Leader discusses implications of tutoring, emphasizing benefits to tutor. (Helps become better self-learner by

developing thinking skills: setting goals, making plans, using resources, evaluating, revising.)

Materials

Listing of Swahili dialogue (with aids to pronunciation and English translation):

	Swahili Spelling	Pronunciation	English Meaning
1ST PERSON	Hu Jambo!	Hoo Jahmbo!	Hello!
2ND PERSON	Si Jambo!	See Jahmbo!	Hello!
1ST PERSON	Habarigani!	Hahbahree Gahnee!	How are things with you?
2ND PERSON	Njama Asanti, Santi.	En Jaymah Asahntee, Sahntee.	Very well, Thanks, and you?
1ST PERSON	Njama.	En Jaymah.	Very well, thanks.
2ND PERSON	Tutaonana!	Tootah Oh Nahnah!	Goodbye!
1ST PERSON	Tutaonana!	Tootah Oh Nahnah!	Goodbye!

FORM 5
TUTOR INTERVIEW OF TUTEE*

Interviewer's Name _____

* Adapted from: Lippitt, Peggy; Lippitt, Ronald; Eiseman, Jeffrey, *Cross-Age Helping Program: Orientation, Training and Related Material*, Ann Arbor, Center for Research on Utilization of Scientific Knowlege, Institute of Social Research, University of Michigan: 1971.

Instructions to tutor: (1) Tell your name.

(2) Tell why you are doing this.

(3) Make child comfortable.

(4) Ask for his help.

1. What is your name? _____

2. How old are you? _____

3. How many sisters do you have? ____ How old are they? _____

4. How many brothers do you have? ____ How old are they? _____

5. Do you have any pets? ____ What kind? _____

6. What is your favorite T.V. program? _____

7. What do you like to do in school? _____

_____

8. What do you hate to do in school? _____

_____

9. What kind of work do you have to do at home? _____

_____

10. How do you feel about older kids? _____

_____

11. How does your best friend feel about school? _____

_____

12. How do you feel about school? _____

_____

13. What did you do in school today that you liked? _____

_____

14. What did you do in school today that you didn't like? _

_____

15. What is the most important thing you are going to do after school today? _____

_____

16. What would you like to know about me? _____

_____

FORM 6
TUTOR ANALYSIS OF TUTEE DATA SHEET

How do you think the younger student feels about:

Himself?   What makes you think this?

Other children?   What makes you think this?

School?   What makes you think this?

Teachers?   What makes you think this?

How do you think he
is doing in school?   What makes you think this?

FORM 7
TUTOR OBSERVING A YOUNGER STUDENT IN CLASS

Your Name: _____

Younger Student's Name: _____

Date: _____

1. Was student working well most of the time?
    YES   NO

2. How did he seem most of the time?
    HAPPY   UNHAPPY

3. Did the teacher talk to him or help him very often?
    YES   NO

4. How did the teacher seem most of the time?
    NOT BUSY   BUSY   DOING WHAT?

Write down anything special you observed.

_____

_____

_____

_____

FORM 8
TUTOR READING KIT

Instructions to Tutor

SMILE!   BE FRIENDLY!   USE FIRST NAMES!
PRAISE!   BE HELPFUL!

Word Review Phase

1. Go over outstanding "Don't Know" cards from previous sessions. Place a "1" in corner of word card if learner now knows words. (Praise learner for correct answers.)

2. Place "0" in corner of word card if learner still does not know word.

3. Help learner attack all unknown words. Tell him word and have him repeat it correctly before going to next word.

4. Word becomes "learned" with three correct answers in succession (three 1's in corner of word card). Circle

word on Word List. Remove flash card and give it to learner.

Reading Phase

1. Review part of story read the previous time. (Ask questions to refresh learner's memory about what has happened.)

2. Learner reads; tutor listens for correctness.

3. Learner misses word; tutor helps learner sound out word, then says word aloud. Learner repeats the word and rereads sentence with missed word.

4. Tutor prints word and page number on the Word List. Learner spells word as tutor writes it.

5. Continue to read until five words are missed (or time is up).

6. Ask questions about story learner has read. (Learner may tell part of story in own words.)

Word Study Phase

1. Tutor makes flash card for all new missed words on the list. Spells each word aloud as learner watches and listens.

2. Tutor tests learner on new words; holds up flash cards and has tutee say word. Tutor praises learner for correct answer. If incorrect, tutor says word and has tutee repeat. Tutor places word in "Don't Know" section of Tutor Kit.

Supplementary Activity Phase

Stop 10 minutes before the end of the tutoring period, or

when a learner finishes a book or story. Engage in a supplementary fun activity; e.g., one of the learning games.

Evaluation Phase

Enter comments on Daily Log about learner's progress and attitude. Keep a diary for additional comments.

Word List		
Word	**Story**	**Page**

Tutor's Daily Log

John Jones		Paul Smith	
Tutor		*Learner*	

MON	TUES	WED	THURS	FRI
Nov.3 Book—The White House Pages 22-27 Extra Activity—Baseball Card Game	Nov. 4	Nov. 5	Nov. 6	Nov. 7

Tutoring (entry in large box)	*Attitudes* (small box in upper right-hand corner)
1. Book and page numbers.	+ Very Good
2. Extra activities.	= OK
	— Not Good

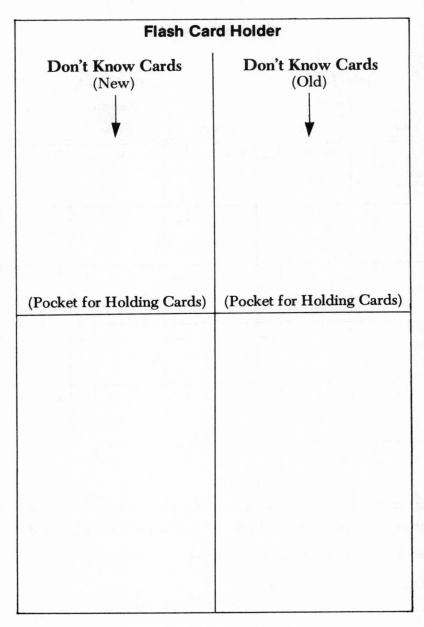

Flash Card Holder

Don't Know Cards
(New)

Don't Know Cards
(Old)

(Pocket for Holding Cards)   (Pocket for Holding Cards)

FORM 9
PAIRED TEACHERS' TUTORING PLAN

To the left of each item record the date when the decision was made. Enter decisions in the blanks.

_____ 1. When will we hold regular planning meetings? (When will the two of us get together regularly to plan, evaluate, revise?)

   Day _____ *Time* _____ *Place* _____

_____ 2. How many tutors will be involved to start with?

   _____

_____ 3. Criteria for selecting learners _____

   _____

   Criteria for selecting tutors _____

   _____

   Criteria for pairing tutors and learners _____

   _____

_____ 4. When will tutoring take place?

Time _____ Days _____ Place _____

_____ 5. Where will tutoring materials be located? _____

_____

_____ 6. When and how will both teachers observe tutor-
          ing? _____

_____

_____ 7. What will students not involved in tutoring be
          doing? _____

_____ 8. When and where will tutor training take place?
          _____

_____ 9. When will tutoring begin? _____

_____

_____ 10. When will ongoing teacher-tutor meetings take
          place? _____

_____ 11. What records of progress will be kept by the tutor
          and learner? _____

FORM 10
TEACHER OBSERVATION OF TUTOR

Tutor _____ *Date* _____
Teacher _____

A. Does tutor ESTABLISH A FRIENDLY AT-
    MOSPHERE? (Calls learner by name,
    smiles, acts friendly)   YES NO

B. Does tutor SUPPORT LEARNER? (Praises
    correct answers, handles errors con-
    structively)   YES NO

C. Does tutor ENCOURAGE INDEPENDENCE in
    learner? (Helps learner find answer in-
    stead of giving it; praises the learner for
    following the steps without being told)   YES NO

D. Does tutor TAKE RESPONSIBILITY? (Deals
    with problems; comes on time, is
    aware of his own strengths and weak-
    nesses; asks for help when necessary)   YES NO

E. Does tutor FOLLOW TUTORING STEPS?
    (Word review, reading, word study,
    supplementary activities, evaluation)   YES NO

Tutor Strengths: _____

_____

_____

Training and/or Improvement needed: _____

_____

_____

Comments: _____

_____

_____

_____

FORM 11
OBSERVATION OF TUTORING BY TCP COORDINATOR

1. Does the tutoring period begin smoothly?

2. Are materials prepared and available?

3. Does the teacher circulate?

4. Does the teacher help tutors and learners with problems?

5. Does the teacher give support, encouragement, praise?

6. Does the teacher take notes?

7. Are the teacher and tutors friendly with each other?

8. Are tutors and learners friendly with each other?

9. Do tutors follow tutoring steps?

10. Do tutors give support, encouragement, praise?

11. Do tutors encourage independence in learners?

12. Are tutors attentive to learners?

13. Does tutoring period end smoothly?

14. Any evidence of going beyond minimal program?

15. Are any especially innovative practices being used?

16. Is anything going on that would be especially worth sharing with other teachers?

COMMENTS: _____

FORM 12
STAFF RESPONSIBILITIES FOR TUTORING EFFECTIVENESS

Sending and Receiving Teachers

- Emphasize value of children learning by themselves and from each other; assume role as guide and facilitator.
- Give high priority to tutoring program as central instructional procedure rather than as an appendage to traditional program.
- Meet regularly and work closely and cooperatively to improve program as a paired team and as part of a teacher resource group.
- Attend training workshop.
- When experienced, assist in training of teachers new to program.
- Plan classroom program that supports tutoring.
- Provide orientation training for tutors (sending) and tutees (receiving). Sending and receiving teachers work together on specific training.
- Develop or obtain materials that facilitate tutoring.
- Observe tutoring regularly.
- Conduct weekly tutoring feedback sessions with tutors.
- Develop methods of evaluating progress.
- Establish friendly relations with children in both classes.
- Keep parents informed of program development and children's progress; provide opportunities for parent participation.

TCP Coordinator

- Assume role as a guide and facilitator in helping teachers promote children's self-learning and learning from each other.
- Conduct training workshops for teachers.
- Assist teachers in training or helping inexperienced teachers develop tutoring program.
- Assist teachers with all major elements of tutoring program.
- Assist teachers in developing or obtaining materials to facilitate tutoring.
- Attend paired teachers planning meetings.
- Coordinate the Teacher Resource Group meetings.
- Assist teachers in developing methods of evaluating progress.
- Provide feedback, encouragement, and on-the-spot assistance to teachers.
- Encourage and stimulate new ideas.
- Document progress in program development and report to faculty and parents.

Principal

- Subscribe fully to major TCP concepts being developed and keep school community informed as to progress in program development.
- Establish climate for change; support and encourage risk-taking and experimentation by staff.
- Provide enthusiastic leadership in helping to solve problems as they arise and in suggesting new ideas.
- Assist teachers in solving logistical problems.

• Become thoroughly knowledgeable about program so as to be capable of performing any of coordinator's tasks.

• Actively participate in program activities (paired teachers planning and resource meetings, teacher training workshop, observing tutoring, etc.).

• Provide feedback and encouragement to teachers.

TCP Consultants

(These could be persons from the school district with experience in TCP.)

• Provide initial orientation and training for key personnel (TCP coordinator, principal, faculty chairman, parent officers, etc.).

• Assist key personnel in training others.

• Assist key personnel in research and development.

FORM 13
GROUP PROCESS QUESTIONNAIRE

Group Performance

1. What objectives were formulated?

2. To what extent were objectives achieved?

3. Were goals realistic or unrealistic? Why?

4. How clearly was the plan for achieving goals formulated?

5. How closely was the plan followed (time, place, materials, personnel, etc.)?

6. What caused deviations from the plan? Were they beneficial or detrimental?

7. How well did the group stick to its job of:

   selecting?

   planning?

   anticipating problems and ways to overcome them?

8. How clearly did the group understand its function? Establish goals?

9. Did the group get adequate information?

10. How well did the group use the information?

11. Did the group plan a procedure for working together?

12. How effectively did the group perform its function? How was this determined?

13. How well did they test for agreement?

14. How well did they accommodate for differences among members?

15. Was the discussion dominated by two or three members?

16. Did the group bring certain matters to a formal vote when necessary?

17. What form of decision-making was used: consensus, majority rule, unilateral executive decision? Was this appropriate for the importance and level of risk in-

volved in the decision?

18. What factors facilitated the group's effectiveness?

19. What factors hindered the group's effectiveness?

20. What changes should the group make in order to be more effective next time?

21. What kind of help does the group need? How can it be obtained?

Individual Performance

1. What did you like most about the experience? Least?

2. Did you have any feelings of irritation with other members during the discussion? With yourself? Why? What did you do with those feelings?

3. Did you have an opportunity to talk as often as you wished?

4. Did you hold back on saying things that you were thinking?

5. What did you like and not like about your own performance?

6. What did you learn about your own working habits, attitudes, learning process, etc.?

7. What changes do you feel are indicated?

8. What kind of help do you need to do a better job next time? How can you get it?

FORM 14
SEQUENCE OF STEPS IN DEVELOPING SHARED PLANNING-AND-DECISION-MAKING

Phase I: Basic Foundations—Faculty and Key Personnel

(Trained facilitator used in this phase.)

1. Orientation to shared planning-and-decision-making (for administrator, faculty, staff, PTA officers).

2. Training in theory and practice of team building, action planning, leadership techniques (for key personnel).

3. Action planning applied within existing groups (School Community Advisory Council—SCAC, Faculty, PTA). If school does not have an SCAC, it is organized during Phase I.

4. Plans developed to establish a TCP Committee (a broadly representative group including the principal, teachers, parents, staff, and. later, students) and a Personnel Committee (responsible for recruiting, interviewing and selecting new teachers).

Phase II: Expanded Activities

(Trained facilitator use continued.)

1. Personnel and TCP committees are activated. One fifth and one sixth grade student are appointed to each committee by teachers at those grade levels.

2. Training in theory and practice of team building and

action planning (for members of Personnel and TCP committees).

3. Using action planning methods, both committees establish goals and priorities for the year and begin to implement them.

4. All teachers receive initial action planning training.

Phase III: Students as Proprietors

(Trained facilitator used minimally, only for assistance with Student Council and classroom shared management activities.)

1. Student Council organized (fifth and sixth grade students elected by their respective classes).

2. Student Council receives training in action planning and team building.

3. Student Council members select representatives for Personnel and TCP Committees to replace those previously appointed by teachers.

Phase IV: Self Direction and New Directions

(Trained facilitator phased out completely.)

1. Student Council expanded to include all grades.

2. Schoolwide elections (simulating real elections) held as a social studies and self-government experience.

3. Parent tutoring teams have regular contact with major committees.

4. School personnel serve as resources for other schools wishing to implement TCP.

FORM 15
RESPONSIBILITIES OF MAJOR SCHOOL COMMITTEES

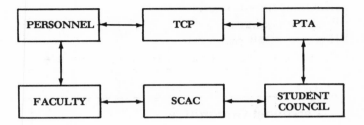

Planning and Policy Making

Faculty

Act as forum for schoolwide issues
Recommend changes
Approve schoolwide changes
Establish sub-committees for support activities

School Community Advisory Council

Establish broad policies and goals
Formulate long-range plans
Identify needs
Evaluate progress
Recommend changes
Approve schoolwide changes

Action and Implementation

Student Council

Identify student needs
Propose changes
React to adult proposals
Provide representatives to other committees

Personnel Committee

Recruit, screen, hire new staff
Evaluate probationary teachers
Discuss personnel problems and make recommendations

TCP Committee

Plan and implement change
Carry out approved recommendations
Coordinate all committees
Act as clearing house for ideas and problems needing action

PTA

Recommend and obtain resources
for school: funds, materials, volunteers
Sponsor social functions

FORM 16
ACTION PLANNING WORKSHEET

Name of Group ————   *Date* ————
Persons Present:

Topic/ Item	Discussion Points	Action Plan	Who Will Do It	When Will It Be Done

FORM 17
COMMITTEE TASK DESCRIPTION

Name of Committee _____

1. Description of Purpose/Procedures (brief).

2. Time Requirements. (Briefly indicate approximate meeting schedule and amount of time required to accomplish the tasks.

3. Materials and Assistance Needed (e.g., student help 2 hours per week, clerical assistance 4 hours per semester.)

4. Training needed. (Briefly indicate type of training a new, inexperienced chairman and/or new committee members would need and how they would get it—from prior chairman, principal, university course, reading, prior membership on the committee.)

FORM 18
COMMITTEE EVALUATION
(End of Year Report)

Date of Report _____   *Period Covered* _____

NAME OF COMMITTEE _____

COMMITTEE CHAIRMAN _____

COMMITTEE MEMBERS _____

MAJOR ACCOMPLISHMENTS FOR THE YEAR _____

_____

_____

TIME SPENT (approximate hours each member spent planning and implementing tasks) _____

_____

FACILITATING FACTORS (things liked and/or which helped achieve committee goals) _____

_____

BLOCKING FACTORS (things not liked and/or which hindered achieving committee goals) _____

_____

SUGGESTIONS FOR NEXT YEAR (members, time, materials, training) _____

_____

_____

FORM 19
TIME UTILIZATION LOG

Name: *Date:*

Committee:

Time	Activity	Priority Rating	Remarks

FORM 20
NASA EXERCISE

Goals

To compare the results of individual decision-making with the results of group decision-making.

To diagnose the level of functioning in a task-oriented group.

Group Size

Between six and twelve participants. Several groups may be directed simultaneously.

Time Required

Approximately one hour.

Materials

Individual work sheets.

Group work sheets.

Answer sheets containing rationale for decisions.

Direction sheets for scoring.

Physical Setting

Participants should be seated around a table. (Avoid a rectangular table because it gives too much control to persons seated at the ends.)

Process

Each participant is given a copy of the individual work sheet and has fifteen minutes to complete the exercise.

One group work sheet is handed to each group. The participants have thirty minutes in which to complete the group work sheet. A member of the group records group consensus on this sheet. Individuals *are not* to change any answers on their individual sheets as a result of group discussion.

Each participant is given a copy of the direction sheet for scoring. Participants should take seven to ten hinutes to score their individual work sheets. They will then give their scores to the recorder, who will compute the average of the individual scores. The recorder will then score the group work sheet.

The group will compare the average score for individuals with the group score and discuss the implications of the experience. This phase of the experience should take seven to ten minutes.

Results are posted on the chart below, and the facilitator directs a discussion of the outcomes of consensus-seeking and the experience of negotiating agreement.

	GROUP 1	GROUP 2	GROUP 3
Consensus Score			
Average Individual Score			
Range of Individual Scores			

NASA Exercise Worksheet

Instructions: You are a member of a space crew originally scheduled to rendezvous with a mother ship on the lighted surface of the moon. Due to mechanical difficulties, however, your ship was forced to land at a spot some 200 miles from the rendezvous point. During landing, much of the equipment aboard was damaged, and, since survival depends on reaching the mother ship, the most critical items available must be chosen for the 200-mile trip.

Below are listed the 15 items left intact and undamaged after landing. Your task is to rank order them in terms of their importance to your crew in allowing them to reach the rendezvous point. Place the number 1 by the most important item, the number 2 by the second most important and so on, through number 15, the least important. *You have 15 minutes to complete this phase of the exercise.*

_____ Box of matches

_____ Food concentrate

_____ 50 feet of nylon rope

_____ Parachute silk

_____ Portable heating unit

_____ Two .45 calibre pistols

_____ One case dehydrated Pet milk

_____ Two 100-lb. tanks of oxygen

_____ Stellar map (of the moon's constellation)

_____ Life raft

_____ Magnetic compass

_____ 5 gallons of water

_____ Signal flares

_____ First aid kit containing injection needles

_____ Solar-powered FM receiver-transmitter

After each participant has completed the exercise, the group discusses the list and rank orders the items together. Suggested answers and reasons for the ranking are given here. The answers arrived at by the group may differ. The important focus is on the factors involved in group decision making.

NASA Exercise Answer Sheet

SUGGESTED RANKING: RATIONALE:

15 BOX OF MATCHES   No oxygen

4 FOOD CONCENTRATE   Can live only for limited time without food

6 50 FEET OF NYLON ROPE   For travel over rough terrain

8 PARACHUTE SILK   As a carrying bag

13 PORTABLE HEATING UNIT   Useful if landing was on dark side of moon. Lighted side of moon is hot.

11 TWO .45 CALIBRE PISTOLS   Could be used to make propulsion device

12 ONE CASE DEHYDRATED PET MILK   Would need to be mixed with H_2O

1 TWO 100-LB. TANKS OF OXYGEN   No air on moon, need own source

3 STELLAR MAP (OF MOON'S CONSTELLATION TION)   Needed for navigation

9 LIFE RAFT   Some value for shelter or as a carrying bag

14 MAGNETIC COMPASS   Probably no magnetized poles

2 5 GALLONS OF WATER — You can't live long without water

10 SIGNAL FLARES — Useful if they contain own oxygen supply

7 FIRST AID KIT CONTAIN-ING INJECTION NEEDLES — First aid kit might come in handy, but needles are useless

5 SOLAR-POWERED FM RECEIVER -TRANSMITTER — For communication

NASA Exercise Direction Sheet for Scoring

To compare individual decision making with group decision making, the following scoring procedure is suggested:

1. Score the net difference between your individual answers and the group's answers. For example, if your answer was 9 and the group was 12, your individual score for that particular item is 3.

2. Compute your total individual score.

3. Add up the total individual scores of all the participants and divide by the number of participants to arrive at an average individual score.

4. Compare your individual score with the average individual score.

5. Score the net difference between group answers and the suggested answers for each item. Total these scores for a group score.

6. Compare the average individual score with the group score.

7. Compare your individual score with the group score.

RATINGS   0-20 Excellent

20-30 Good

30-40 Average

40-50 Fair

over 50 Poor

NASA Exercise—Follow-Up

The following procedure is recommended for analyzing the group interaction.

Influence:

1. Using a scale from one to X (number of people in the group), with one being the strongest and X the weakest, each individual places himself according to the influence he thinks he exerted on group decision.

2. Group examines placements. Anyone can move anyone else.

3. Continue until group is roughly satisfied

Sharing:

1. Distribute flowers to two participants who facilitated.

2. Distribute onions to two participants who hindered group process.

Discussion:

1. Range of individual scores

2. Group effectiveness factors:

Planning procedures, testing for consensus (acquiescence vs. agreement), inclusion, participation, openness to ideas.

Use of group's resources, leadership.

3. Participation:

Rank order participants according to most and least facilitating.

How did individuals feel about own participation, others, reactions of others toward own participation?

FORM 21
GROUP DEVELOPMENT*

The following selection is excerpted from William C. Schutz' theory of interpersonal behavior.

... the formation and development of two or more people into an interpersonal relation (that is, a group) always follow the same sequence ... interaction begins with inclusion, is followed by control, and finally by affection ...

Inclusion Phase

The inclusion phase begins with the formation of the group. When people are confronted with one another they first find the place where they fit. This involves being in or out of the

---

* Excerpted from Schutz, William *The Interpersonal World*, Palo Alto, California: Science and Behavior Books, 1966.

group, establishing one's self as a specific individual, and seeing if one is going to be paid attention to and not be left behind or ignored.

This anxiety area gives rise to individual-centered behavior, such as overtaking, extreme withdrawal, exhibitionism, recitation of biographies, and other previous experience. At the same time the basic problem of commitment to the group is present. Each member . . . is asking, "How much of myself will I devote to this group? How important will I be in this setting? Will they know who I am and what I can do, or will I be indistinguishable from many others?" . . . He is, in effect, primarily deciding on his preferred amount of inclusion . . . —just how much actual contact, interaction, and communication he wishes to have . . .

Control Phase

. . . Once members are fairly well established as being together in a group, the issue of decision-making procedures arises, which involves problems of sharing responsibility and its necessary concomitant, distribution of power and control. Characteristic behavior at this stage includes a leadership struggle . . . The primary anxieties at this phase revolve around having too much or too little responsibility, and too much or too little influence . . .

Affection Phase

Finally, following a satisfactory resolution of those problems of control, problems of affection become focal . . . At this stage it is characteristic to see much behavior as expression of positive feelings, direct personal hostility, jealousies, pairing behavior, and, in general, heightened emotional feeling between pairs of people. The primary anxieties in this stage have to do with not being liked or not being close enough to people, and with too much intimacy. Each member . . . is deciding how to get close enough to receive warmth yet far enough away to avoid the pain of possible rejection . . .

Discussion

These are not distinct phases. The group development postulate asserts that these problem areas are emphasized at certain points in a group's growth. All three problem areas are always present but not always of equal salience. Similarly, some persons do not always go along with the central issue for the group. For certain individuals a particular problem area will be so personally potent that it will transcend the current group issue. For any person, his area of concern will be the resultant of his individual problem areas and those of the group's current phase . . .

FORM 22
EXERCISES DEMONSTRATING FIRO B CONCEPTS

Newmark has developed the following group participation exercises to illustrate FIRO B concepts of inclusion, control and affection:

Inclusion Task—Choosing Up Sides For Teams

Goals

To explore participants' feelings about being included in a group activity and about including others.

Group Size

Group may be broken up into teams of between 6-8 members.

Time

15-45 minutes for team selection, discussion, and self-ratings.

Process

SELECTION   Two persons are appointed by facilitator as team captains for a debate on an educational subject. Depending on size of the total group, there may be three or more teams and team captains.

Each captain, in turn, selects a team member from the remaining group participants. Person selected can join that team, decline to be on it, or state that he does not wish to participate in the debate at all.

After each captain has made two choices, group is told that a member can volunteer for each team. The captain can accept or reject him. (Persons who declined at first may change their minds.)

Selection then continues until all but 10% to 20% of total group have been included.

Discussion

Group then discusses feelings and attitudes towards inclusion. Did they want to be selected for a team? How did they feel about being selected early, late, not at all? Did they volunteer for a team when they had the opportunity? Why? Why not? Were they rejected? How did the rejector feel, the rejectee, the others?

Do they have any recollections of childhood incidents of being included in, or excluded from, things? What were the feelings? How do they compare with now?

Do they have any recent experiences of being included or excluded?

Follow-Up

On a 10 point scale participants rate themselves on need to:

> Express inclusion (how much do you initiate social interactions instead of waiting for others to do it? try to be with others rather than alone? try to be in the center of things with others rather than on the fringe?)

> Desire inclusion (how much do you want others to invite you to do things with them, to be aware of you and think you are important enough to want to include you in their activities?)

Control Task—Thumb Wrestling

Goals

To examine one's need to win or exercise control in a competitive situation.

To examine one's passive/aggressive tendencies in regard to controlling or being controlled by others.

Group Size

Group forms into pairs.

Time

10-20 minutes.

Process

PAIRED COMPETITION   Facilitator demonstrates for group with one individual.

Group divides itself into pairs.

Each pair locks fingers of one hand, with thumbs free above. Only thumbs can move. Object is to pin down other person's thumb under yours and hold for a quick count of three. First person to pin other person's thumb down twice wins.

Pairs compete.

Discussion

Group discusses feelings and attitudes towards the exercise in control.

> Whom did you select to compete with? Why?

> Were you aggressive or passive0 did you throw yourself into it?

> How important was winning to you?

> Did you cheat?

> Did you win or lose? How did you feel about it?

> Do you have any recollections of childhood incidents involving winning or losing with an individual or a group? Being powerful or powerless? What were your feelings? How do they compare with your feelings now?

> Have you had any recent experience of feeling powerful and influential, or powerless and inconsequential? What were your feelings? How do they compare with your feelings now?

Follow-Up

On a 10 point scale, participants rate themselves on need to:

Express influence, control (how much do you try to influence others? try to take charge in social situations? try to have things done in the way you want them? try to be first over others?).

To be influenced, controlled (how much do you let others influence you? want others to lead and take charge? depend on others rather than resisting influence from them?).

Affection Task—Strength Bombardment

Goals

To explore each participant's readiness to give and receive affection.

To explore participant's feelings about giving and receiving affection.

Group Size

10-15.

Time

15-30 minutes.

Process

BOMBARDMENT   Group sits in a circle.

One person states two things he likes about self.

Each member of the group, in turn, states one thing he likes about the person under consideration.

This process continues until each member has received feedback.

Discussion

Group discusses feelings and attitudes towards the exercise in affection.

> How did you feel about stating something you liked about self? How difficult was this for you? Were you spontaneous or did you screen? How personal were you, or did you state something you liked to do? Was your positive statement made unequivocally or was it qualified? Did it come out negative? Did you feel awkward or embarrassed? Were you honest? What did you notice about others' reactions (verbal and non-verbal)?

> How did you feel about the feedback you received? Did you protest or shake your head or did you accept it? Did you believe it? Did it make you feel good or uneasy? Did you feel it was true or did you feel unworthy? Did you notice others' reactions, verbal and non-verbal?

Follow-Up

On a 10 point scale participants rate themselves on need to:

> Express closeness, affection (how much do you try to have close emotional relationships with others? to be personal, informal, and confiding rather than distant and guarded?).

> Receive closeness, affection (how much do you want others to try to have an emotionally close, personal and confiding relationship with you?).

FORM 23
SEQUENCE OF STEPS IN IMPLEMENTING THE PARENT INVOLVEMENT PROGRAM

Phase I: Basic Foundations—Teacher/Parent Contacts

1. Teacher's Introductory Note (1st week).

2. Paired Teachers' Introductory Note (2nd or 3rd week)

3. Teacher Telephone Contact (within 1st month).

4. Regular Telephone Contact (every 6 to 8 weeks).

5. Paired Teacher Get Acquainted/Orientation Activity (beginning of year).

6. Parent Telephone Tree (3rd or 4th week).

7. Recruiting a Parent Classroom Coordinator (within first 3 to 6 weeks).

8. Student-Class Progress Notes Sent Home (monthly).

9. Examples of Student Work Sent Home (monthly).

10. Student Thank-you Notes for Parent Assistance (as necessary).

11. Written feedback from Parents (every 10 weeks).

Phase II: Expanded Parent/Teacher Contacts

1. School Visitation Days (1 to 2 days per week).

2. Parent-Student-Teacher Conference (once per semester).

3. Home Visitation (once per year).

4. Class Program (one per year).

Phase III: Parent Assistance/Mutual Support

1. Home Tutoring/Involvement Team.

2. Classroom Advisory Council (core group).

3. Assisting in Classroom.

4. Assisting with Trips.

5. Assisting at Home.

6. Parent Paired Classroom Social.

Phase IV: Parent Involvement—Schoolwide

1. Principal's Welcoming Note (1st week).

2. Welcoming New Parents (1st day of school).

3. School Information Booklet (beginning of year).

4. Know Your Faculty/Staff Booklet (beginning of year).

5. School Newsletter (monthly).

6. Community News Bulletin Board.

7. Principal's Open Forum (weekly, semi-monthly or monthly).

8. Attendance at Committee Meetings.

9. Community Nights.

10. Parent Written Feedback.

11. Suggestion Box.

12. Contributions to Newsletter.

13. Hallway Displays.

14. Invite a Teacher to Dinner or Lunch.

FORM 24
SAMPLE INTRODUCTORY NOTE TO PARENTS

Dear Mr. and Mrs. _____ ,
    Welcome to room # _____ . I am _____ ,
your child's __*(grade)*__ teacher. I am looking forward to a
happy and successful year working with you and your child. It
is important for children that we work together. I hope we can
get to know each other better during the year.

    I will be in contact with you from time to time to chat
about your child. Please feel free to contact me if you have any
questions or need any information. I like to have my parents
visit the classroom at least once each semester. Of course, you
are welcome at any time. And we hope you will visit often.

    There will be a special Parents' Night in a few weeks. I, or
one of our parents, will contact you regarding this meeting. I
look forward to meeting you in person.

                    Sincerely,

                    _____

P. S. Here is some information about me which may be of
      interest to you. I am married and have ____ children,
      aged ____ . I live at _____ . I went
      to high school in _____ , and college at
      _____ . I have been teaching for
      ____ years. My favorite pastimes and hobbies
      are _____ .

FORM 25
INVOLVING CHILDREN IN INVOLVING PARENTS

Purpose

1. Underscore team concept and role of children in getting parents involved in school.

2. Increase parent responses to school communications.

3. Enhance student language skills.

4. Increase students' understanding of purpose of the communication and the importance of their participation in eliciting a response from parents.

Activities

1. The teacher discusses with the children the content of a note to be sent home. They discuss the importance of parents receiving the communication and responding to it. Some response from the parent to the communication is sought (usually in written tear-off form).

2. Child interviews parents after they have read the communication; obtains parents' response; records response on paper; and returns completed assignment to teacher.

3. The teacher keeps visible classroom chart of parent responses. Children who fail to return parents' response are reminded by teacher and given a second note to deliver.

FORM 26
SAMPLE PAIRED TEACHERS' INTRODUCTORY
NOTE TO PARENTS

Dear Parents,

Our school is engaged in developing a new idea in education—a tutorial community school. We are attempting to introduce and extend the concept of cooperative learning, which we hope will change the total climate of learning in our school. Students at every grade level will work with one another as both tutor and learner. Everyone learns to teach and teaches to learn. We work as a community—helping and receiving help from one another. Through tutoring both tutor and tutee achieve more, become better self-learners and have a more positive attitude towards school, learning, others, and self.

The children in room _____ , grade _____ , and room _____ , grade _____ , are working as partners this year. Your child, in one way or another, will be participating. We would like you to attend a meeting where we will be explaining and discussing the program on ____*(date)*____ , at ____*(place)*____ .

If you have any questions or need further information, please let us know.

Sincerely,

_____
(Signature of sending teacher)

Room _____ Grade _____

_____
(Signature of receiving teacher)

Room _____ Grade _____

FORM 27
SAMPLE TEACHER NOTE ABOUT TELEPHONE CONTACT

Dear Parents,

We have a mutual interest: YOUR CHILD! From time to time I would like to talk with you about your child's progress and about how we can help your child get the most out of school. I have set aside a special time for a chat. Please call me. I will be at home on _____ between ____ and ____ p.m. If my telephone is busy, please try again during these hours. I will try to limit my conversations with each parent to three minutes so that I can talk to as many of you as possible.

Thank you for your interest and cooperation.

My telephone number is: Teacher's name:

_____   _____

                                 Room number:

                                 _____

....

Please tear off and return to classroom.

Telephone Hours

____   I have read the message and noted the day and time.

____   I will be unable to call at that time.

____   But you can call me. I am available on _____ between ____ and ____ p.m.

Parent's Name _____

Child's Name _____

Room Number _____

FORM 28
TEACHER REPORT ON TELEPHONING PARENTS

1. *Purpose:* To establish positive contacts with each parent by telephone without overburdening teachers' time.

2. *Number of parents contacted:* twenty-five out of thirty.

3. *Total Time Involved:* a little over three hours. It averaged out to about seven minutes per parent. Some initial calls took 15 to 20 minutes. Eventually the calls averaged about three minutes per call.

4. *Parent Reactions:* The parents were all pleased that I called. They appreciated that I cared enough to call when there was no problem. They were especially delighted when I had a word of praise for their children. Two parents discussed a problem they had with their children but had never told a teacher about. They were very relieved to have had a chance to talk about it. One mother's older child was kicked out of junior high school the day I called. She cried, from relief, when she found out that her other child was doing well in school. I had never before realized how important it is to talk to the parents of the children who do well.

5. *Children's Reactions:* The children were very happy that I called. Comments made were: "I got a big hug and kiss from my mother." "Boy, is my mother happy with me." One boy brought me a thank you card and a box of candy.

6. *My reactions:* I felt I knew each parent much better. Some of the parents I had never talked to before. I would like some way worked out to be able to communicate with the non-English speaking parents. I am sure the calls can be kept to an average of 3 minutes if done on a regular basis. The time spent is very worthwhile.

FORM 29
SAMPLE PAIRED TEACHERS' INVITATION TO GET ACQUAINTED EVENING

Dear Parents,
  Please join us for a GET ACQUAINTED EVENING.

  Date:

  Time:

  Room #:

We will be discussing what your child learns in school, focusing on goals for the year and how we can work together to reach these goals. You will have an opportunity to ask questions and discuss the program. It should be an informative and enjoyable evening. This is a chance for all of us to get to know each other. We are looking forward to seeing you.

————————————
(teacher's signature)

————————————
(teacher's signature)

Please sign and return this portion.

_____ I will be able to attend.

_____ I will not be able to attend.

Parent's signature _____

Child's name _____

Room # _____

FORM 30
SAMPLE FOLLOW-UP NOTE TO PARENTS NOT ATTENDING MEETING

Dear _____ ,
    I was sorry that you were unable to attend
_____*(event)*_____ . It was an enjoyable and pro-
ductive meeting.
    I hope that we will be able to get together very soon. Please contact me if you have any questions or need any information. We hope you will vist the class soon; we'd like to get to know you better.

                        Sincerely,

_____
               (teacher's signature)

FORM 31
SUGGESTED ACTIVITIES FOR PARENT INVOLVEMENT

At School

1. Visit classroom and school; observe; discuss observations with teachers and principal.

2. Assist teachers in classroom through storytelling, tutoring, grading papers, clerical work, supervising interest center activities, etc.

3. Share talents with class. (Perform or demonstrate some skill, profession or hobby; lead discussion on it; involve kids in learning more about it, or in acquiring the skill.)

4. Help escort class on field trips.

5. Coach team games during recess, lunch, and P.E.; help supervise the yard.

6. Sponsor or supervise enrichment clubs during lunch or after school.

7. Assist in library.

8. Co-lead Junior Great Books discussion group.

9. Assist with safety patrol as students go to and from school.

10. Beautify the school, i.e., construction, painting, gardening, hall displays.

11. Participate in parent Saturday workshops; prepare materials, duplicate, etc.

12.   Serve as a parent representative on a special committee.

13.   Periodically attend committee meetings and school functions.

At Home

1.   Survey parents and community for furniture, rugs, lumber, and other materials needed, and arrange to obtain them.

2.   Prepare teaching materials (tutor reading kit, games, etc.)

3.   Organize field trips for classmates without teacher.

4.   Serve on telephone tree to keep parents informed.

5.   Recruit volunteers for construction, transporting, painting, and tutoring.

6.   Grade papers and do other clerical work.

7.   Share in cooperative baby-sitting to permit other parents to attend school meetings on a rotating basis.

FORM 32
USE OF TELEPHONE TREE TO OBTAIN
MATERIAL FOR CLASSROOM PROJECT

The teacher may telephone the parent telephone tree chairman, who will then call the telephone tree coordinators. The latter then call all the parents on their branch, reading the items to each parent and asking for an immediate yes or no. Or the teacher may send the written list home with each child, mentioning that a telephone call to each parent will be made as a follow-up.

These are the supplies that our class will need for our cooking program. Any items that can be donated to the program by parents would be appreciated. Parents may bring them to school or send them with child.

Paper napkins	Paper towels
Plastic spoons	Paper cups (2 or 5 oz. size)
Small paper plates	Vanilla extract
Honey	Salad oil
Pie pans	Bread pans
Salt and pepper shakers	Hot pad holders
Plastic sink strainers	Dishwashing detergent
Plastic dish pansy	Large pot with lid
Plastic mixing bowls	Egg beaters
Spatulas (long-handled)	Wooden spoons (long-handled)
Cutting boards	Plastic cereal bowls

FORM 33
SAMPLE NOTE TO PARENTS ABOUT CLASS ACTIVITIES AND INDIVIDUAL CHILD'S PROGRESS

Dear _____ ,

This week we are reviewing our math. The children are making up math problems. They will exchange these problems with one another. Some of the children have come up with some unique ideas and problems. We will send home examples of these problems at the end of the week.

We are taking our first walking field trip to the library.

The children divided themselves into three teams for their reading assignments: (1) transportation by land, (2) transportation by sea, and (3) transportation by air. The teams will decide what kind of project they want to do (e.g., history, use, or changes in the particular mode of transportation chosen).

Perhaps you could ask your child what team he chose and what ideas he has about the project. When the projects are finished, they will be displayed for a week in the classroom. We'll let you know the dates. The children and I would like you to visit the class and see the project.

Looking forward to seeing you soon.

Sincerely,

_____

Your child's teacher

P. S.   Your son, John, is moving ahead very rapidly in math and doing excellent work. He has also been very effective as a tutor in reading with a second grade student. He is really using his imagination to make reading games that are interesting to his pupil.

FORM 34
SAMPLE NOTE TO PARENTS FROM CHILD

Dear Dad and Mom,

This week we started our science project. We are studying plants—what is good for them, what will help them grow. We are learning the parts of flowers and what each part is called and what they do. We are going to grow some plants in light and some in the dark. For homework we have to look at plants at home and in the yards. We are to count how many different ones we see.

I can start some plants at home if I use carrot tops, beans. They grow fast.

Your child,

_____

FORM 35
SAMPLES OF POSITIVE NOTES TO PARENTS
ABOUT CHILDREN

_____ is an independent worker. He read for over an hour by himself yesterday and wrote a report on the short story he read.

_____ has respect for property. He cleaned up his area very well after an art project.

_____ is very helpful. She finished her math problems early and helped other children who were having difficulty.

FORM 36
GUIDELINES FOR VISITING PARENTS

Dear Parent:
    Welcome to your child's classroom! The children and I are very pleased to have you visit frequently. Your observations

and comments about what you see will be most welcome. The following is a guide to help make your visit more meaningful.

Classroom Philosophy

I view the classroom as a community—a place where children live and learn together. The children must feel that it is their classroom and that they share the responsibility to make it a great place to be and to learn.

Among our main goals are that students continuously improve in self-learning and in learning with other children (both giving and receiving help). Thus, most of the day the students work alone, in pairs, and in teams. They take the responsibility for their own learning.

I act as a facilitator and a resource, to guide, suggest, diagnose, answer questions. Sometimes I tutor individuals or pairs of children, and sometimes I work with small groups and teams. I occasionally present material to the whole class. My role is to help children learn by themselves and from each other and to reduce their dependence on the teacher.

As you wander around the room, feel free to sit down with any child or team to watch them work. Do not hesitate to ask any questions you wish. Please write down any observations, comments or questions you have so that we can discuss them at the end of your visit.

Questions to Keep in Mind

Here are some things you might want to look for:

1. Do most of the children seem to be content?

2. Do most of the children seem to be actively engaged in some learning activity; or are they passively sitting around doing nothing?

3. How do you find the general classroom atmosphere:

   Tense, cold, unfriendly, with frequent conflicts and disruptions?

   Or, calm, pleasant, active, warm, friendly?

4. Do the students seem to be cooperating or competing with each other?

5. Are most students working alone, with other children or with the teacher?

6. Did the day start in an interesting, enjoyable way; or was it routine and dull?

7. Did the day end in an interesting, enjoyable way; or was it routine and dull?

8. Do students who are working together seem to know what they are doing?

9. Are tutors and learners friendly with each other?

10. Are the teacher and tutors friendly with each other?

11. Does the teacher circulate, observe and help students; or is he off by himself?

12. Does the teacher take notes?

13. Does the teacher give support, encouragement, praise?

14. Do tutors give support, encouragement, praise to the learners?

15. If you observed a tutor feedback session, how did it go? Did the tutors frankly express their problems, concerns, complaints, need for help, etc.?

Did the teacher dominate the session? Did most of the students participate? Was the interaction mainly between student and teacher, or was there considerable exchange between students?

16. Do you have any questions?

17. What suggestions do you have for us?

FORM 37
SAMPLE NOTE ON FIELD TRIPS

Dear Parents:

We are now ready to start our field trip program. We have planned many trips. Some will be by bus; some will be walking trips. We will need parent assistance on both types of trips. Having extra adults along makes the trip easier and more enjoyable for everyone. Please let us know if you will be able to accompany us on any of the trips listed below.

PLEASE PUT UP SCHEDULE AT HOME SO YOUR CHILD CAN USE IT AS A REMINDER.

We will be walking to the library each Wednesday at 10:00 A.M. We will return at 11:45A.M.

Other trips scheduled are:

DATE	TIME	PLACE

. . . .

Please complete and return.

____ I will be able to accompany class on the
following trip(s):

____ I have read the notice, but I will not be able
to participate.

Parent's name _____

Child's name _____

Room number _____

FORM 38
INVITATION TO CONTRIBUTE TO HALLWAY DISPLAYS

Dear Parents,

We want to use our walls and hallways to make our school look more interesting, exciting, and beautiful, and also as a means of getting to know each other better and to show what is going on throughout the school.

Each class has a designated hallway territory. How about bringing in something of yours to display so we can get to know you better? Your display would be in your child's class territory.

Please contact me about getting involved. Your ideas and participation will be most welcome and helpful.

_____

(Teacher)

_____

(Room No.)

FORM 39
SEQUENCE OF STEPS IN IMPLEMENTING A FEEDBACK PROGRAM

Phase I: Basic Foundations, Faculty and Key Personnel

(Trained facilitator used in this phase.)

1. Training in Theory and Practice of Feedback Sessions—Administrator, Key Personnel, Teachers.

2. Teacher Feedback Sessions (Faculty and Principal).

3. Training in Theory and Practice of Student Feedback.

4. Limited Student Feedback Sessions (Some Teachers).

Phase II: Expanded Feedback Activities

(Trained facilitator use continued; group members serve as co-facilitators.)

1. Training in Theory and Practice of Feedback Sessions—Support Staff, Parents.

2. Nonteaching Staff and Parents Join Teacher Feedback Groups.

3. Training in Theory and Practice of Small Group Facilitation (Administrator, Key Personnel, Teachers).

4. Beginning Student Feedback Sessions (All Teachers).

5. Advanced Student Feedback Sessions (Some Teachers).

6. Key Personnel Feedback Sessions (Occasional).

Phase III: Self-Directed Sessions and Special Groups

(Trained facilitator no longer used.)

1. Key Personnel Feedback Sessions (Regularly).

2. Peer Group Feedback Sessions (SCAC, PTA, Nonteaching Staff, Student Council).

3. Advanced Student Feedback Sessions (All Teachers).

FORM 40
THE JOHARI WINDOW/
A GRAPHIC MODEL OF
AWARENESS IN INTERPERSONAL RELATIONS*

Like the happy centipede, many people get along fine working with others, without thinking about which foot to put forward. But when there are difficulties, when the usual methods do not work, when we want to learn more—there is no alternative but to examine our own behavior in relation to others. The trouble is that, among other things, it is so hard to find ways of thinking about such matters, particularly for people who have no extensive backgrounds in the social sciences.

When Harry Ingham and I first presented the Johari Window to illustrate relationships in terms of awareness (at W.T.L., in 1955), we were surprised to find so many people, academicians and nonprofessionals alike, using and tinkering with the model. It seems to lend itself as a heuristic device to speculating about human relations. It is simple to visualize the four quadrants which represent The Johari Window.

---

* *Joseph Luft.* This article is reprinted from NTL's *Human Relations Training News,* 1961, 5(1), 6-7. A more complete exposition of Johari Window concepts may be found in Joseph Luft's *Group Processes: An Introduction to Group Dynamics* and *Of Human Interaction,* Mayfield Publishing Co., formerly National Press Books, 1970.

	Known to Self	Not Known to Self
Known to Others	I **Area of Free Activity**	II **Blind Area**
Not Known to Others	III **Avoided or Hidden Area**	IV **Area of Unknown Activity**

THE JOHARI WINDOW

Quadrant I, the area of free activity, refers to behavior and motivation known to self and known to others.

Quadrant II, the blind area, where others can see things in ourselves of which we are unaware.

Quadrant III, the avoided or hidden area, represents things we know but do not reveal to others (e.g., a hidden agenda or matters about which we have sensitive feelings).

Quadrant IV, area of unknown activity. Neither the individual nor others are aware of certain behaviors or motives. Yet we can assume their existence because eventually some of these things become known, and it is then realized that these unknown behaviors and motives were influencing relationships all along.

The Quadrants and Changing Group Interaction

In a new group, Quadrant I is very small; there is not much free and spontaneous interaction. As the group grows and matures, Quadrant I expands in size; and this usually means we are freer to be more like ourselves and to perceive others as they really are. Quadrant III shrinks in area as Quadrant I grows larger. We find it less necessary to hide or deny things we know or feel. In an atmosphere of growing mutual trust there is less need for hiding pertinent thoughts or feelings. It takes longer for Quadrant II to reduce in size, because usually there are "good" reasons of a psychological nature to blind ourselves to the things we feel or do. Quadrant IV perhaps changes somewhat during a learning laboratory, but we can assume that such changes occur even more slowly than do shifts in Quadrant II. At any rate, Quadrant IV is undoubtedly far larger and more influential in an individual's relationships than the hypothetical sketch illustrates.

The Johari Window may be applied to *intergroup* relations. Quadrant I means behavior and motivation known to the group and also known to other groups. Quadrant II signifies an area of behavior to which a group is blind; but other groups are aware of this behavior, e.g., cultism or prejudice. Quadrant III, the hidden area, refers to things a group knows about itself but which are kept from other groups. Quadrant IV, the unknown area, means a group is unaware of some aspect of its own behavior, and other groups are also unaware of this behavior. Later, as the group learns new things about itself, there is a shift from Quadrant IV to one of the other quadrants.

Principles of Change

1. A change in any one quadrant will affect all other quadrants.

2. It takes energy to hide, deny, or be blind to behavior which is involved in interaction.

3. Threat tends to decrease awareness; mutual trust tends to increase awareness.

4. Forced awareness (exposure) is undesirable and usually ineffective.

5. Interpersonal learning means a change has taken place so that Quadrant I is larger and one or more of the other quadrants has grown smaller.

6. Working with others is facilitated by a large enough area of free activity. It means more of the resources and skills in the membership can be applied to the task at hand.

7. The smaller the first quadrant, the poorer the communication.

8. There is universal curiosity about unknown areas, but this is held in check by custom, social training, and by diverse fears.

9. Sensitivity means appreciating the covert aspects of behavior in Quadrants II, III, and IV and respecting the desire of others to keep them so.

10. Learning about group processes as they are being experienced helps to increase awareness (larger Quadrant I) for the group as a whole, as well as for individual members.

11. The value system of a group and its membership may be noted in the way *unknowns* in the life of the group are confronted.

A centipede may be perfectly happy without awareness, but after all, he restricts himself to crawling under rocks.

FORM 41
JOHARI WINDOW SELF-RATING EXERCISE

1. Participants form groups of three.

2. Using the Johari Window Self-Rating Sheet, each person marks an X where he thinks he belongs on the horizontal (solicits feedback) and vertical (gives feedback) scales. He then completes his window by drawing in the intersecting vertical and horizontal lines.

3. Each person then draws a window for the other two people in the triad.

4. Each person compares his self-rating with how the other two triad members rated him.

5. Each person states his reactions to the information gained about himself. Group interpretation and discussion follow.

JOHARI WINDOW SELF-RATING SHEET

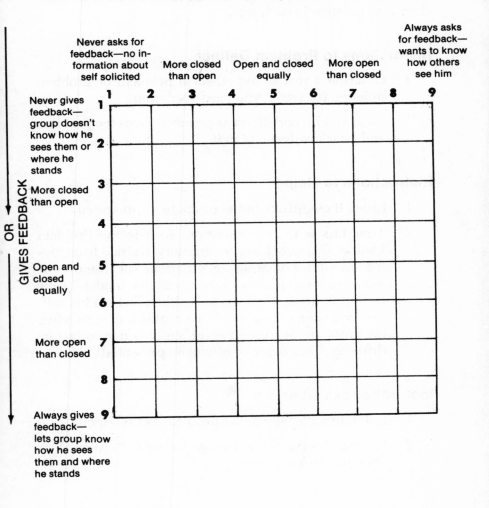

FORM 42
THE HELPING TRIOS EXERCISE

The group divides up into groups of three. Each person takes a role as Problem Definer, Helper or Observer. The exercise is conducted three times so that each member of the triad has a chance to function in each role.

Instructions to Problem Definer

1. Describe a real or hypothetical problem or problem situation for which you need a solution.

2. Be as candid and direct as possible about the problem and your involvement in it.

Instructions to Helper

1. Listen thoughtfully to the problem as presented.

2. Your task is to raise questions to help the Problem Definer diagnose his own difficulty. Refrain from giving any advice or citing any experience of your own or of others. Keep probing to bring out new angles. Leave responsibility for answers to Problem Definer himself. You will have succeeded if you enable him to redefine his problem, or to see the difficulty is due to factors different from those he originally presented.

Instructions to Observer

1. Listen thoughtfully to the problem as presented.

2. As you observe the exchange between Problem Definer and Helper, note:

    a. What do you think were the unspoken feelings of each as the talk went on?

    b. What questions seemed to be helpful? Why? Which not helpful? Why?

    c. What did the Helper do that seemed to bring insight? What did he do that seemed unproductive?

3. Act as timekeeper, following this approximate schedule:

    a. Allow brief time—two or three minutes—for the Problem Definer to organize his thoughts.

    b. Five minutes for the Problem Definer to explain his problem.

    c. Ten minutes for the Helper to discuss problem with the Problem Definer and try to help him.

    d. Five minutes for Observer to share his observations along lines suggested above.

FORM 43
COMMITMENTS FOR DEVELOPING A TUTORIAL COMMUNITY SCHOOL

Action by District Superintendent's Office

1. Approve basic plan and statement of commitments. Arrange for briefing of Area Superintendents.

2. Designate school as experimental and provide local autonomy.*

---

* Action to be taken either at district or area level, as appropriate.

3.   Assist Area Superintendents in effecting transfer of personnel into and out of designated school.

4.   Publicize orientation and screening program in district media.

5.   Appoint a full-time TCP coordinator at designated school.*

6.   Provide funds for staff development, community involvement, purchase of materials.*

7.   Make other assignments available to teachers who don't work out at TCP school.

Action by Area Superintendent's Office

1.   Confirm approval of basic plan and statement of commitments.

2.   Recommend principals and schools.

3.   Assist in final selection of school and principal.

4.   Publicize screening and orientation program in area media.

5.   Arrange for transfer of teachers into and out of designated school.

Action by Parents

1.   Attend briefings and workshop on TCP.

2.   Confirm approval of basic plan and statement of commitments.

---

* Action to be taken either at district or area level, as appropriate.

3. Formally request TCP at school through Area Superintendent.

4. Participate in the planning and development of the TCP program.

5. Become involved in the implementation of TCP through participation in:

    Assisting in the classroom.

    School feedback sessions.

    Parent home tutoring team.

    The community advisory council and/or its activities.

    PTA activities.

Action by Teachers

1. Work towards changing role in the classroom to a guide and facilitator, helping children to learn by themselves and from each other.

2. Accept self-learning and student tutoring not as appendages to the regular program, but as the major instructional procedures around which the educational program is developed.

3. Provide regular opportunities for children to express honest feelings and thoughts (both negative and positive) about the teacher, school, class activities, self, and others.

4. Encourage and promote student self-management in the classroom.

5. Participate in and support regular open, frank sessions with other teachers, parents and administrators, giv-

ing and taking honest feedback about things blocking or facilitating achievement of school goals.

6. Improve knowledge of the community and the out-of-school life of students.

7. Increase and improve contacts, information flow and interpersonal relations and communications with parents through home visitation, class visits by parents, informal social functions, feedback sessions, and the like.

8. Encourage and participate in joint planning-and-decision-making by parents, teachers, administrators, and students.

9. Maintain an experimental attitude—a willingness to specify objectives, try new things, evaluate results, and revise plans.

10. Assist in developing peer accountability and cooperation among teachers—offering and accepting criticism and help, sharing ideas, materials, and so forth.

11. Continuously strive to improve knowledge and skills that contribute to achievement of the TCP goals and that create an exciting and effective learning environment.

12. Agree that first two years are a trial period and consent to transfer out without prejudice if it doesn't work out.

Action by the Principal

1. Attend briefings and workshops on TCP.

2. Subscribe fully to the major TCP concepts.

3. Confirm approval of basic plan and statement of commitments.

4. Support and encourage risk-taking and experimentation among staff members.

5. Actively participate in TCP activities, such as feedback groups, community involvement programs, and others.

6. Establish mechanisms and procedures which insure real, and not superficial, shared planning-and-decision-making among students, parents, teachers, support staff and administrators.

7. Assure that when decisions are made the goal of developing a Tutorial Community School receives number one priority.

FORM 44
EVALUATION OF FACTORS CONTRIBUTING TO STUDENT PROGRESS

Parent Form

The following form should be completed by the parent prior to the three way conference between parent, child, and teacher.

*Name of Child*_____ *Date*_____

Parent's Estimate of Child's Progress During Period

Academic Skills

Has done well in the following areas:

Needs help in the following areas:

Social Skills

Has done well in the following areas:

Needs help in the following areas:

Child's Efforts to Improve

What I like most about my child's effort during this period:

What I like least:

How my child could change or improve his efforts:

Parent's Self-Evaluation

What I like most about my efforts to help my child's learning during this period:

What I like least about my efforts:

What I think I should do differently in the future:

Parent's Evaluation of School and Classroom Climate

What I like best about the school climate or my child's classroom during this period:

What I like least:

What I would like to see changed at the school or in my child's classroom:

Parent's Evaluation of Teacher

What I like best about the efforts of the teacher to help my child during this period:

What I like least:

How I would like to see my child's teacher change:

Student Form

The following form should be completed by the student prior to the three-way conference between parent, child, and teacher.

*Name of Child*_____ *Date* _____

Child's Estimate of Own Progress During Period

Academic Skills

I have done well in the following areas:

I need help in the following areas:

Social Skills

> I have done well in the following areas:
>
> I need help in the following areas:

Efforts to Improve

> What I like most about my efforts to learn during this period:
>
> What I like least:
>
> What I think I should do differently in the future:

Child's Evaluation of School and Classroom Climate

> What I like best about the school climate or my classroom during this period:
>
> What I like least:
>
> What I would like to see changed at the school or in my classroom:

Child's Evaluation of Teacher

> What I like best about the efforts of my teacher to help me during this period:
>
> What I like least:

What I would like to see my teacher change is:

Child's Evaluation of Parents

What I like most about my parents' efforts to help me during this period:

What I like least:

How I would like to see my parents change:

Teacher Form

The followinng form should be completed by the teacher prior to the three-way conference between parent, child, and teacher.

*Name of Child*_____ *Date*_____

Teacher's Estimate of Child's Progress During Period

Academic Skills

Has done well in the following areas:

Needs help in the following areas:

Social Skills

Has done well in the following areas:

Needs help in the following areas:

Child's Efforts

What I like most about the child's efforts to improve during this period:

What I like least:

How I would like to see the child change in his efforts:

Teacher Self-Evaluation

What I like most about my efforts to facilitate this child's learning during this period:

What I like least:

What I think I should do differently in the future:

Teacher's Evaluation of School and of Own Classroom Climate

What I like best about the school climate or my classroom during this period:

What I like least:

What I would like to see changed at the school or in my classroom:

Teacher's Evaluation of Parent

What I like best about the efforts of this child's parents during this period is:

What I like least:

How I would like to see this child's parents change:

FORM 45
PARENT-CHILD-TEACHER CONTRACT TO
IMPROVE INSTRUCTIONAL CLIMATE

After the three-way conference between parent-student-teacher, they all come to an agreement about the goals for the next period, and about the responsibilities of each of them for achievinng these goals. The following is completed.

THE GOALS FOR _____
                    (Name of Child)

FOR THE PERIOD _____ ARE AS FOLLOWS

Academic Skills:

Social Skills:

ACTIONS TO BE TAKEN

By the Teacher:

By the Parent:

By the Child:

*Date*_____

_____
Teacher's Signature

_____
Child's Signature

_____
Parent's Signature

FORM 46
QUESTIONS MOST FREQUENTLY ASKED ABOUT FEEDBACK*

1. What is the value of the feedback program?

    The value of feedback is that it builds the values of a democratic society—participation, involvement and responsibility.

    It promotes a spirit of scientific inquiry which stresses the need to examine human interaction in order to guide such interaction into constructive outlets.

    It makes for a healthy organization, which, like a healthy individual, is aware of its own behavior and the reasons for its actions.

---

* Prepared jointly with Dr. Lawrence Solomon, TCP consultant on Feedback and Shared Planning.

It enhances interpersonal competence by enabling individuals to receive frank and accurate information regarding the impact of their behavior upon others. Such knowledge provides the power to make any needed changes.

2. What is the purpose of the basic feedback session?

To share information that can be used as the basis for corrective action to improve personal and organizational functioning.

To reveal to participants the relationship between their own behavior and the achievement of organizational objectives.

To clarify objectives and examine behavior that may be promoting or frustrating achievement of these goals.

3. What does the individual get out of a feedback session? Each participant in a feedback session should expect to increase his awareness of:

The impact of his own behavior upon the functioning of others.

The role he plays in contributing to the achievement of organizational objectives and as a member of an interdependent team.

Participants learn to be more open in communicating their feelings and reactions, and more secure in accepting the frank and open expressions of other people's reactions to them. In the long run, the individual should become more effective, productive and happier in his work.

400 THIS SCHOOL BELONGS TO YOU & ME

4. What makes a session good? A good session is one in which the participants:

> Truly listen to each other; listen to understand and empathize, rather than to defend or explain.

> Speak openly, honestly and spontaneously.

> Deal with specific, task-related behaviors.

> Openly inquire into ways in which they might improve their working together as a team.

> Actively engage each other and do not permit a few persons to monopolize the session.

5. What makes a session bad? A bad session is one in which the participants:

> Are defensive, constantly explaining, justifying.

> Use "hurt feelings" as a defense against understanding.

> Share information strategically; i.e., say only what they think others want to hear, use information as a weapon to achieve hidden objectives.

> Deal with deep personality factors which are not task-relevant, or are not amenable to modification.

> Allow one or two persons to dominate the session while the others act as spectators.

6. Would a neurotic person benefit from feedback sessions, or would they tend to emphasize his problems?

> That depends on the degree of disturbance. If the person is psychotic, then he would not be likely to benefit from task-oriented feedback sessions; but then neither is it likely he would be a member of an operat-

ing team in an organizational setting. Within the broad range of normal functioning that characterizes the majority of the population, everyone can theoretically benefit from feedback sessions. The focus is on task relevant behaviors rather than on the analysis of personality.

7. Can feedback sessions be harmful?

Properly conducted feedback sessions are no more stressful than many other forms of human interaction; they are not nearly as stressful, for example, as the conventional social institutions of marriage and graduate school. Sometimes a participant may receive feedback that makes him uncomfortable. Most often, however, when given the choice, an individual would rather be informed honestly than live in ignorance with false self-concepts.

For most of us, psychological growth and maturity are painful processes. We may have to relinquish idealized and exaggerated beliefs about ourselves or others. It is almost universally reported that, in the pursuit of self-knowledge, one simultaneously experiences the need to know and the fear of knowing. Yet for most the pain of growth is preferable to the stagnation of self-deception.

There is considerable evidence that honest, open feedback is a liberating, freeing, and growth producing experience. More harm is done by repression and by leading a quiet life of desperation than by openness.

8. How is feedback helpful?

Feedback, when properly given (not as an accusation, but as a statement about how your behavior affects me or the task at hand) can be extremely helpful to the recipient. Such information can help the individual to become more effective in his interpersonal relations, in his on-the-job behavior and task accomplishment. If a person's behavior is not having the intended or desired effects, then he can change it, once this fact is known. Without feedback, the impact of one's behavior upon others may never be fully or accurately known. Feedback enables a person to change self-defeating behavior and strengthen and expand constructive behavior. Feedback is essential if an individual is to make things happen as he wishes them to happen. Feedback closes the loop in a communication cycle, allowing an individual accurately to assess the consequences of his own behavior.

9.   Is a feedback experience always beneficial?

If one goal of the feedback experience is to establish inquiry as a norm, and to enable participants to learn how to learn, then in that sense every feedback experience can be beneficial. Whether or not a participant feels personally benefited by the experience will depend upon a variety of factors, such as:

The openness of the individual to new learning.

The salience of the information for that individual.

The payoff when new behaviors are tried as a consequence of the feedback received.

Individuals will not necessarily feel uplifted or pleased after every feedback session. However, some of the most valuable learning occurs after having experienced some distress. In the long run, the benefits are numerous and powerful, leading to greater energy and happiness.

10. How does the verbal expression of strong negative feelings toward someone help that person?

> The expression of any strong feelings verbally is a form of emotional honesty. When such feelings are expressed openly, they may be dealt with directly in a straightforward manner. If not expressed openly, strong feelings do not go away; they merely go underground and come out in indirect and disguised ways, making coping with them effectively extremely difficult. The recipient of a feeling message knows exactly where he stands with the other person and can respond on a reality level to the honest emotions present in their relationship. Otherwise, their interaction takes on the characteristics of shadow-boxing, with neither participant facing squarely what is actually occurring between them.

11. Does the honest expression of feelings have to be hostile?

> Feedback is not limited to expressions of hostility. Positive feelings of respect, approval and affection are also an important part of feedback sessions.

12. Is it possible to discuss attitudes and feelings involving children and teaching without discussing personal lives?

> Certainly it is possible. However, it should be recognized that behavior at school is merely a small sample of each participant's behavior elsewhere in his life. What a teacher does in the classroom, at the faculty meeting, and in his interactions with others in the school setting reflects that person's habitual ways of being; and these ways of being are pervasive throughout one's personal, social, and professional life. Often it is helpful for a participant to see the connection between behavior at school and at home or elsewhere.

Enhancing one's interpersonal competence as a member of an operating team in an organizational setting redounds in improved interpersonal functioning in other walks of life. Since each individual is a unity, it is unavoidable that sometimes organizational feedback sessions deal with subject matter that may appear personal. However, emphasis is on task accomplishment, and the group will usually avoid totally unrelated personal matters. Nor will personal topics be discussed without the willingness of the participant involved.

13.   Can feedback sessions be harmful if there is no trained facilitator or if participants are people who work together?

Properly conducted feedback sessions contain minimal potential for harm. A trained facilitator is important in the early stages of feedback training to insure that the ground rules and guidelines become established as norms. Once such norms have become internalized within the group, the presence of a trained facilitator is no longer essential.

People who work together tend to build up, over time, a set of implicit contracts by which individuals tacitly agree to avoid confronting many of the real issues that face them as members of a team. An outside, trained facilitator is necessary at the beginning to help the group confront these contracts, to open them for examination and legitimate change. Once the norm of inquiry and the ground rules are established, the group can monitor their own functioning to the mutual benefit of all members.

14.   Why shouldn't problems, complaints, differences be settled on a one-to-one basis rather than in a group setting?

In a highly complex, interdependent socio-technical system like a school, no problem exists in isolation. Problems which develop within a group context require the group for their solution. Additionally, dealing with issues in a group setting enriches the problem-solving process; many different perspectives and experience backgrounds may be brought to bear upon the issues. Such richness is absent in a one-to-one setting.

15. How do you prevent a principal from "getting even" with a teacher who has criticized him strongly in a feedback session? Can this threat ever be removed?

It cannot be removed, but it can be dealt with directly when it is treated as a realistic issue for the group to resolve. Holding all group members accountable for the enforcement of agreed upon guidelines may help to reduce this problem. A principal who violates his pledge to the group may retain the role power he has by virtue of his position but he will lose his real social power. Honest discussion in the group should aid against retaliation by the principal. The group feedback session actually acts as a safeguard against unwarranted, vindictive behavior on the part of the principal because his apparently retaliatory action can be brought back to the group. Feedback serves as a self-correcting mechanism.

16. What do you do about individuals who use the feedback sessions to attack others viciously?

This type of behavior is not common. Most teachers are not vicious and do not behave that way. If it does happen, it is handled by the group. The constructive approach is to give that individual feedback about how his viciousness makes others feel. An honest sharing of such feelings should provide the support needed by the person who may be under attack; and should create a climate of inquiry within which the attacker may begin to explore the reasons for his viciousness. Such exploration is important because the person may be acting similarly in the classroom with children.

17. Can people who work together and give each other negative feedback still remain friends?

Yes. Cooperative and friendly bonds should be re-established between individuals who have been in conflict with one another or who have been exchanging negative feedback in a group session. If a person holds a grudge, the preferred approach is to explore the consequences of that behavior and to make it the issue around which feedback is focused. Remember, more often than not, an honest expression of feelings, even negative feelings, serves to clear the air and brings individuals into closer relationship with one another. In establishing the initial ground rules for feedback, there should be agreement to look favorably on confrontation, and to want to restore friendly attitudes and behavior afterward. This norm must be continuously reemphasized throughout the life of the group. An atmosphere should be created where conflict and differences are not regarded as threatening and people become comfortable with them.

The reverse question might be appropriate, "Can persons who keep negative feelings to themselves, or hold grudges, be friends without dealing with their differences openly?"

BIBLIOGRAPHY

Ford Foundation; Film: "Tomorrow, We'll See What Happens." (Documentary film about the Tutorial Community Project at three public elementary schools in the Los Angeles City School System [30 min., b/w, 16 mm sound]. May be obtained from: Films Incorporated, 1144 Wilmette Avenue, Wilmette, Illinois 60091.

Tutorial Community Project Publications. May be obtained for cost of duplication and mailing from: Educational Communications Corp., 1910 Ocean Front, Santa Monica, Calif. 90406, Attn: Dr. Gerald Newark.

Ford Foundation; *About TCP.* New York, 1974 (an overview of TCP in question and answer format).

Melaragno, Ralph J. *Tutoring with Students.* Englewood Cliffs, N.J.: Educational Technology Publications (in press).

Melaragno, Ralph J., and Newmark, Gerald. *A pilot study to apply evaluation-revision procedures to first-grade Mexican-American classrooms.* Pacoima, Calif.:Tutorial Community Project, 1968.

Melaragno, Ralph J., and Newmark, Gerald. *A proposed study to develop a tutorial community in the elementary school.* Pacoima, Calif.: Tutorial Community Project, 1968.

Newmark, Gerald, and Melaragno, Ralph J. *Tutorial Community Project—Report of the first year (May 1968-June 1969).* Pacoima, Calif.: 1969.

Melaragno, Ralph J., and Newmark, Gerald. *Tutorial Community Project—Report of the second year (July 1969-August 1970).* Pacoima, Calif.: 1970.

Newmark, Gerald, and Melaragno, Ralph J. *Tutorial Community Project—Report of the third year (September 1970-October 1971).* Pacoima, Calif.: 1971.

Melaragno, Ralph J. *Tutorial Community Project—Progress Report—Pacoima Elementary School (August 1971-July 1972).* Pacoima, Calif.: 1972.

Melaragno, Ralph J. *Tutorial Community Project—Progress Report—Pacoima, Plainview and Norwood Elementary Schools (September 1972-December 1973).* Pacoima, Calif.: 1973.

Melaragno, Ralph J. *Tutorial Community Project—Progress Report—Pacoima, Plainview, and Norwood Elementary Schools (September 1973-December 1974).* Pacoima, Calif.: 1974.

Newmark, Gerald. *Tutorial Community Project—Progress Report—Wilshire Crest and Dublin Avenue Elementary Schools (August 1971-July 1972).* Los Angeles, Calif.: 1972.

Newmark, Gerald. *Tutorial Community Project—Progress*

Report—Wilshire Crest and Dublin Avenue Elementary Schools (September 1972-December 1973). Los Angeles, Calif.: 1973.

Newmark, Gerald. *Tutorial Community Project—Progress Report—Wilshire Crest and Dublin Avenue Elementary Schools (September 1973-December 1974).* Los Angeles, Calif.: 1974.

Watson, Donald and Rosenberg, Sarah. *An Interschool Tutoring Program.* Pacoima, Calif.: Pacoima Elementary School, 1973.

TUTORING AND SELF-LEARNING

Cloward, Robert. "Studies in Tutoring." *The Journal of Experimental Education* 36, no. 1 (Fall 1967), pp. 14-25.

Durrell, Donald D., and Palos, Viola A. "Pupil study teams in reading." *Education for May,* 1956, pp. 552-556.

Ebersole, Elbert H., and DeWitt, Donlu. "The Soto pupil-team program for reading." *Improving Human Performance,* 1972, vol. 1, no. 4, pp. 39-42.

Faucette, Betty. *Synanon Infant School.* Santa Monica, California: Synanon Foundation, May 1973.

Gartner, Alan; Kohler, Mary; and Riessman, Frank. *Children Teach Children.* New York: Harper and Row, 1971.

Harrison, Grant V. "Tutoring: A Remedy Reconsidered." *Improving Human Performance,* 1972 (a), vol. 1, no. 4, pp. 1-7.

Harrison, Grant V. *Supervisors Guide for the Structured Tu-*

torial Reading Program. Provo: Brigham Young Univ. Press, 1972(B).

King, Hopson P. *Individualized Instruction: Games that Teach.* Encino, California. International Center for Educational Development, 1971.

Lippitt, Peggy, "Children Can Teach Other Children." *The Instructor,* no. 9 (May 1969), pp. 41ff.

Lippitt, Peggy; Lippitt, Ronald; and Eiseman, Jeffrey. *Cross-Age Helping Program.* Ann Arbor: Center for Research on Utilization of Scientific Knowledge, Institute for Social Research, 1971.

Lippitt, Peggy and Lohman, John E., "Cross-Age Relationships—an Educational Resource." *Children,* vol. 12, no. 3 (May-June 1965).

Lorton, Mary B. *Workjobs: Activity-Centered Learning for Early Childhood Education.* Menlo Park, California: Addison-Wesley Publishing Company, 1972.

Mainiero, John. *A cross-age teaching resource manual.* Ontario-Montclair School District. Ontario, California, 1971.

Glasser, Joyce F. *The Elementary School Learning Center for Independent Study.* West Nyack, New York: Parker Publishing Co., Inc. 1971.

Group for Environmental Education Inc., *Yellow Pages of Learning Resources,* Philadelphia, 1972.

Melaragno, Ralph J. "Intergrade tutoring on a school-wide basis." *Improving Human Performance,* 1972(a), vol. 1, no. 4, pp. 22-26.

National Commission on Resources for Youth:

"For the Tutor." New York: NCRY, 1970.

"Tutoring Tricks and Tips." New York: NCRY, 1970.

"Youth Tutoring Youth—A Tutor's Handbook." New York: NCRY, 1970.

Youth Tutoring Youth—A Manual for Trainees." New York: NCRY, 1970

"Supervisor's Manual—Youth Tutoring Youth." New York: NCRY, 1968.

Orlick, Gloria. *The Reading Helper Series*. New York: Book-Lab, Inc., 1970.

Popham, W. James. *Evaluating Instruction*. Englewood Cliffs: Prentice-Hall, 1973.

Stohl, Dona K., and Anzalone, Patricia. *Individualized Teaching in Elementary Schools*. West Nyack, New York: Parker Publishing Co., Inc., 1971.

Thelen, Herbert A. *Learning by Teaching*. Report of a conference on the helping relationship in the classroom, Stone-Brandel Center. University of Chicago, 1968.

Vermont Department of Education. "Vermont Design for Education," Montpelier: 1968.

SHARED PLANNING-AND-DECISION-MAKING

Addison-Wesley Series on Organization Development. Reading, Mass.: Addison-Wesley, 1969.

Bennis, Warren G. *Organization Development: Its Na-*

ture, Origins, and Prospects.

Beckhard, Richard. *Organization Development: Strategies and Models.*

Black, Robert R., and Mounton, Jane S. *Building a Dynamic Corporation Through Grid Organization Development.*

Lawrence, Paul R., and Lorsch, Jay W. *Developing Organizations: Diagnosis and Action.*

Schein, Edgar H. *Process Consultation: Its Role in Organization Development.*

Walton, Richard E. *Interpersonal Peacemaking: Confrontation and Third-Party Consultation.*

Fox, Robert S. *Diagnosing Professional Climate of Schools,* NTL Learning Resources, Fairfax, Virginia, 1973.

Gordon, William, J. *Synetics.* New York: Collier Books, 1961.

Handbook for School-Community Advisory Councils, Los Angeles Unified School District, October 1971.

Lassey, R. W. (ed.) *Leadership and Social Change.* Iowa City: University Associates Press, 1971.

Novotney, Jerold M. (ed.) *The Principal and the Challenge of Change.* Melbourne: Florida Institute for the Development of Educational Activities, Inc., 1968.

Nylen, A., J. R. Mitchell, A. Stout (eds.) *Handbook of Staff Development and Human Relations Training.* Washington, D. C., NTL Institute for Applied Behavioral Science, 1967.

Schmuck, Richard A., et al. *Handbook of Organization De-*

velopment in Schools. Palo Alto: National Press Books, 1972.

DeFranco, Ellen B., and Pickarts, Evelyn M. *Parents, Children, and Reading: A Handbook for Teachers.* New York: American Book Company, 1972.

Dolch, Edward W. *Helping Your Child With Reading.* Champaign, Illinois: Garrard Publishing Company, 1956.

Dolch, Edward W. *Helping Your Child With Spelling.* Champaign, Illinois: Garrard Publishing Company, 1956.

Dolch, Edward W. *Helping Your Child With Arithmetic.* Champaign, Illinois: Garrard Publishing Company, 1956.

Los Angeles City Schools Division of Planning and Research. *Conferencing: an approach to reporting pupil progress.* Los Angeles, Calif.: 1971.

National School Public Relations Association. *How to Help your Child Learn—a Handbook for Parents of Children in Kindergarten through Grade 6.* Washington, D. C.: NSPRA, 1960.

Newman, Sylvia. *Guidelines to Parent-Teacher Cooperation in Early Childhood Education.* New York: Book-Lab, Inc., 1971.

Russell, David H., and Karp, Etta E. *Reading Aids Through the Grades.* New York: Teachers College Press, 1938.

Russell, David H., Russell, Elizabeth F. *Listening Aids Through the Grades.* New York: Teachers College Press, 1959.

Schindler-Rainman, Eva, and Lippitt, Ron. *The Volunteer Community—Creative Use of Human Resources.* Washington, D. C. NTL Institute for Applied Behavioral Science, 1971.

PARENT INVOLVEMENT

DeFranco, Ellen B., and Pickarts, Evelyn M. *Dear Parents: Helping Your Child to Read.* New York: American Book Company, 1972.

TASK ORIENTED FEEDBACK

Association for Supervision and Curriculum Development. *Perceiving, Behaving, Becoming—A New Focus for Education,* Washington, D. C.: 1962.

Bessell, Harold, and Palomares, Uvaldo H. *Methods in Human Development.* San Diego: Human Development Training Institute, 1967.

Egan, Gerald. *Face to Face: The small group experience and interpersonal growth.* Monterey, Calif.: Brooks/Cole Publishers, 1973.

Gordon, Tom. *Parent Effectiveness Training.* New York: Wyden, 1970.

Howe, Leland W., and Howe, M. Martha. *Personalizing Education: Values Clarification and Beyond.* New York: Hart Publishing Company, 1975.

Pfeiffer, J. W. and Jones J. E. *Annual Handbook for Group Facilitators.* La Jolla, California: University Associates Publishers, Inc. (1972, 1973, 1974, 1975).

Rogers, Carl. *Freedom to Learn.* Columbus: Charles E. Merrill, 1969.

Rogers, Carl R. *Carl Rogers on Encounter Groups.* New York: Harper & Row, 1970.

Schutz, William C. *The Interpersonal Underworld* (a reprint edition of *FIRO*). Palo Alto, California: Science and Behavior Books, 577 College Avenue, 1966 (paperback).

Simon, Steve. *The Synanon Game* (reprint of a lecture). Santa Monica, California: Synanon Foundation, 1973.

Schmuck, Richard A., and Schmuck, Patricia A. *A Humanistic Psychology of Education: Making the School Everybody's Home.* Palo Alto: National Press Books, 1974.

Solomon, L. N. and Berzon, B. (eds.) *New Perspectives on Encounter Groups.* San Francisco: Jossey-Bass, 1972.

IMPLEMENTATION STRATEGY

Endore, Guy. *Synanon: The Learning Environment* (Pamphlet). Santa Monica, California.

Fantini, Mario D. *Public Schools of Choice.* New York: Simon and Schuster, 1974.

Gardner, John W. *Self-Renewal.* New York: Harper & Row, 1963.

Gardner, John. *How to Prevent Organizational Dry Rot.* Harpers Magazine, October, 1965.

Sarason, Seymour B. *The Culture of the School and the Problem of Change.* Boston: Allyn and Bacon, Inc., 1971.

INDEX

416

GERALD NEWMARK

"Jerry Newmark has the ability to combine common sense and the scientific method in a way that is both beautiful and rare." This was the way Dr. Gerald Newmark was described at an educational conference in Berlin in 1966.

Dr. Newmark received his Ph.D. in Instructional Technology from the University of Southern California. He has had extensive teaching experience at all levels of education: elementary, secondary, junior college, and university. He has also been a research scientist at the Rand Corporation and the System Development Corporation. Dr. Newmark's particular talents lie in helping organizations change from unresponsive, impersonal bureaucracies to dynamic groupings whose members feel a sense of community, involvement, and ownership.

During the past thirteen years, much of Dr. Newmark's professional effort has been concentrated in research work to develop new models of education. *This School Belongs to You and Me* is the direct result of his work in Los Angeles public schools under a six-year grant from the Ford Foundation.